New Testament Commentary

I0154538

Romans
and
Corinthians

F B Hole

Scripture Truth Publications

ROMANS AND CORINTHIANS

First published as articles in the magazine "Edification" 1930-32.

Hardback edition first published in July 1979 as "Paul's Epistles (Volume One)" by Central Bible Hammond Trust Limited, Wooler.

Reprinted in April 1995 as "Paul's Epistles (Volume 1): Romans - 2 Corinthians" with ISBN-10: 0-901860-12-3 by Scripture Truth Publications, Wooler.

Transferred to Digital Printing 2007

ISBN: 978-0-901860-43-9 (paperback)

ISBN: 978-0-901860-47-7 (hardback)

A publication of Scripture Truth

Published by Scripture Truth Publications
Coopies Way, Coopies Lane,
Morpeth, Northumberland, NE61 6JN

Scripture Truth is an imprint of Central Bible Hammond Trust, a charitable trust

Printed and bound by Lightning Source

CONTENTS

———

ROMANS

INTRODUCTION

THE GREAT THEME of the Epistle to the Romans is the Gospel of God, as is indicated in its opening words. It seems to fall quite naturally into three main sections, as follows:—

1. The Gospel fully unfolded, and expounded in orderly fashion, for the instruction of believers. (Chaps. i.-viii.).

2. God's dealings with men, in sending forth the Gospel to Gentiles, reconciled with His previous dealings, which were exclusively with Israel. (ix.-xi.).

3. Instructions and exhortations as to the conduct that befits the Gospel on the part of those who have received it. (xii.-xvi.).

It is one thing to carry the Gospel as a herald to sinful men, and quite another to set it forth in detail for the establishment of saints. The former is the work of the evangelist, the latter that of the teacher. If we wish to hear Paul preaching the Gospel, whether to Jews or to the heathen, we turn to the Acts. If we wish him to instruct us in its fulness and glorious power, we read the Epistle to the Romans.

CHAPTER 1

IT IS VERY fitting therefore that the opening words of the epistle should give us a brief summary of the Gospel. Jesus the Christ, who is God's Son, and our Lord, is the great theme of it, and it particularly concerns Him as the One who is risen from the dead. He truly came here as a real Man, so that He was David's seed on that side; yet He was not merely that, for there was another side, not what He was "according to the flesh," but "according to the Spirit of holiness." He was the Son of God in power, and the resurrection of the dead declared it; whether it was His own resurrection, or His wielding the power of resurrection while still on earth.

From that same powerful Son of God Paul derived his apostleship and the grace to fulfil it, for he was set apart to herald forth the glad tidings. The scope of that message was not limited as the law had been. It was for all nations; and those who received the message, by obeying it, were revealed as the called ones of Jesus Christ. Such were the Romans to whom he wrote.

The Apostle evidently knew many of the saints living in Rome, who had doubtless migrated there from the lands further to the east, but as yet he had not personally visited the great metropolis; hence what he says in verses 8 to 15. They had a good report and Paul longed and prayed that he might see them, but had hitherto been hindered. His desire was their thorough establishment in the faith by his imparting to them things of a spiritual nature. He explains what he means in verse 12; the gifts were to be in the nature of mutual upbuilding in the faith, rather than the bestowing of great abilities, miraculous powers, and the like. It is better to be godly than gifted.

From verse 15 it would appear that not all the believers in Rome had as yet heard the Gospel unfolded in all its fulness, as Paul was commissioned to set it forth. Hence, since the Lord had specially committed the Gospel to him as regards the Gentiles, he felt he was in their debt. He was ready to discharge that obligation, and since he had been hindered as to bodily presence, he would do it by letter.

Now the Gospel was in reproach. It has always been so from the earliest days, yet the Apostle had not an atom of shame in regard to it because of its power. Only let a man believe it, no matter whether he be Jew or Gentile, and it proves itself to be God's mighty force or energy to his salvation. It is exactly so today. Men may ridicule it in theory but only the wilfully blind can deny its power, which is most manifest when those who believe it have been living in the depths of degradation.

And observe, it is the power of God because there is revealed in it the righteousness of God. Here we are face to face with a truth of first-rate importance—*there is no salvation apart from righteousness*; nor would any right-minded person wish there to be.

But let us make sure that we catch the drift of verse 17. "Righteousness *of God revealed*" is in contrast with the law, the leading feature of which was righteousness *from man required*. The Gospel's righteousness is "from faith." The preposition *from* is a little unfortunate. It is rather *by*. The righteousness which the law demanded from men was to be by (or, on the principle of) works. The righteousness of God which the Gospel reveals is to be reached by faith. Then again the Gospel reveals God's righteousness *to* faith whereas all that the law brought it revealed to sight. The first occurrence of the word, faith, stands in contrast to *works*, the second to *sight*. In the book of Habakkuk there is a prophecy which is fulfilled in the Gospel, "The just shall live by faith." The preposition here translated "by" is just the one translated "from" immediately before. Not by works but by faith.

The Gospel, then, reveals *the righteousness of God*, and proves itself to be *the power of God* unto salvation, but it has behind it as a dark background, *the wrath of God*, of which verse 18 speaks. Righteousness and power unite today for the salvation of the believer. In the coming day they will unite in adding terror to His wrath. The wrath is not yet executed, but it is revealed as coming from heaven without distinction upon all man's evil, whether it be open evil or the more subtle evil of "holding the truth in unrighteousness," as was done, for instance, by the Jew.

From this point the Apostle proceeds to show that all men are hopelessly lost and subject to the judgment and wrath of God. First of all—verse 19 to the end of chapter i.—he deals with the Barbarians, of whom he had spoken in verse 14. They at least had the witness of creation, which testified to the eternal power and Godhead of the Creator and makes them to be without excuse.

Here we have the passage that deals with the vexed question of the responsibility of the heathen. What about the heathen?—how often is that question asked! Certain facts stand out very distinctly.

1. Those peoples that are now heathen *once knew God.* Man's course has not been from polytheism to monotheism, as some dreamers would have us imagine, but the other way round. They have sunk out of light into the darkness. Once "they knew God", (v. 21) but the fact is, "they did not like to retain God in their knowledge." (v. 28.).

2. The root cause of their fall was that they did not wish to yield to God the glory that was his due, for they wished to pose as wise themselves —as we see in verses 21 and 22. In short, *pride* was the root and God has allowed them to make fools of themselves.

3. Their descent has been *gradual.* First vain thinkings: then, darkened understandings, gross idolatry, to be followed by outrageous sins in which they fell below the level of the beasts. Each generation went beyond the follies of their predecessors, thus ratifying for themselves the previous departure.

4. Their plight has been reached under *the government of God.* Three times over do we get the phrase (with slight variations) "God gave them up to . . ." If men object to thinking of God and give Him up, they have no ground of complaint when He gives them up. And if they give up God, and consequently good, they naturally find themselves given up to everything that is evil and degrading. There is an ironic justice about God's government.

5. The final item in this dreadful tragedy is that they know their practices are wrong and worthy of death, and yet they not only go on with them but are utterly fascinated by them. *They delight in them* to such an extent that they find pleasure in others sinning even as they do themselves.

If we really allow this fearful picture of human depravity to imprint itself on our minds we shall have no difficulty in acquiescing in the Divine verdict that all such are *"without excuse."* (v.20.).

CHAPTER 2

THE HEATHEN WORLD of nineteen centuries ago had however in its midst a number of peoples who were highly civilized. The apostle Paul knew that he was as regards the Gospel as much a debtor to the Greek who was wise, as to the Barbarian who was unwise. As we open chapter ii., we find him turning from the one to the other. His style becomes very graphic. It is almost as if at this point he saw a highly refined and polished Greek standing by, and quite approving of his denunciation of the enormities of the poor Barbarians. So he wheeled round and boldly charged him with doing in a refined way the very same things as in their grosser forms he condemned in the Barbarian. Thereby he too stands before God without excuse, for in judging others he condemned himself.

Under the term, Greek, the Apostle included all those peoples who at that time had been educated and refined under the influence of Grecian culture. The Roman himself would come under the term. They were fine fellows externally, brainy, intelligent and fond of reasoning. In the first eleven verses of this chapter Paul reasons with them as to righteousness and judgment to come, and where can you match these verses for pungency and brevity and power?

The Greeks had a certain code of outward morality. They loved beauty and strength and cultivated their bodies to these ends. This alone preserved them from the deadly excesses of the barbarians. Yet they knew how to indulge themselves discreetly, how to sin scientifically. The same feature marks our age. A present day slogan in the world might be, "Don't sin coarsely and clumsily, sin scientifically." Under such circumstances it is very easy for men to deceive themselves; very easy to imagine that, if only one approves good things in theory, and avoids the grosser manifestations of evil, one is secure oneself from the judgment of God.

Take note of three steps in Paul's argument:—
1. "The judgment of God is *according to truth*." (v. 2). Truth means reality. No unreality will stand in the presence of God, but everything be manifested as it is. A poor prospect for the Greek, whose virtues were only skin deep.
2. There is too the "revelation of the *righteous* judgment of God." (v. 5). A wretched criminal may have the truth of his crime dragged into the light, yet if the presiding judge be incompetent or unrighteous he may escape. The Divine judgments are righteous as well as according to truth.
3. "There is *no respect of persons* with God." (v. 11). In some countries today respect of persons provides the undoubted criminal with an avenue of escape. Favouritism does its work, or other influences behind the scenes, or even bribery is set in motion, and the offender escapes the penalty he deserves. It will never be thus with God.

There is, then, no avenue of escape for the refined sinner or mere moralist. Indeed, it would appear that he will come in for severer condemnation. His very knowledge heightens his guilt, for repentance is the goal to which the goodness of God would lead him, but he despises God's goodness in the hardness of his heart and so treasures up wrath to himself.

The statements of verses 6 to 11 present a difficulty to some minds inasmuch as in them no mention is made of faith in Christ. Some read verse 7, for instance, and say, "There! So after all you have only got to keep on doing good and seeking good, and eternal life will be yours at the end." We have only to read on a little further however, and we discover that no one does good or seeks good, except he believes in Christ.

4

ROMANS

The ground of judgment before God is *our works*. If anyone does truly believe in the Saviour he experiences salvation, and hence has power to do what is good and to continue in it. Moreover the whole object of his life is changed, and he begins to seek glory and honour and that state of incorruptibility which is to be ours at the coming of the Lord. On the other hand there are all too many who, instead of obeying the truth by believing the Gospel, remain slaves of sin. The works of these will receive well-merited condemnation in the day of judgment.

At this point in the argument someone might wish to say, "Well, but all these people had never had the advantage of knowing God's holy law, as the Jew had. Is it right to condemn them like this?" Paul felt this, and so added verses 12 to 16. He stated that those who have sinned under the law will be judged by the law in the day when God judges by Jesus Christ. Whereas those who have sinned without having the light of the law will not be held responsible for that light:—nevertheless they will *perish*. Verses 13 to 15 are a parenthesis, you notice. To get the sense you read on from verse 12 to verse 16.

The parenthesis shows us that many things which the law demanded were of such a nature that men knew they were wrong in their hearts without any law being given. And further men had the warning voice of conscience as to these things even when they had no knowledge of the law of Moses. Go where you will you find that men, even the most degraded, have a certain amount of natural light or instinct as to things that are right or wrong. Also they have conscience, and thoughts which either accuse or excuse. Hence there is a ground of judgment against them apart from the law.

When God judges men by Jesus Christ there will be a third ground of judgment. Not only *natural conscience*, and *the law*, but also "according to *my Gospel*." Judgment will not be set until the fulness of gospel testimony has gone forth. Those who are judged and condemned as having been in the light of the Gospel will fare far worse than those condemned as in the light of the law or of conscience. And in that day the *secrets* of men are to be judged, though their condemnation will be on the ground of works.

Oh, what a day will the day of judgment be! May we have a deep sense of its impending terrors. May we earnestly labour to save at least some from ever having to face it.

Having dealt with the Barbarian and the Greek, proving that both alike are without excuse and subject to the judgment of God, the Apostle turns to consider the case of the Jew. The graphic style with which he started chapter ii. continues to the end of the chapter. He seems to see a Jew standing by as well as a Greek, and in verse 17 he turns from the one to address the other.

The Jew not only possessed the witness of creation, and of natural conscience, but also of the law. The law brought him a knowledge of God and of His will, which placed him far above all others in religious matters.

5

ROMANS

He made, however, one great mistake. He treated the law as something in which he could boast, and therefore it ministered to his pride. Says the Apostle, "thou . . . restest in the law, and makest thy boast of God." He did not realize that the law was not given to him as something in which to *rest*, but as something to act as a *test*.

The test is applied to him from verse 21 to the end of the chapter. He comes out of it with his reputation utterly shattered. True he had the form of knowledge and truth in the law, but it all acted as a two-edged sword. He had been so busy turning its keen edge against other people that he entirely overlooked its application to himself. He viewed it for others as a standard—as a plumb-line or spirit level—but for himself he thought it a personal adornment, a feather to be stuck in his cap.

Do not let us be at all surprised at his doing this, for it is just what we all do naturally. We pride ourselves upon our privileges and forget their corresponding responsibilities.

Each question in verses 21, 22 and 23 is like a sword-thrust. To each implied accusation the Jew had to plead guilty. He had the law truly, but by breaking it he dishonoured God, whose law it was. Indeed, their guilt was so flagrant that the Gentiles looked at the Jews and blasphemed God, whose representatives they were.

This being the state of affairs it was useless their falling back upon the fact that they were God's circumcised people. The argument of verses 25 to 29 is very important. It is not official position, which is an outward thing, that counts before God and puts right what is wrong. It is the inward thing that God values. God would have respect to the one who obeys, even were he an uncircumcised Gentile. He would reject the disobedient, even were he the circumcised Jew.

CHAPTER 3

PAUL KNEW WELL that all this would be very objectionable in Jewish ears, and that they would indignantly charge him with belittling and setting aside all that God had done in calling Israel out of Egypt to be His people. Hence the questions that he raises in the first verse of chapter iii. His answer is that it was indeed profitable to be a Jew, and chiefly in this, that he had the Word of God.

Let us at this point make a present-day application. The position of privilege held in the former day by the Jew is now held by Christendom. There is an undoubted advantage in being born and bred in a "Christian" land, yet at the same time tremendous responsibilities. Also, it is sadly true that the awful sins of Christendom only provoke the heathen to blaspheme. The unconverted professor of the Christian religion will be judged according to the high standard he has professed, and hence merit severer judgment.

The oracles of God today cover not only the Old but also the New Testament—not only the word of His law but also the word of His grace. But let us specially underline that word, *committed.* Of old the oracles of God were committed to the Jews; today they are to the Church. That is the true position. The Church is not the *producer* of the oracles, nor is she, as so many falsely assert, the only authorized *teacher* of them; she is simply the *custodian* of them. They are committed to her that by them the Spirit may be her Teacher.

In the beginning of our third chapter only the Jew and the law are in question. The Apostle knew well the quibbles raised by Jewish minds. He was aware too of slanderous reports that they circulated as concerning his teaching. Hence what he says in verses 3 to 8. He makes it perfectly plain that no amount of human unbelief can nullify or alter what God has said. "The faith of God" is, of course, *all that which God has revealed,* in order that men may receive it in faith.

Again, God is so supremely above man's evil and unbelief that He knows how to turn it ultimately into a kind of dark background whereon to display the brightness of His righteousness and truth. Does this in any way compromise Him, or make it wrong for Him to judge the sinner? It does not: nor does it furnish any kind of excuse for those who would like to seize upon it as a reason for further wrong-doing, saying, "If my evil can thus be made to serve God's glory, I will proceed to accomplish more evil." The judgment of such will be certain and just.

What then is the position? Let us be sure that we understand it. Verse 9 raises this question. The position is, that though the Jew had certain great *advantages* as compared with the Gentile, he was no *better* than the Gentile. The Apostle had proved this before, especially in chapter ii. Both Jew and Gentile are "under sin." He was not however, in the case of the Jew, going to rest content with proving it by reasoning. He proceeds to quote directly against him his own Scriptures.

Verse 10 begins, "As it is written." And there follows down to the end of verse 18 a series of quotations from the Psalms and one from Isaiah, six in all. They describe in full the real state into which mankind is sunk.

The first quotation (vv. 10-12) is a passage found twice in the Psalms (xiv. and liii). Its repetition would seem to indicate that its statements are most important and on no account to be missed by us; though they are of such a nature that we should be very glad to miss them, if we had our way. This quotation contains six statements of a general and comprehensive and sweeping nature. Four are negative statements and two positive. Four times we find "none," and twice "all," though the second time it is implied and not expressed. Let us face the sweeping indictment.

The first count is this: *None righteous*—not even one. This embraces us all. The statement is like a net, so capricious that it takes all in, so sound that not the smallest fish can find a rent that permits it to escape. No one of us is right in our relations with God.

7

Someone who is contentious might reply, "That seems exaggerated. But even if true, man is an intelligent creature. He only has to be told, for him to put things right." But the second count is to the effect that *nobody does understand* their state of unrighteousness. They are incapable of fathoming their plight, or even a fraction of it. This considerably aggravates the position.

"Oh, well," says the contentious one, "if man's understanding is astray, there are his instincts and feelings. These are all right, and if followed will surely lead him after God." But count No. 3 confronts us—*there is no one who seeks after God.* Is that really so? It is indeed. Then what does man seek after? We all know, do we not? He seeks after self-pleasing, self-advancement, self-glory. Consequently he seeks money, pleasure, sin. What he seeks when the power of God has touched his heart is another matter. The point here is what he seeks according to his fallen nature, and apart from the grace of God.

Man's *state* is wrong. His *mind* is wrong. His *heart* is wrong. This third count clinches the matter and seals his condemnation. It shows there is no point of recovery *in himself.*

Out of this flow the three counts of verse 12. All are astray. All, even if massed together, are unprofitable; just as you may add noughts to noughts in massed thousands, and it all amounts to nothing. And lastly, all man's works, as well as his ways are wrong. He may do a thousand things which upon the surface look very fair. Yet are they all wrong because done from a totally wrong motive. No work is right but that which springs from the seeking of God and his interests. And that is precisely what man never seeks, but rather his own interests, as we have just seen.

It is very striking how the words, "No, not one," occur at the end of the first and last of the counts. They have been translated, "Not even one . . . not so much as one," which is perhaps even more striking. Well then, may they strike home to all our hearts. We are not going to suppose that the Christian reader wishes to quarrel with the indictment—we should at once doubt his Christianity if he did—but we are sure that many of us have accepted and read these words without at all fully realizing the state of the ruin, irremediable apart from the grace of God, which they reveal. It is most important that we should realize it, for except we correctly diagnose the disease we shall never properly appreciate the remedy.

The objector however may still have something to say. He may complain that all these six statements are of a general nature, and he may remind us that when lawyers have a weak case they indulge in much talk of a general sort so as to avoid being compelled to descend to particulars. If he speaks thus, he is immediately confronted by verses 13 to 18, in which particulars are given. These particulars relate to six members of man's body: his throat, tongue, lips, mouth, feet and eyes. It is in the body that man sins, and deeds done in the body are to be judged in the day that is before us all. Notice that of the members mentioned no less than four have to do with what we *say*. One refers to what we *do*, and one to what we *think*; for the eye is the window of the mind.

What an awful story it is! And what language! Take time that it may soak in. An "open sepulchre" for instance! How terribly expressive! Is man's throat like the entrance to a cave filled with dead men's bones and all uncleanness and stench? It is. And not only is there uncleanness and stench but deceit and poison, cursing and bitterness. His ways are violence, destruction, misery. No peace is there, whilst God and His fear have no place in his mind.

Now all this was specially and pointedly said to the Jew. Paul reminds them of this in verse 19. They were the people under the law to whom the law primarily addressed itself. They might wish to brush it all aside, and make believe that it only applied to the Gentile. This was inadmissible. The laws of England address themselves to the English; the laws of China to the Chinese; the law of Moses to the Jew. Their own Scriptures condemn them, shutting their mouths and bringing in against them the sentence— Guilty before God.

This completes the story. Barbarian and Greek had before been proved guilty and without excuse. *All the world* is guilty before God. Moreover there is nothing in the law to extricate us from our guilt and judgment. Its part the rather is to bring home to us the knowledge of our sin. It has done this most effectually in the verses we have just considered.

Where then is hope to be found? Only in the Gospel. The unfolding of the Gospel starts with verse 21, the opening words of which are, "But now . . ." In contrast with this story of unrelieved darkness there has now come to light another story. Blessed be God, ten thousand times ten thousand, that there is another story to tell. And here we have it told in an order that is divine, and in words that are divinely chosen. That word NOW is emphatic. We shall meet with it again several times in reference to various details of the Gospel message. Anticipate what is to come to the extent of reading the following verses, and observing its use:—v. 9; v. 11 (marginal reading); vi. 22; vii. 6; viii. 1.

The first word in connection with the Gospel is, "the righteousness of God," and not as we might have expected, the love of God. The fact is that man's sin is a direct challenge to God's righteousness, and hence that righteousness must in the first place be established. The whole Gospel scheme is founded in divine righteousness. What news can be better than that? It guarantees the stability and endurance of all that follows.

The Gospel then is, in the first place, the manifestation of the righteousness of God, altogether apart from the law, though both law and prophets had borne witness to it. That righteousness has been manifested, not in rightful legislation, nor in the execution of perfectly just retribution upon the transgressors, but in Christ and in the redemption that is in Him. In the death of Christ there was a complete and final settlement, upon a righteous basis, of every question which man's sin had raised. This is stated in verse 25. Propitiation has been made. That is, full satisfaction has been rendered to the righteousness of God; and that not only in regard to the sins of those who are believers in this Gospel age, but also in regard to those of all previous ages. The "sins that are past," are the sins of those who lived before Christ came—past, that is, from the standpoint of the cross of Christ, and not from the standpoint of your conversion, or my conversion, or anybody's conversion.

That righteousness of God, which has been manifested and established in the death of Christ, is "*unto* all," but is only "*upon* all them that believe." Its bearing is unto or towards everybody. As far as God's intention in it is concerned, it is for all. On the other hand only those who actually believe receive the benefit. Then the righteousness of God is upon them in its realized effect, and they stand right with God. God Himself is the Justifier of the one who believes in Jesus, however great his guilt has been, and He is just in justifying him. This is stated in verse 26.

This glorious justification, this complete clearance, is the portion of all who believe in Jesus, whether Jew or Gentile. All have sinned, so that there is no difference as to guilt. In the same way there is no difference in the way of justification. Faith in Christ, and that alone, puts a man right with God. This is stated in verse 30.

This way of blessing, as is evident, shuts out all boasting on the part of men. It is wholly excluded. Here is the reason why proud men hate the idea of the grace of God. We are justified freely by His grace. Grace gave Jesus to die. Grace is the way of God's acting in justification, and faith is the response upon our part. We are justified by faith apart from the works of the law. This is the conclusion to which we are led by the truth we have been considering.

The last verse of our chapter meets the objection, which might be raised by a zealous Jew, that this Gospel message cannot be true because it falsifies the law, indubitably given of God at an earlier time. "No," says Paul, "far from making the law null and void, we establish it by putting it in the place God always intended it to occupy."

Never was the law so honoured and established as in the death of Christ. The Gospel honours it by allowing it to do its proper work of bringing in the knowledge of sin. Then the Gospel steps in and does what the law was never intended to do. It brings complete justification to the believer in Jesus.

CHAPTER 4

THE FOURTH CHAPTER is practically a parenthesis. In verse 28 of chapter iii. the conclusion is reached that a man is justified by faith without the deeds of the law. To exactly the same point are we brought back in verse 1 of chapter v., and then—but not till then—does the Apostle carry us on further into the blessings of the Gospel. In chapter iv. he develops at considerable length certain Old Testament scriptures which support his thesis, that before God a man is justified by faith alone.

When, in chapter iii., the Apostle aimed at convincing the Jew of his sinfulness, that he equally with the Gentile was subject to the judgment of God, he clinched his argument by quoting what the law had said. Now the point is to prove that justification is by faith, with the deeds of the law excluded, and again the Old Testament is appealed to. In days of long ago the faith of the Gospel was anticipated; and this was the case, whether before the law was given, as in the case of Abraham, or after it was given, as in the case of David.

The first question asked is, What about Abraham? He is spoken of as "the father of circumcision," in verse 12, and as such the Jew boasted very greatly in him. He was also "the father of all that believe," as verse 11 states. Had he been justified by works he would have had something in which to glory, but not *before God*. Note the two words italicized, for they plainly indicate that the point of this passage is, what is valid before God and not what is valid before men. Herein lies an essential difference between this chapter and James ii., where the word is, "Shew me thy faith" (verse 18). We may also point out that whereas Paul shows that the works *of the law* must be excluded, James insists that the works *of faith* must be brought in.

We may put the matter in a nutshell thus:—Before God a man is justified by faith without the deeds of the law; whereas, to be accepted as justified before men, the faith that is professed must evidence its vitality by producing the works of faith.

The case is very clear as to both Abraham and David. We have but to turn to Genesis xv. on the one hand, and to Psalm xxxii. on the other, in order to see that faith was the way of their justification and that works were excluded. The wonder of the Gospel is that God is presented as, "Him that justifieth the ungodly." The law contemplated nothing more than this, that the judges, "shall justify the righteous, and condemn the wicked" (Deut. xxv. 1). That the ungodly should be justified was not contemplated. But this is what God does in the Gospel, on the basis of the work of Christ, since "Christ died for the ungodly." This opens the door into blessing for sinners such as ourselves.

We get the expression, "this blessedness," in verse 9. It refers to faith being "counted for righteousness," or "reckoned for righteousness," or righteousness being "imputed." These, and similar expressions, occur a number of times in the chapter. What do they mean? Whether referring to Abraham or David or to ourselves who believe today, they mean that God accounts us as righteous before Him in view of our faith. We must not imagine that all virtue resides in our faith. It does not. But faith establishes contact with the work of Christ, in which all the virtue does reside. In that sense faith justifies. Once that contact is established and we

11

stand before God in all the justifying virtue of the work of Christ, we are of necessity justified. It could not righteously be otherwise. God holds us as righteous in view of our faith.

The question raised in verse 9 is this:—Is this blessedness for the Jew only or is it also for the Gentile who believes? The Apostle knew right well the determined way in which the bigoted Jew sought to place all the condemnation upon the Gentile while reserving all the blessing for himself. The answer is that the case of Abraham, in whom they so much boasted, proves that it is for ALL. Abraham was justified before he was circumcised. Had the order been reversed, the Jew might have had some ground for such a contention. As things were, he had none. Circumcision was only a sign, a seal of the faith which justified Abraham.

Abraham then in his justification stood clean outside the law. The law indeed only works wrath, as verse 15 says. There was plenty of sin before the law came in, but there was not transgression. To transgress is to offend by stepping over a clearly defined and forbidden boundary. When the law was given the boundary was definitely raised, and sin became transgression. Now "sin is not imputed when there is no law" (v. 13). That is, so long as the evil had not been definitely forbidden God did not put the evil down to man's account, as He does when the prohibition has been issued. This then was the work of the law. But long before the law was given Abraham had been justified by faith. Does not this display how God delights in mercy? Justification was clearly indicated four hundred years before the urgent need of it was manifested by the law being given.

"Therefore it is of faith that it might be by grace." Had it been by works it would have been a matter of debt and not grace, as verse 4 told us. On the principle of faith and grace the blessing is made "sure to all the seed;" that is, the true spiritual seed of Abraham or in other words, true believers. For Abraham is, "the father of us all." "US all" be it noted—ALL true believers.

This fact being established, the last nine verses of chapter iv. apply the principles of Abraham's justification to the believer of today.

Abraham's faith had this peculiarity, that it was centred in God as the One who was able to raise the dead. If we turn to Genesis xv. we discover that he believed God when the promise was made as to the birth of Isaac. He believed that God would raise up a living child from parents who, as regards the process of reproduction, were dead. He believed in hope when it was against all natural hope that such a thing should be.

Had Abraham been weak in faith he would have considered all the circumstances, which were against it. He would have felt that the promise was too great and consequently have staggered at it. He did neither. He took God at His word with the simplicity of a little child. He believed that God would do what He had said He would do. And this, be it noted, is what here is called strong faith. Strong faith then is not so much the faith that performs miracles as that faith which implicitly trusts God to do what He has said, even though all appearances and reason and precedent should be against it.

Now these things have not been written for Abraham's sake alone but also for us. The same principles apply exactly. There is however one important difference. In Abraham's case he believed that God *would* raise up life out of death. We are not asked to believe that God *will* do it, but that He *has done it*, by raising up Jesus our Lord from the dead. How much simpler to believe that He has done it, when He has done it, than to believe that He will do it, when as yet He has not done it. Bearing this in mind it is easy to see that as regards the texture or quality of faith we cannot hope to produce as fine an article as Abraham did.

Where however the case of Abraham is far surpassed is in the glorious facts that are presented to our faith, the glorious light in which God had made Himself known. Not now the God who will raise up an Isaac, but the God who has raised up Jesus our Lord from the dead. Christ, who was delivered for our offences and was raised again for our justification, is presented as the Object of our faith. And by Him we believe in God.

It is possible of course to believe on Him that raised up the Lord Jesus, without at all realizing what is involved in this wonderful fact. The last verse of the chapter states what is involved in it. Let us pay great attention to it, and so make sure that we take it in. Twice in the verse does the word "our" occur. That word signifies believers, and believers only.

Jesus our Lord has died. But He did not die for Himself, but for us. Our offences were in view. He was the Substitute, and assuming all the liabilities incurred, He was delivered up to judgment and death on their account.

He has been raised again by the act of God. But it is equally true that His resurrection was not simply a personal matter, and on His own account. We still view Him as standing on our behalf, as our Representative. He was raised representatively for us. God raised Him with our justification in view. His resurrection was most certainly *His own personal vindication* in the face of the hostile verdict of the world. Equally certainly it was *our justification* in the face of all the offences, which apart from His death were lying to our account.

His death was the complete discharge of all our dread account. His resurrection is the receipt that all is paid, the God-given declaration and proof that we are completely cleared. Now justification is just that—a complete clearance from all that which once lay against us. Being then justified by faith we have peace with God. We must read on from the end of chapter iv. into chapter v. without any break whatever.

CHAPTER 5

WE MAY USE the words, "justified by faith," in two senses. By simple faith in Christ, and in God who raised Him from the dead, we are justified, and this whether we have the happy assurance of it in our hearts or not. But then, in the second place, it is by faith that we know that we are justified. Not by feelings nor by visions or other subjective impressions, but by faith in God and in His Word.

As the result of our justification we have peace with God. Observe the distinction between this and what is stated in Colossians i. 20. Christ has made peace by the blood of His cross. Thereby He removed every disturbing element. This He did once for all, and because that work is done peace becomes the enjoyed portion of each who is justified by faith. We enter into it one by one. When Paul knew by faith that he was justified, peace with God was his. When I knew that I was justified peace was mine. When you knew, peace was yours. And until we did know peace was not ours. Instead of having peace with God we had doubts and fears, and probably plenty of them.

Peace stands first amongst the blessings of the Gospel. It heads the list but does not exhaust the list. Faith not only conducts us into peace but also gives us access into the grace or favour of God. We *are* in the favour of God. We know it and enter upon the enjoyment of it by faith. It is not stated here what the character of this favour is. We know, from Ephesians i. 6, that it is the favour of the Beloved. No favour could be higher and more intimate than that.

This favour is a present reality. We shall never be more in favour than we are now, though our enjoyment of it will be greatly increased in the day when our hope materializes. Our hope is not merely glory but the glory *of God*. Who would not rejoice with such a hope as that!

As to all the guilt of our past we are justified and at peace with God. As to the present we stand in divine favour. As to the future we rejoice in hope of the glory of God. But what about the difficulties and tribulations which bestrew our way to glory?

In these too we rejoice, wonderful to say: for the word translated "glory" in verse 3 is the same as that translated "rejoice" in the preceding verse. Paul is still setting before us the proper and normal effects of the Gospel in the hearts of those who receive it. The secret of our ability to rejoice in that, which naturally is so distasteful to us, is that we know what it is designed to work.

Tribulations are not in themselves pleasant but grievous, yet they help to set in motion a whole sequence of things which are most excellent and blessed—patience, experience, hope, the love of God shed abroad in our hearts by the Holy Spirit. Tribulations, to the believer, have become a set of spiritual gymnastics which greatly promote the development of his spiritual constitution. Instead of being against us they are turned into a source of profit. What a triumph of the grace of God this is!

Did you ever meet some dear old Christian who at once struck you as being full of calm endurance, very experienced, filled with hope in God, and irradiating love of a divine sort? Then you would find pretty surely

14

ROMANS

that such an one had gone through many a tribulation with God. Paul recognized this and hence he rejoiced in tribulation. If we see things in this light—which is the true light—we shall rejoice in them too.

You will notice that here, for the first time in this unfolding of the Gospel, the Holy Spirit is mentioned. The Apostle does not pause to tell us exactly *how* He is received. He only refers to the fact that He *is* given to believers, and that His happy work is the shedding abroad in our hearts of the love of God. Ephesians i. 13 shows us plainly that He is given when we have believed the Gospel of our salvation; and that of course is just the point to which we have been conducted at the beginning of Romans v. Very appropriately therefore the first mention of the Spirit comes in here.

Our hearts would be dark indeed were not the bright beams of the love of God shed abroad in them by the Holy Spirit. As it is they are bright indeed. Yet the light that shines into them has its source outside them. If we start searching our own hearts for the love, we make a great mistake; as great a mistake as if we tried searching the bright face of the moon to find the sun. True, moonlight is reflected sunlight—second-hand sunlight. Still the sun is not there. Just so all the light of the love of God which shines in the heart of a believer shines from the great sun which is outsiae himself. And that sun is the death of Christ.

In verses 6-8 therefore His death is again set before us; and this time as the final and never to be repeated expression of the love of God—a love which rises far above anything of which man is capable. God loved us when there was nothing about us to love, when we were without strength, ungodly and sinners, and even enemies, as verse 10 reminds us.

That death has brought us not only justification but reconciliation also. The guilt of our sins has been removed, and also the alienation which had existed between us and God. That being so a twofold salvation is bound to be ours.

A day of wrath is coming. Twice before in the epistle has this been intimated (i. 18; ii. 5). We shall be saved from that day through Christ. From other Scriptures we know that He will save us from it by taking us from the scene of wrath before the wrath bursts.

Again, being reconciled we shall be saved by His life. This is a salvation which we need continually, and shall need as long as we are in the world. He lives on high for us His people. When Moses went up the hill and interceded for Israel they were saved from their foes (See, Exod. xvii.). Just so are we saved by our Lord, who lives in the presence of God for us.

The Epistle opened by telling us that the Gospel is the power of God unto salvation to every one who believes. We now discover that when we speak of being saved we are using a word of very large meaning. It is not only true that we have been saved by belief of the Gospel, but also that we shall be saved from the spiritual dangers and conflicts of this present age, and from the wrath of the age to come.

15

In verses 9-11 we get not only salvation but also justification and reconciliation. These are words of greater definiteness and more limited meaning. There is no future aspect in connection with them. They are entirely present realities for the believer. "*Now* justified by His blood" (verse 9). "We have *now* received the reconciliation" (verse 11). We shall never be more justified than we are today. We shall never be more reconciled than we are today, though we shall presently have a keener enjoyment of the reconciliation which has been effected. But we shall be more fully saved than we are today, when in the age to come we are in glorified bodies like Christ.

Believing the Gospel, we receive the reconciliation today, and consequently are able to find our joy in God. Once we feared Him and shrank from His presence, as did Adam when he hid behind the trees of the Garden. Now we make our boast in Him and rejoice. And this is all God's own doing through our Lord Jesus Christ. What a triumph of grace it is!

Thus far the Gospel has been set before us in relation to our sins. Our actual offences have been in view, and we have discovered the way God has of justifying us from them and bringing us into His favour. There was more than this involved in our fallen condition however. There was what we may call the racial question.

For our racial head we have to go back to Adam, and to Adam in his *fallen* condition, for only when fallen did he beget sons and daughters. His fall came about by an act of sin, but that act induced a state or condition of sin which permeated his very being. Thereby his whole spiritual constitution was altered so fundamentally as to affect all his descendants. He could only beget children "in his own likeness, after his image" (Gen. v. 3)—the likeness and image of a fallen man. Heredity of this sort is a terrible fact, borne witness to by Scripture. Does God in the Gospel propose any remedy for this awful blight which lies upon the human race? Can He deal with the nature from which the acts of sin spring: with the root which produces the hideous fruits, as well as with the fruits themselves?

He can. Indeed, He has done so, and chapter v. from verse 12 onwards, unfolds to us the effects of what He has done. Just what He has done is not stated in so many words, though it is plainly inferred. The passage is admittedly a difficult one, and this is one element of its difficulty. Another element in its difficulty is that in several verses the translation is obscure, and even slightly defective. A third difficulty is that this side of matters is one that all too often is overlooked; and, where that has been the case, we plunge into unfamiliar waters and easily get out of our depth.

To begin with, notice that verses 13 to 17 are a parenthesis, and are printed as such, being enclosed in brackets. To get the sense we read on from verse 12 to verse 18, when at once we can see that the main drift of the passage is the contrast between one man who sinned, involving others in the results of his transgression, and Another who accomplished a righteousness, into the blessed effects of which others are brought. The whole passage emphasizes a tremendous contrast, a contrast which centres in Adam on the one hand and Christ on the other. If Adam stands at the head of a fallen race lying under death and condemnation, Christ is the Head of a new race standing in righteousness and life.

We may say then that what God has done is to raise up a new Head for men in the Lord Jesus Christ. Before He formally took the place of Head He accomplished perfect righteousness by obedience unto death. By virtue of His death and resurrection believers stand no longer connected with Adam but with Christ. They have been, so to speak, grafted into Christ. They are no longer in Adam but "in Christ." This is the underlying fact which the passage infers, whilst it elaborates the glorious consequences flowing therefrom.

Look again at verses 12, 18 and 19. Particularly scrutinize verse 18. If you have Darby's New Translation read it in that. You will see that the words inserted in italics in the Authorized Version can come out, and that the marginal reading is the better: also that the twice repeated word, "upon" should be rather, "towards." The contrast is between the one offence of Adam, the bearing of which was condemnation towards all men, and the one righteousness of Christ, completed in His death, the bearing of which is justification of life towards all men.

We ponder this quietly for a few moments, and then probably observe to ourselves that though all men have come under the condemnation not all by any means have come under the justification. Exactly, for this verse only states the general bearing of the respective acts, and it is true that, as far as God's intention in the death of Christ is concerned, His death is for all. The next verse goes on to the realized effects of the respective acts, and only many—or more accurately, "the many"—are in view.

By "the many" we understand those, and only those, who are under the respective headships. In Adam's case "the many" does of course cover all men, for by nature we are all of his race. In the case of Christ not all men are of His race, but only all believers. All men were constituted sinners by Adam's disobedience. All believers are constituted righteous by Christ's obedience, even unto death.

So in the three verses we are considering we have this sequence. On the one hand, one man Adam, one offence, all men constituted sinners, all sinning, consequently death and condemnation upon all. On the other hand, one Man Christ, one righteousness in obedience unto death, those under His headship constituted righteous in justification of life.

Now observe the five verses included in the parenthesis. The first two of these meet a difficulty that might arise in the minds of those very familiar with the law. Adam sinned against a definite commandment, hence his sin was a transgression. After that some 2,500 years had to roll away before the law of Moses was given, when once more transgression became possible. Between those points there was no transgression, for there was no law to transgress. Yet there was sin universally, as proved by the universal reign of death. The practical difference lay here, that sin is not "imputed" when there is no law: that is it is not put to our account in the same way. Only those who have known the law will be judged by the law, as we saw when reading chapter ii.

This being admitted, it is still true that sin and death have reigned universally. All Adam's posterity are involved in his fall. This being so, the contrast between Adam and Christ is worked out in verses 15 to 17. Each verse takes up a different detail, but the general point is stated at the beginning of verse 15; viz., the free gift through Christ in no sense falls short of the offence through Adam, indeed it goes beyond it.

In verse 15 the word many occurs twice just as we noticed it does in verse 19. In this verse too it is more accurately, "the many," that is, those who come under the respective headships. Adam brought in death upon all those under his headship, which as a matter of fact means all men without exception. Jesus Christ has brought in the grace of God and the free gift of grace to the many who are under Him; that is, to all believers.

Verse 16 brings in the contrast between condemnation and justification. In this connection the gift surpasses the sin. The condemnation was brought in by one sin. The justification has been triumphantly wrought out by grace in the teeth of many offences.

A further contrast confronts us in verse 17. The condemnation and justification of the previous verse are what we may call the immediate effects. Immediately anyone comes under Adam he comes under condemnation. Immediately anyone comes under Christ he comes into justification. But what are the ultimate effects? The ultimate effect of Adam's sin was to establish a universal reign of death over his posterity. The ultimate effect of Christ's work of righteousness is to bring in for all who are His abundance of grace, and righteousness as a free gift, so that they may reign in life. Not only is life going to reign but we are going to reign in life. A most astounding thing surely! No wonder that the free gift is stated to go beyond the offence.

Verses 20 and 21 recapitulate and sum up what we have just seen. The law was brought in to make man's sin fully manifest. Sin was there all the time but when the law was given sin became very visible as positive transgression, and offence, definitely put down to man's account, abounded. The law was followed, after a due interval, by the grace which reached us in Christ. We can discern therefore three stages. First, the age before the law when there was sin though no transgression. Second, the age of law when sin abounded, rising to Himalayan heights. Third, the incoming of grace through Christ—grace which has risen up like a mighty flood overtopping the mountains of man's sins.

In the Gospel grace not only super-abounds, but it reigns. We who have believed have come under the benign sway of grace, a grace which reigns through righteousness, inasmuch as the cross was pre-eminently a work of righteousness. And the glorious end and consummation of the story is eternal life. Here the boundless vista of eternity begins to open out before us. We see the river of grace. We see the channel of righteousness, cut by the work of the cross, in which it flows. We see finally the boundless ocean of eternal life, into which it flows.

And all is "by Jesus Christ our Lord." All has been wrought by Him. He is the Head under whom, as believers, we stand, and consequently the Fountain-head from whom all these things flow to us. It is because we are in His life that all these things are ours. Our justification is a justification of life, for in Christ we have a life which is beyond all possibility of condemnation—a life in which we are cleared not only from all our offences, but also from the state of sin in which we formerly lay as connected with Adam.

CHAPTER 6

THAT WHICH WE have thus far learned of the Gospel from this epistle has been a question of what God has declared Himself to be on our behalf, that which He has wrought for us by the death and resurrection of Christ, and which we receive in simple faith. In it all God has been having, if we may so say, *His say* toward us in blessing. Chapter vi. opens with the pertinent question, "What shall *we say* then?"

This signalizes the fact that another line of thought is now about to open before us. Nothing can exceed the wonder of what God has wrought on our behalf, but what are we in consequence thereof going to be for Him? What is to be the believer's response to the amazing grace that has been shown? Is there through the Gospel the bringing in of a power which will enable the believer's response to be one worthy of God? As we open chapter vi. we begin to investigate these questions and to discover the way in which the Gospel sets us free to spend lives of practical righteousness and holiness.

If men attain a merely head knowledge of the grace of God, their hearts remaining unaffected, they may easily turn grace into licence and say, "Well, if God's grace can abound over our sin, let us go on sinning that grace may go on abounding." Does the Gospel in any way countenance such sentiments? Not for one moment. The very reverse. It tells us plainly that we are dead to sin. How then can we still live in it? Once we were terribly alive to sin. Everything that had to do with our own lawless wills— with pleasing ourselves, in other words—we were keenly set on, whilst remaining absolutely dead to God and His things. Now an absolute reversal has taken place and we are dead to the sin to which formerly we were alive, and alive to the things to which formerly we were dead.

Have we been ignorant as to this, or only dimly conscious of it? It should not have been so, for the fact is plainly set forth in Christian baptism, a rite which lies at the threshold of things. Do we know, or do we not know, what our baptism means?

There is perhaps a previous question which ought to be raised. It is this, Have you been baptised? We ask it because there seems to be in some quarters distinct carelessness as to this matter, engendered we suspect by the over-emphasis placed on it in former days. If we neglect it we do so to our very distinct loss. In baptism we are buried with Christ, as verse 4 states, and not to have been buried with Him is a calamity. Moreover, if not amongst "so many of us as were baptised" the Apostle's argument in verses 4 and 5 loses its force as far as we are concerned.

What then is the significance of baptism? It means identification with Christ in His death. It means that we are buried with Him, and that the obligation is placed upon us to walk in newness of life, even as He was raised up into a new order of things. This is its meaning and this the obligation it imposes, and our loss is great if we know it not. We greatly fear that the tremendous controversies which have raged over the manner and the mode and the subjects of baptism have led many to overlook entirely its *meaning*. Argumentations about baptism have been carried on in a very unbaptised way, so that no one would have thought the contestants "dead to sin."

Baptism is however a rite, an outward sign. It accomplishes nothing vital, and alas, millions of baptised persons will find themselves in a lost eternity. It points however to that which is vital in the fullest sense, even the Cross, as we shall see.

Let us notice the closing words of verse 4, "newness of life," for they give a concise answer to the question with which the chapter opened. Instead of continuing in sin, which is in effect continuing to live the old life, we are to walk in a life which is new. As we go through the chapter we discover what the character of that new life is.

Our baptism was our burial with Christ—in figure. It was "the likeness of His death," and in it we were identified with Him; for that is what the rather obscure expression, "planted together" means. We submitted to it in the confidence that we are to be identified with Him in His risen life. The newness of life in which we are to walk is in fact connected with the life of resurrection in which Christ is today.

In verse 3 we were to know the meaning of our baptism; now in verse 6 we are called upon to know the meaning of the cross in relation to "our old man," and "the body of sin." The cross is that which lies behind baptism, and without which baptism would lose its meaning.

We have already had before us the death of Christ in its bearing upon our sins and their forgiveness. Here we have its bearing upon our sinful nature, whence have sprung all the sins that ever we committed.

It is not perhaps easy to seize the thought conveyed by "our old man." We may explain it by saying that the Apostle is here personifying all that we are as the natural children of Adam. If you could imagine a person whose character embraced all the ugly features that have ever been displayed in all the members of Adam's race, that person might be described as, "our old man."

All that we were as children of fallen Adam has been crucified with Christ, and we are to know this. It is not a mere notion but an actual fact. It was an act of God, accomplished in the cross of Christ: as much an act of God, and as real, as the putting away of our sins, accomplished at the same time. We are to know it by faith, just as we know that our sins are forgiven. When we do know it by faith certain other results follow. But we begin by knowing it in simple faith.

What God had in view in the crucifixion of our old man was that "the body of sin" might be "destroyed," or rather, "annulled," so that henceforth we might not serve sin. This again is a statement not easy to understand. We must recall that sin formerly dominated us in our bodies, which in consequence were in a very terrible sense bodies of sin. Now it is not that our literal bodies have been annulled, but that sin, which in its fulness dominated our bodies, has been, and thus we are freed from its power. It has been annulled by the crucifixion of our old man, the result of our identification with Christ in His death, so that His death was ours also.

Take note of the closing words of verse 6. They give us quite clearly the light in which sin is viewed in this chapter. Sin is a master, a slave-owner, and we had fallen under its power. The point discussed in the chapter is not the presence of sin *in us* but the power of sin *over us*. We have got our discharge from sin. We are justified from it, as verse 7 states.

Our discharge has been effected by the death of Christ. But it is very important to maintain the connection between His death and His resurrection. We saw this when considering the last verse of chapter iv., and we see it again here. Our *death* with Christ is in view of our *living* with Him in the life of the resurrection world.

We get the word *know* for the third time in verse 9. We should know the meaning of baptism. We should know the bearing of the death of Christ as relating to our old man. Thirdly we should know the bearing of the resurrection of Christ. His resurrection was not a mere resuscitation. It was not like the raising of Lazarus—a coming back to life in this world for a certain number of years, after which death again supervenes. When He arose He left death behind Him for ever, entering another order of things, which for convenience sake we call the resurrection world. For a brief moment death had dominion over Him, and that only by His own act in subjecting Himself to it. Now He is beyond it for ever.

His death was a death unto sin once and for ever. It is sin here, you notice, and not sins; the root principle which had permeated our nature and assumed the mastery of us, and not the actual offences which were its product. Moreover, it is not death *for* sins but *unto* sin. Sin never had to say to Him in His nature as it had with us. But He had to say to it, when in His sacrifice He took up the whole question of sin as it affected the glory of God in His ruined creation, and as it affected us, standing as a mighty barrier against our blessing. Having had to say to it, bearing its judgment, He has died to it, and now He lives to God.

Let us pause and test ourselves as to these things. Do we really know this? Do we really understand the death and resurrection of Christ in this light? Do we realize how completely our Lord has died out of that old order of things dominated by sin, into which once He came in grace to accomplish redemption; and how fully He lives to God in that new world into which He has entered? It is important that we should realize all this, because verse 11 proceeds to instruct us that we should *reckon* according to what we *know*.

If we do not know rightly, we cannot reckon correctly. No tradesman will rightly reckon up his books if he does not know the multiplication tables. No skipper can rightly reckon the position of his vessel if he does not know the principles of navigation. Just so no believer is going to rightly reckon out his position and attitude either in regard to sin or to God, if he does not know the bearing of the death and resurrection of Christ upon his case.

When once we *do* know, the reckoning enjoined in verse 11 becomes perfectly plain to us. Our case is governed by Christ's, for we are identified with Him. Did He die to sin? Then we are dead to sin, and so we reckon it. Does He now live to God? Then we now live to God, and so we reckon it. Our reckoning is not mere make-believe. It is not that we try to reckon ourselves to be what in point of fact we are not. The very reverse. We are dead to sin and alive to God by His own acts, accomplished in the death and resurrection of Christ (to be made effectual in us by His Spirit, as we shall see later on) and that being so, we are to accept it and adjust our thoughts to it. As things *are*, so we are to reckon.

Before we were converted we were dead to God and alive to sin. We had no interest in anything that had to do with God. We did not understand His things; they left us cold and dead. When however it was a question of anything that appealed to our natural desires, of anything that fed our vanity and self-love, then we were all alive with interest. Now by the grace of God the situation is exactly reversed as the fruit of our being in Christ Jesus.

Having adjusted our reckoning, in accordance with the facts concerning the death and resurrection of Christ which we know, there yet remains a further step. We are to *yield* ourselves to God in order that His will may be practically worked out in detail in our lives. The word yield, occurs, you will notice, five times in the latter part of the chapter.

Being dead to sin it is quite obvious that the obligation rests upon us to refuse sin any rights over us. Formerly it did reign in our mortal bodies and we were continually obeying it in its various lusts. This is to be so no

22

longer, as verse 12 tells us. We have died to sin, the old master, and its claim upon us has ceased. Being alive from the dead, we belong to God, and we gladly acknowledge His claims over us. We yield ourselves to Him.

This yielding is a very practical thing, as verse 13 makes plain. It affects all the members of our bodies. Formerly every member was in some way enlisted in the service of sin and so became an instrument of unrighteousness. Is it not a wonderful thing that every member may now be enlisted in the service of God? Our feet may run His errands. Our hands may do His work. Our tongues may speak forth His praise. In order that this may be so we are to yield ourselves unto God.

The word, yield, occurs twice in this verse, but the verb is in two different tenses. A Greek scholar has commented upon them to this effect:—that in the first case the verb is in the present in its continuous sense. "Neither yield your members." It is at no time to be done. In the second case the tense is different. "Yield yourselves to God." Let it have been done, as a once accomplished act.

Let us each solemnly ask ourselves if indeed we have done it as a once accomplished act. Have we thus definitely yielded ourselves and our members to God, for His will? If so, let us see to it that at no time do we forget our allegiance and fall into the snare of yielding our members even for a moment to unrighteousness, for the outcome of that is sin.

Sin, then, is not to have dominion over us, for the very reason that we are not under the law but under grace. Here is the divine answer to those who tell us that if we tell people that they are no longer under the regime of law, they are sure to plunge into sin. The fact is that nothing so subdues the heart and promotes holiness as the grace of God.

Verse 15 bears witness to the fact that there have always been people who think that the only way to promote holiness is to keep us under the tight bondage of law. There were such in Paul's day. He anticipates their objection by repeating in substance the question with which he opened the chapter. In reply to it he restates the position in a more extended way. Verses 16 to 23 are an extension and amplification of what he had just stated in verses 12 to 14.

He appeals to that practical knowledge which is common to us all. We all know that if we yield obedience to anyone, though not nominally their servant we *are* their servant practically. That is the case also in spiritual things, whether it be serving sin or God. Judged by this standard, we were without a question once the slaves of sin. But when the Gospel "form of doctrine" reached us we obeyed it, thanks be to God! As a result we have been emancipated from the thraldom of sin, and have become servants of God and righteousness. Well then, being now servants of righteousness, we are to yield our members in detail so that God may have His way with us.

This yielding then is a tremendously important business. It is that to which our knowledge and our reckoning lead up. If we stop short of it our knowledge and our reckoning become of no effect. Here doubtless we have the reason of so much that is feeble and ineffectual with Christians who are well instructed in the theory of the thing. They stop short at yielding themselves and their members to God. Oh, let us see to it that if as yet we have never had it done, as a once accomplished act, we have it done at once! Having it done we shall need and find grace for the continuous yielding of our members in the service of God.

All this supposes that the old master, sin, is still within us, only waiting for opportunities to assert itself. This makes the triumph of grace all the greater. It also increases to us the value of the lessons we learn. We learn how to yield our members servants to righteousness unto holiness, even while sin is lurking within, eager to reassert itself. In serving righteousness we serve God, for to do the will of God is the first element of righteousness. And righteousness in all our dealings leads to holiness of life and character.

Instead, then, of continuing in sin, as those enslaved by its power, we are set free from it by being brought under the sway of God. Twice do we get the words, "made free from sin" (verses 18 and 22). Formerly we were "free from righteousness." We have escaped the old power and come under the new. This is the way of holiness and life.

Everlasting life is here viewed as the end of the wonderful story. In the writings of the Apostle John we find it presented as a present possession of the believer. There is no conflict between these two views of it. That which is ours now in its essence, will be ours in its full expanse when eternity is reached.

The last verse of our chapter, so well known, gives us a concise summary of the matter. We cannot serve sin without receiving its wages, which is death. Death is a word of large meaning. In one sense death came in upon man when by sin he was utterly separated from God. The death of the body occurs when it is separated from the spiritual part of man. The second death is when lost men are finally separated from God. The full wages of sin includes death in all three senses.

In connection with God no wages are spoken of. All is gift. The very life in which we can serve Him is His own gift through Jesus Christ our Lord. Thus at the end of the chapter we come back to the thought with which the previous chapter closed. We may well make our boast in the eternal life which is ours by God's free gift, and heartily embrace all the consequences to which it leads.

CHAPTER 7

THE OPENING WORDS of chapter vii. direct our minds back to the 14th and 15th verses of the previous chapter, where the apostle had plainly stated that the believer is not under law but under grace. A tremendous controversy had raged around this point, to which the Acts bears witness—especially chapter xv.

That point was authoritatively settled at Jerusalem as regards the Gentile believers. They were not to be put under the law. But was the point as clear when Jewish believers were in question?

It was evidently by no means clear to the Jewish believers themselves. Acts xxi. 20, proves this. It was very necessary therefore that Paul should make the matter abundantly plain and definite; hence his recurring to the theme as he opens this chapter. The words enclosed in brackets in verse 1 show that he is now specially addressing himself to his Jewish brethren. They alone *knew* the law, in the proper sense of the term. Gentiles might know something about it as observers from without: Israel knew it from within, as having been put under it. This remark of Paul's furnishes us with an important key to the chapter, indicating the point from which things are viewed.

The first six verses of this chapter are doctrinal in nature, showing the way by which the believer is delivered from the bondage of law and brought into connection with Christ. From verse 7 onwards, we have a passage which is highly experimental. The actions of the law, on the heart and conscience of one who fears God, are detailed. We are given an insight into the experimental workings of law which ultimately prepare the believer for the experience of the deliverance found in Christ and in the Spirit of God. It is a remarkable fact that in all chapter vii. there is not one mention of the Holy Spirit; whereas in chapter viii. there is probably more mention of Him than in any other chapter of the Bible.

The Apostle's starting point is the well known fact that law extends its sway over a man as long as he lives. Death, and death only, terminates its dominion. This is seen very clearly in connection with the divine law of marriage, as stated in verses 2 and 3.

The same principle applies in spiritual things, as verse 4 states, though it does not apply in exactly the same way. The law is in the position of husband and we who believe are in the position of wife. Yet it is not that death has come in upon the law, but that *we have died*. Verse 4 is quite plain as to this. Verse 6 appears to say that the law has died, only here the correct reading is found in the margin of reference Bibles. It is not, "that being dead . . . ," but rather, "being dead to that . . ." The two verses quite agree.

We have become dead to the law "by the body of Christ." This at first sight seems somewhat obscure. Paul refers, we believe, to that which was involved in our Lord taking the body prepared for Him, and thereby becoming a Man. He took that body with a view to *suffering death*, and hence the body of Christ is used as signifying His death. It is the same figure of speech as we have in Colossians i. 22., where we are said to be reconciled "in the body of His flesh, *through death*."

We have died from under law's dominion in the death of Christ. In this way our connection with the first husband has ceased. But all is in view of our entering into a new connection under the risen Christ. Every Jew found the old husband—the law—very stern and unbending, a wife-beater in fact; though they had to admit they richly deserved all they got. We, Gentiles, can hardly imagine how great the relief when the converted Jew discovered that he was now under Christ and not under law. "Married" to Christ, risen from the dead, the standard set was higher than it ever was under law, but now an unbounded supply flowed from Him of the grace and power needed, and hence fruit for God became a possibility. As Husband, Christ is the Fountain-head of all support, guidance, comfort and power.

How striking the contrast which verse 5 presents! Indeed the verse itself is very striking for it names four things that go together:—flesh, law, sins, death. Of old the law was imposed upon a people "in the flesh." In result it simply stirred into action the sin which ever lies latent in the flesh. Consequently the "motions" or "passions" of sins were aroused and death followed as God's judgment upon all. "Flesh" here is not our bodies, but the fallen nature which has its seat in our present bodies. Every unconverted person is "in the flesh;" that is, the flesh dominates them and characterizes their state. But you notice that for believers that state has passed away. The Apostle says "*when we were* in the flesh."

Another contrast confronts us when we turn to verse 6. "*when we were . . . But now.*" Having died with Christ, we are not only dead to sin, as chapter vi. enforces, but dead also to the law and therefore delivered from it. Consequently we can now serve God in an entirely new way. We not only do new things, but we do those new things in a new spirit. In the previous chapter we read of "newness of life." (verse 4.) Now we read of "newness of spirit."

We read of people in Old Testament days who turned from lives of recklessness and sin to the fear of God—Manasseh, King of Judah, for instance, as recorded in 2 Chronicles xxxiii. 11-19. It might perhaps be said of him that he walked in newness of life during the last years of his reign. Yet he could only serve God according to the principles and ways of the law-system under which he was. It was impossible for newness of *spirit* to mark him. If we want to see service in newness of spirit we must turn to a converted Jew of this present period of grace. He may once have done his best to serve God in the spirit of strict law-keeping. Now he discovers himself to be a son and heir of God in Christ Jesus, and he serves in the spirit of a son with a father—a spirit which is altogether new.

An employer may set two men to a certain task, one of them being his own son. If the young man in any degree realizes the relationship in which he stands he will set about the work in a spirit altogether different to that of a hired servant. Our illustration would perhaps have been even nearer the mark had we supposed the case of a wife serving her husband's interests. Delivered from the law by death, the death of Christ, we are linked with the risen Christ in order to fruitfully serve God in a spirit that is new.

Teaching such as this most evidently brings Christ into prominence and puts the law into the shade. Does it in any way cast an aspersion on the law? Does it even infer that there was something wrong with *it*? This point is taken up in verses 7 to 13, and it is made abundantly clear that the law was perfect as far as it went. The mischief was not with the law but with the sin which rose up against the law, finding in the law indeed that which provoked it, and also that which condemned it.

Verse 7 tells us how the law exposed and condemned sin. Before the law came we sinned but did not realize what sinners we were. Directly the law spoke we discovered the true state of the case. Just as a plumbline reveals the crookedness of a tottering wall, so the law exposed us.

Yet it was sin and not law that wrought the mischief, as verse 8 states; though sin somewhat camouflaged itself by springing into activity directly it was confronted with the definite prohibition of the law. The very fact that we were told not to do a thing provoked us to do it!

As a matter of fact then the law affected us in two ways. First, it stirred up sin into action. It drew a line and forbade us to step over it. Sin promptly stirred us up to transgress by stepping over it. Second, in the presence of this transgression the law solemnly pronounced the death sentence upon us. True, the law set *life* before us; saying, "This do, and thou shalt live." Yet in point of fact all it ever did in regard to us was to condemn us to *death*, as failing utterly to do what it commanded. These two results of the law are tersely stated at the end of verse 9:—"Sin revived, and I died."

This being the state of the case, no blame of any kind attaches itself to the law, which is "holy, and just, and good." Sin, not the law, is the culprit. Sin worked death, though it was by the law that the sentence of death was pronounced. Sin indeed was working before ever the law was given, but directly it was given sin had no excuse and its defiance became outrageous. Sin by the commandment coming became *exceeding sinful*, as verse 13 tells us.

We have now got to a part of the chapter where the Apostle speaks in the first person singular. In verses 5 and 6 it was "we . . . we . . . we . . ." after the question with which verse 7 opens it is all "I . . . I . . . me . . . I . . ." This is because he now speaks *experimentally*, and when experience is in question each must speak for himself.

The opening words of verse 14 may seem to be an exception to what we have just said but they are not. It is a *fact* that the law is spiritual, and not a mere matter of experience—and it is stated as a fact which we know. In contrast with it stands what "I am," and this has to be learned as a matter of sad experience, "carnal, sold under sin."

How do we learn what we are? Why, by making a genuine effort to conform to the spiritual demand which the law makes. The more earnest we are about it the more effectively is the lesson burned into our souls. We learn our sinfulness in trying to be good!

Let us recall what we learned in chapter vi. for there we were shown the way. Realizing by faith that we are identified with Christ in His death we understand that we are to reckon ourselves dead to sin and alive to God, and consequently we are to yield ourselves and our members to God for His will and pleasure. Our souls fully assent to this as right and proper, and we say to ourselves, with considerable enthusiasm perhaps, "Exactly! that is what I am going to do."

We essay to do it, and lo! we receive a very disagreeable shock. Our intentions are of the best but we somehow are without power to put these things into practice. We see the good and approve it in our minds, yet we fail to do it. We recognize the evil of which we disapprove, and yet we are ensnared by it. A very distressing and humiliating state of affairs, which we find stated in verse 19.

In verses 14 to 23 we get "I" no less than 24 times. "Me" and "my" occur 10 times. The speaker evidently describes an experience, during which he was simply swamped in self-occupation. All his thoughts were turned in upon himself. This is not surprising for this is exactly the normal effect of the law upon an awakened and conscientious soul. As we examine those verses, we can see that the exercises recorded resulted in valuable discoveries.

1. He discovered by experience the good and holy character of the law. It *is* good as verse 9 states; but he now has to say "*I consent* unto the law that *it is good*."

2. He discovered by experience his own fallen state: not only "carnal" but "sold under sin." Anyone who has to confess that he is so overpowered to be compelled to avoid what he wishes and practice what he hates, and so be in the humiliating position of continually disowning his own actions (verse 15) is indeed *enslaved*. We are like slaves sold in the market to a tyrannical master:—*sold under sin*.

3. Yet he learns to distinguish between what has been wrought in him by God—what we call "the new nature"—and the flesh which is the old nature. Verse 17 shews this. He recognizes that there is his true "I" connected with the new nature, and an "I" or a "me" which he has to repudiate, as being the old nature.

4. He learns by experience the true character of that old nature. If it be a question of "me," that is, "the flesh" (here you see, it is the old "me" that he has to repudiate) in that no good is found, as verse 18 tells us. *Good* simply is *not there*. So it is useless searching for it. Have some of us

spent weary months, or even years, looking for good in a place where it is non-existent?

5. He learns further that though he is now possessed of a new nature, an "inward man" (verse 22) yet that *in itself* bestows no strength upon him. The inward man may delight in God's holy law; his mind may consent to the law that it is good, but all the same there is a more powerful force working in his members that enslaves him.

What a heart breaking state of affairs! Some of us have known it bitterly enough. Others of us have a taste of it now. And if any as yet have not known it they may well be alarmed, for it at once raises a question as to *whether they are as yet possessed of a new nature*. If there is nothing but the old nature, struggles and exercises such as these must in the nature of things be unknown.

Such exercises are of great value as preparing the soul for the gladness of *a divinely wrought deliverance*.

As we draw near to the end of chapter vii. it is important for us to notice that in this passage the word *law* is used in two senses. In the great majority of instances it refers of course to the law of God formulated through Moses. In verses 2 and 3 however we get "the law" of a husband; in verse 21, "a law"; in verses 23 and 25, "another law," "the law of my mind," and "the law of sin." In these cases the word is evidently used to signify a power or force which acts uniformly in a given direction: in just the sense in which we use the word when we talk of "the laws of nature."

If then we read again the above verses, substituting the words, "controlling force" for the word, "law," we may gain a somewhat clearer view of what the Apostle is saying. Take verse 23. The controlling force with each of us should be our minds: our bodies should be held in the subject place. This should be so in a very special way with those whose minds have been renewed by the power of God. But there is sin to be reckoned with, which exerts its controlling force in our members. The terrible fact has to be faced by us, and experimentally learned, that if left to ourselves, sin proves itself the stronger force, assumes control and we are held in captivity.

No wonder the Apostle in the remembrance of it cries out in anguish, "O wretched man that I am!" We too know something of this wretchedness, surely. Have we never felt ourselves to be like a wretched seagull bedraggled from head to tail with filthy oil discharged from passing motor-ships? The law of its mind, the law of air both without and within its feathers, is totally overcome by the horrid law of sticky oil! And who shall deliver it? It has no power in itself. Unless someone captures and cleanses it, it must die.

Verse 24 contains not only the agonized exclamation but also that important question, "Who shall deliver me?" The form of the question is important. Earlier in the story, when the speaker was passing through the experiences detailed in verses 14 to 19 for instance, his question would have been, "How shall I deliver myself?" He was still searching for something *within* himself which would accomplish it, but searching in vain. Now he is beginning to look *outside* himself for a deliverer.

When not only our self-confidence but our self-hope also is shattered, we have taken a big step forward. We inevitably then begin to look outside ourselves. At first perhaps we only look for *help*, and consequently look in wrong directions. Yet sooner or later we discover it is not help that we need, but rather a positive *deliverance* by a power that is not of ourselves at all. Then, very soon, we find the answer to our cry. Deliverance is ours through Jesus Christ our Lord, thanks be to God! He is as able to deliver us from the slavery of sin as He is from the guilt of our sins.

CHAPTER 8

BUT HOW DOES this deliverance work? How is it accomplished? We find an answer to these questions when we commence to read chapter viii. At the end of chapter vii. the law of sin and death proved itself far more powerful than the law of the renewed mind. In the opening of chapter viii. the law of the Spirit, who is now given to the believer, proves itself far more powerful than the law of sin and death. The Apostle can exultingly say, It has "made me free."

Not only have we life in Christ Jesus but the Spirit of that life has been given to us. Thereby a new force enters our lives. Coming under the controlling power of the Spirit of God we are released from the controlling power of sin and death. The greater law overrides the lesser.

The point may be illustrated by many happenings in the natural world which surrounds us. Here, for instance, is a piece of iron. It lies motionless upon the ground, held to the spot by the law of gravitation. An electric magnet is placed above it and the current is switched on. Instantly it flies upward, as though suddenly possessed of wings. A new controlling power has come on the scene which, under certain conditions and in a limited sphere, has proved itself stronger than the power of gravitation.

The Holy Spirit has been given to us that He may control us, not that we may control Him. How does He exert His influence? He works within the believer, but it is in connection with an attractive Object without— Christ Jesus our Lord. He is here not to speak of Himself or to glorify Himself, but to glorify Christ. He indwells us, not that He may foster the old life, the life of the first Adam; the life of which He is the Spirit is the life of Christ, the last Adam. We are "in Christ Jesus," as the first verse shows, and we are that without any qualification whatever, for the words which close the verse in our Authorized Version should not be there, having evidently crept in from verse 4, where they rightly occur.

There is nothing to condemn in Christ Jesus, and nothing to condemn for those in Christ Jesus. The reason for this is two-fold. Verses 2 and 3 each supply a reason, both beginning with "for." Verse 2 gives the practical or experimental reason. The believer under the control of the Spirit is set free from the control of that which formerly brought the condemnation in. Being a statement of a liberty which has to be experimentally realized the Apostle speaks still in a personal and individual way—"hath made *me* free."

Verse 3, on the contrary, is a statement of what has been accomplished by God in a judicial way at the cross of Christ. The law had been proved to be weak through the flesh, though in itself holy and just and good. It was like a skilful sculptor set to the task of carving an enduring monument —some thing of beauty intended to be a joy for ever—out of a great heap of dirty mud. A heart-breaking, a hopeless task, not because of any defect in the sculptor but because of the utterly defective material with which he had to deal. The law could condemn the sinner, but it could not so condemn sin in the flesh that men might be delivered from servitude to sin and, walking after the Spirit, be found fulfilling what the law had righteously required.

But what the law could not do God has done. He sent forth His own Son, who came in the likeness of sinful flesh—only in the *likeness* of it, be it noted, for though perfectly a Man He was a perfect Man, without the slightest taint of sin. God sent Him "for sin," that is, as a sacrifice for sin; so that in His death sin in the flesh might be condemned. Sin is the root principle of all that is wrong with man; and the flesh is that in man which furnishes sin with a vehicle in which to act, just as the electricity generated in a power station finds a vehicle for its transmission and action in the wires that are carried aloft.

We know that sin had its primary origin in the heavens. It began with Satan and the fallen angels, yet Christ did not come to die for angels and consequently it was not sin in the nature of angels which was condemned. He died for men, and it was sin in the flesh that was condemned. It was *condemned*, you notice, not forgiven. God does indeed forgive sins, which spring forth as the fruits of sin in the flesh; but sin—the root principle— and the flesh—the nature in which sin works—are not forgiven but unsparingly condemned. God has condemned it in the cross of Christ. We must learn to condemn it in our experience.

We are to judge as God judges. We are to see things as He sees them. If sin and the flesh lie under His condemnation then they are to lie under our condemnation. Sin and the flesh being judged in the cross, the Holy Spirit has been given to us that He may energize the new life that is ours. If we walk in the Spirit then all our activities, both mental and bodily, will be under His control, and as a consequence we shall be found doing what the law requires.

Herein, of course, is a marvellous thing. When under the law and in the flesh we were struggling to fulfil the law's demands and continually failing. Now that we are delivered from the law, now that we are in Christ Jesus and indwelt by the Spirit of God, there is a power which can enable us to

31

fulfil it. And as we do walk in the Spirit and not in the flesh, and according to the measure in which we so walk, we do actually fulfil what the law has so rightly demanded of us. This is a great triumph of the grace of God. As a matter of fact though, the triumph may be even greater, for it is possible for the Christian "so to walk even as He [Christ] walked" (1 John ii. 6). And the "walk" of Christ went far beyond anything that the law demanded.

We may sum up these things by saying that the Christian—according to the thoughts of God—is not only forgiven, justified, reconciled, with the Spirit shedding abroad in his heart the love of God; but also he sees the divine condemnation of sin and the flesh in the Cross, he finds that his own vital links before God are not with Adam fallen but with Christ risen. Consequently he is in Christ Jesus, with the Spirit indwelling him, in order that, controlling him and filling him with Christ, as an Object bright and fair before his eyes, he may walk in happy deliverance from the power of sin and be gladly fulfilling the will of God.

Nothing less than this is what the Gospel proposes. What do we think of it? We pronounce it magnificent. We declare the whole scheme to be a conception worthy of the mind and heart of God. Then our consciences begin to prick us, reminding us how little these wonderful possibilities have been translated into actualities in our daily experience.

The Apostle Paul, you notice, did not lay down his pen nor turn aside to another theme when he had written verse 4. There is more to be said that may help us to gain a real and experimental entrance into this blessed deliverance so that we may be living out the life of Christ in the energy of the Spirit of God. Verses 5 to 13 continue taking things up from a very practical standpoint.

Two classes are considered. Those "after" or "according to" the flesh and those according to the Spirit. The former mind the things of the flesh: the latter the things of the Spirit. The mind of the flesh is death: the mind of the Spirit life and peace. The two classes are in complete contrast, whether as to nature, character or end. They move in two totally disconnected spheres. The Apostle is of course speaking abstractly. He is viewing the whole position according to the inward nature of things, and not thinking of particular individuals or their varying experiences.

We may very rightly raise the question of our own experiences. If we do, what have we to say? We have to confess that though we are not after the flesh yet we have the flesh still in us. Hence it is possible for us to turn aside from that minding the things of the Spirit, to mind the things of the flesh. And, in so far as we do, we come into contact with death rather than life and peace. But let us make no mistake about it; if we go in for the things of the flesh, we are not seeking things which are properly characteristic of the Christian, but rather wholly abnormal and improper.

The things of the flesh appeal to the mind of the flesh, and *that* is simple enmity against God. This saying which occurs in verse 7 may seem hard, but it is true, for the flesh is essentially lawless. Not only is it not subject but it cannot be. Do we believe that? Let the flesh be educated, refined, religionized; let it be starved, flogged, restrained; it is just the old flesh still. The only thing to do with it is to condemn it and set it aside, and this is just what God has done, as stated in verse 3. May we have wisdom and grace to do likewise.

It is clear that since the mind of the flesh is simply enmity against God, those "in the flesh" cannot please Him. If we would see a complete contrast with this we must turn to 1 John iii. 9. There we find that the one born of God "cannot sin." All who are not born of God are in the flesh; that is, their state is characterized by the flesh and nothing else. There is no new nature with them, and hence the flesh is the source of all their thinkings and doings, and all is displeasing to God. The one who is born of God partakes of the nature of Him of whom he is born.

But not only is the believer born of God, he is also indwelt by the Spirit of God, who seals him as Christ's. This great reality entirely alters his state. Now he is no longer in the flesh but in the Spirit; that is, his state is characterized by the presence and power of the Spirit of God, who is also called in verse 9 the Spirit of Christ. There is but one and the self-same Spirit yet the change in the descriptive title is significant. Christ is He from whom we derive our origin spiritually, the One to whom we belong. If indeed we are His, we are possessed of His Spirit, and consequently should be Christ-like in our spirits, so really so that all may see that Christ is in us.

According to verse 10 He *is* in us if His Spirit indwells us, and hence we are not to be ruled by our bodies. They are to be held as dead, for acting they only lead to sin. The Spirit is to be the Energizer of our lives and then the outcome will be righteousness. To do the will of God is practical righteousness.

Our bodies are spoken of as "mortal bodies" in verse 11. They are subject to death, indeed the seeds of death are in them from the outset. At the coming of the Lord they are to be quickened. The God who raised up Christ from the dead will accomplish this by His Spirit. In this connection we have a further description of the Holy Spirit. He is "the Spirit of Him that raised up Jesus from the dead." Indwelling us in this character, He is the pledge of the coming quickening, whether it reach us in resurrection of the body or in the change to be wrought in the bodies of saints who are alive and remain to the Lord's coming.

The conclusion to be drawn from all that we have just been considering is that the flesh has no claim upon us whatever. It has been judged in the Cross. It is antagonistic to God, irreconcilably so, and we are not "in the flesh." We are indwelt by the Spirit, and "in the Spirit." We are therefore in no way debtors to the flesh that we should live after it, for life according to the flesh has but one end—death. The Spirit is in us that we may live according to Him. That means putting to death the deeds of the body, refusing practically its promptings and desires. That is the way to what is really life according to God.

What great importance all this gives to the indwelling of the Spirit of God. He produces an altogether new state or condition in the believer, and He gives character to the state that He produces. He is the power of Christian life in the believer, the Energy that breaks the power of sin and sets us free. But He is more than this for He is an actual Person indwelling us, and so taking charge of us.

In the bygone dispensation the Jew was under the law as a schoolmaster or tutor. It took him by the hand as though he were a child under age, and led him until such time as Christ came. Now Christ having come we are no longer under the schoolmaster but like sons of full age in our father's house. Not only are we sons but we possess the Spirit of God's Son. All this we find in Galatians iii. and iv. Verse 14 of our chapter refers to this truth.

Those who were in the position of minors were put under law as a schoolmaster, and were led by it. We who have received the Spirit of God and are led by Him are the sons of God. Christ is the Captain of our salvation, gone on high. The Spirit indwells us on earth, as our Leader in the way that goes up to glory. Praise be unto our God! Our hearts should indeed be filled with everlasting praise.

We have in our chapter a wonderful unfolding of truth concerning the Spirit of God. We have seen Him, in verse 2, as the new law of the believer's life. In verse 10, He is presented to us as life, in an experimental sense. In verse 14 He is the Leader, under whose guardianship we have been placed while on our way to glory.

Further He sustains the character of a Witness, as we find in verse 16. Being made sons of God we have received the Spirit of adoption, and two results flow out of this. First, we are able to respond to the relationship which has been established, turning to God with the cry of, "Abba, Father." Second, the Spirit gives us the conscious enjoyment of the relationship. We know in our own spirits that something has happened, which has brought us out of darkness into light. The Spirit corroborates this, bearing witness to what has happened, even that we are now children of God.

The witness goes even beyond this, for if we are children then are we heirs, and that jointly with Christ; for by the Spirit we are united to Christ, though that truth is not developed in this Epistle. What amazing truth is this! How often does our very familiarity with the words blind us to the import of them! Let us meditate on these things so that there may be time for the truth to sink unto our hearts.

The chapter opened with the fact that we are in Christ, if true believers. Then we found that having the Spirit of Christ, Christ is in us. Now we come to the fact that we are identified with Him, both in present suffering and in future glory. The point here is not that we suffer for Christ in the way of testimony and that glory is to be our reward hereafter: that we find elsewhere. The point rather is that being in Him and He in us we share in His life and circumstances, whether here in sufferings or there in glory.

This leads the Apostle to consider the contrast between present sufferings and future glory, which contrast is worked out in the paragraph comprised in verses 18 to 30, though it is at once stated in very forcible words that the sufferings are not worthy of any comparison with the glory.

The same contrast is drawn in 2 Corinthians iv. 17, and even more graphic language is employed; "A far more exceeding and eternal weight of glory." In our passage the matter is considered with greater wealth of detail. The paragraph seems to fall into three sections. First, the character of the coming glory. Second, the believer's comfort and encouragement in the midst of the sufferings. Third, the purpose of God which secures the glory.

First, then, the glory is connected with the manifestation of the sons of God. The sons will be manifested when the Son, who is the Firstborn and Heir, is revealed in His glory. Then the creature (that is, the *creation*) will be delivered from the bondage of corruption and share in "the liberty of the glory of the sons of God." (N.Tr.) It has well been remarked that the creation does not share in the liberty of grace which we enjoy even amidst the sufferings, but it will share in the liberty of the glory. The creation was not made subject to vanity by its own will but rather as the result of the sin of the one to whom it was subject; that is, of Adam. And creation is represented as anxiously looking out in hope of the deliverance which will arrive with the manifestation of the glory. When the sons are publicly glorified the year of release and jubilee will have come for the whole creation. What glory that will be! How do present sufferings look in the light of it?

Still there are these sufferings, whether for the creation as a whole or for ourselves in particular. Verse 22 speaks of the former. Verses 23 and 26 of the latter. We have infirmities, as well as the groans which are the fruit of pain, whether physical or mental. What then, in the second place, have we to sustain us in the midst of it all?

The answer is again that we have the Spirit, and He is presented to us in three further capacities which He fills. He is the Firstfruits (v. 23), the Helper and the Intercessor (v. 26).

We are already sons of God. Yet we wait for "the adoption," that is, for the full state and glory of the position, which will be reached when our bodies are redeemed at the coming of the Lord. We have been saved *in* hope (not, *by* hope) and are consequently put in the position of patient waiting for the promised glory. Saved are we in expectancy of glorious things to come, yet we have the Firstfruits in the Spirit who has been

35

given to us. The firstfruits were offered up in Israel as the pledge and fore-taste of the coming harvest (see, Lev. xxiii. 10, 17, 20), so in the Firstfruits of the Spirit we have the pledge and foretaste of the redeemed body and the glory that is ahead.

Also the Spirit helps our infirmities. This word helps us to see that a clear distinction exists between infirmities and sins, for the Spirit never helps our sins. Infirmity is weakness and limitation, both mental and physical, and therefore if unassisted we may very easily fall victims, ensnared by sin. The help of the Spirit is that we may be strengthened and delivered.

Then again, such is our weakness and limitation that very frequently we find ourselves in circumstances where we simply do not know what to pray for. Then the Spirit indwelling us takes up the role of Intercessor, and utters His voice even in our groanings which baffle utterance. God, who searches all hearts, knows what is the mind and desire of the Spirit, for all His desires and intercessions are perfectly according to the mind of God, whatever our desires might be. God hears according to the Spirit's desires, and not according to ours, and we may well be very thankful that this is so.

We must not miss the connection between verses 26 and 28, though it is not very clear in our version. It is, "We do *not* know what we should pray for as we ought . . . but we *do* know that all things work together for good to them that love God." This thing and that thing may appear to work evil, but together they work for our spiritual good. This must be so, inasmuch as the Spirit indwells us, helping our weaknesses and interceding in our perplexities; and also in the light of the fact that God has taken us up according to His purpose, which nothing can thwart.

This brings us to the third thing: the purpose of God, which secures the glory. Two verses cover the whole statement; its exceeding brevity only enhancing its force.

There are five links in the golden chain of divine purpose. The first is foreknowledge, which is rooted in the very omniscience of God—rooted therefore in eternity. Next comes predestination: an act of the divine Mind, which destined those whom He foreknew to a certain glorious place long before they existed in time. From other scriptures we know that this predestination took place before the foundation of the world.

But predestination was followed by the effectual call which reached us in the Gospel. Here we come down to time, to the moments in our varied histories when we believed. The next step practically coincided in point of time with this; for we were justified, and not only called, when we believed. Lastly "whom He justified them He also glorified." Here our golden chain, having dipped down from eternity into time, loses itself again in eternity.

Yet, as you will notice, it says, "glorified"—the past tense and not the future. That is because, when we view things from the standpoint of divine purpose, we are carried outside all time questions, and have to learn to look at things as God looks at them. He "calleth those things which be not as though they were." (iv. 17). He chooses, "things which are not." (1 Cor. i. 28). Things, which are not to us, exist for Him. We are glorified in the purpose of God. The thing is as good as done, for His purpose is never violated by any adverse power.

See then the point at which we have arrived. In the Gospel God has declared Himself as for us in the wonders of His justifying grace. This came before us up to the close of chapter v. Then the enquiry was made as to what should be our response to such grace; and we have discovered that though we have no power in ourselves to make a suitable response, there is power for it, since we are set in Christ and indwelt by the Spirit of God. We are set free from the old bondage that we may fulfil the will of God. Moreover we have seen how many-sided are the capacities which the Spirit fills as indwelling us. He is "Law," "Life," "Leader," "Witness," "Firstfruits," "Helper," "Intercessor." And then again, we find ourselves in the embrace of the purpose of God, which culminates in glory—a purpose that nothing can frustrate.

No wonder the Apostle returns to his question, as to what *we* shall say, with all these things before him! What can be said but words that breathe the spirit of exultation? The question occurs in verse 31, and from thence to the end of the chapter the answer is given in a series of questions and answers, ejaculated with that rapidity which betokens a burning and triumphant heart. These verses lend themselves not so much to exposition as to meditation. We will just notice a few of the more salient points.

God is for us! Fallen man instinctively thinks of God as being against him. It is far otherwise, as the Gospel proves. His heart is *toward* all men, and He is actively and eternally *for* all who believe. This effectually silences every foe. No one can be effectively against us, however much they would like to be.

The gift of the Son carries with it every lesser gift that we can hold with Him. Notice, in verse 32, the word "freely," and also "with Him." Do we want anything which we cannot have with Him? In our folly or haste we may sometimes want such things. On quiet reflection however we would not have for one moment what would entail separation from Him.

God is our Justifier, not man. In the presence of this no one will succeed in laying so much as one thing to our charge. Even among men, when once the judge has cleared the prisoner it is practically libel to bring the charge against him.

If no charge can be brought there is no fear of condemnation. But if in any way that could be in question there is a perfect answer in Christ, once

ROMANS

dead but now risen, and at the seat of power as an Intercessor on our behalf. Notice that this chapter presents a twofold intercession: Christ at the right hand of God, and the Spirit in the saints below. (vv. 26, 34.)

Could we have a more perfect expression of love, the personal love of Christ, than we have had? We could not. Yet the question may arise— so timorous and unbelieving are our hearts—May not some thing arise, some force appear, which will separate us from that love? Well, let us search and see. Let us mentally ransack the universe in our search.

In this world, which we know so well, there is a whole range of adverse powers. Some of them are exerted directly by evil men, such as persecution or the sword. Others of them are more indirect results of sin in the government of God, such as distress, famine, nakedness or peril. Will any of these things seen and felt, separate us from Christ's love? Not for one moment! Again and again has a timorous convert been assailed by brutal men, who have said in effect, "We'll knock these notions *out* of you." Again and again has the effect of their persecution simply been to knock the truth securely *in*. He has not only won in the conflict but come out of it an immense gainer, and so more than conqueror. By these very things he has been rooted in the love of Christ.

But there is an unseen world—a whole range of things of which our knowledge is very small. Ills, that we know not of, always take on a more fearsome aspect than ills that we know and understand. There are the mysteries of death as well as of life. There are powers of an angelic or spiritual order. There are things that may lie in distant ages or reaches of space that we may yet have to traverse, or creatures that as yet we have not known. What about these?

The answer is that none of these shall for one moment separate us from the love of God. That love rests on us in Christ Jesus our Lord. He is the worthy and all-glorious Object of that love, and we are in it because connected with Him. The love reached us in Him, and we, as now in Him, stand abidingly in that love. If Christ can be removed out of the embrace of that love, we can be. If He cannot be, neither can we. Once grasp that great fact and Paul's persuasion becomes our persuasion. Nothing can separate us, for which eternal praise be to our God!

Our chapter, then, which began with, *"No condemnation"*, ends with, *"No separation."* And in between we discover ourselves to be taken up according to the purpose of God, in which there can be *no violation.*

CHAPTER 9

CHAPTER IX. OPENS another section of the Epistle, a very clearly defined one. In chapters i.—viii. the apostle had unfolded his Gospel, in which all distinction between Jew and Gentile is seen to be non-existent. He knew however that many might regard his teaching as indicating that he had no love for his nation and no regard for God's pledged word relating to them. Consequently we now have three dispensational chapters in which the mystery of God's ways concerning Israel are explained to us.

In the first three verses of chapter ix. Paul declares his deep love for his people. His affection for them was akin to that of Moses, who prayed, "Blot me, I pray Thee, out of Thy book" (Exod. xxxii. 32). Then in verses 4 and 5 he recounts the great privileges which had been accorded to them. Last of these, but not least, there sprang out of them the Christ, whose Deity he plainly states.

How then came it that Israel was in so sorry a plight? Had the Word of God failed? Not for one moment; and the first great fact brought forward to explain the situation is that of the *sovereignty* of God.

Now Israel were the last people in the world who could afford to quarrel with the divine sovereignty, for again and again it had been exercised in their favour. This point comes very clearly before us up to verse 16. God made a sovereign choice in regard to the sons of both Abraham and Isaac. He chose Isaac and Jacob, and set aside Ishmael and Esau. If any wished to object to God making a choice, they would have to obliterate all distinction between themselves and both Ishmaelites and Edomites. This they would not contemplate for one moment. Well then, God was only continuing to do as He had already done, and hence not all who were of Israel by natural descent were the true Israel of God.

Moreover when Israel made the golden calf in the wilderness they would have been blotted out in judgment had the law had its way. Instead God fell back upon His sovereign mercy, according to words from Exodus xxxiii. 19, quoted here in verse 15. This is a third case of God exercising His sovereignty in their favour, even as verse 17 supplies us with an example of God exercising His sovereignty against Pharaoh.

The plain facts are these:—(1) God has a will. (2) He exercises it as He pleases. (3) No one can successfully resist it. (4) If challenged, the rightness of His will can always be demonstrated when the end is reached. God is like the potter and man is like the clay.

How often God's will is challenged! How much reasoning has taken place on the facts stated in our chapter! How slow we are to admit that God has a right to do as He likes, that in fact He is the only one that has the right, inasmuch as He alone is perfect in foreknowledge, wisdom, righteousness and love. Things may often appear inexplicable to us, but then that is because we are imperfect.

Verse 13 has given rise to difficulty. But that statement is quoted from the book of Malachi; words written long after both men had fully shown what was in them; whereas verse 12 records what was said before their birth. Others have objected to God's words to Pharaoh as quoted in verse 17. The answer to such objections lies in our chapter, verses 21 to 23. Men pit themselves against God, hardening their hearts against Him, and in result God makes a signal example of them. He has a right so to do; while others become vessels of mercy, whom beforehand He prepares for glory.

Consequently if any object to what God is doing today, in calling out by the Gospel an elect people both from Jews and Gentiles, the answer simply is, that God is only doing again in our days what He has done in the past. Moreover the prophets had anticipated that He would act thus. Both Moses and Isaiah had foretold that only a remnant of Israel should be saved, and that a people formerly not beloved would be called into favour. This is stated in verses 25 to 29.

The matter is briefly summed up for us in the closing verses. Israel stumbled at that stumblingstone, which was Christ. Further they misused the law, treating it as a ladder by which they might climb into righteousness, instead of a plumb-line by which all their supposed righteousness might be tested. Israel had *missed* righteousness by *law*, and Gentiles had *reached* righteousness by faith.

CHAPTER 10

THIS LEADS THE Apostle, in the early part of chapter x. to contrast the righteousness of the law with that of faith, and once more he expresses his fervent love and desire towards his people. His prayer for them was for their salvation. Very clear proof this, that they were not saved. Religion they had, zeal they had, the law they had, but they were not saved. Wrongly assuming that they were to establish their own righteousness by law-keeping they went about to do it, and miserably failed. And the very zeal with which they went about it blinded them to the fact that Christ was the end of the law, and that God's righteousness was available for them *in Him*.

How much better it is to have God's righteousness than our own, for ours at the best would be only human. Every one that believes has Christ for righteousness, as verse 4 tells us. And Christ is "the end of the law." The word *end* is used here, we believe, just as it is in 2 Corinthians iii. 13., signifying the *object in view*. The law was really given in view of Christ. It paved the way for Him. If only Israel had been able to steadfastly look to the end of the law they would have seen Christ. It is quite true of course that Christ being come, all thought of righteousness being reached by law came to a conclusion. But that is not the primary meaning of verse 4.

Next, we have a striking contrast drawn between the righteousness of law and the righteousness of faith. The former demands the works that are in keeping with its requirements and prohibitions. Words will not do, works must be produced. By those works, if produced, men shall live. Failing to produce them, and to go on failing to produce them, men shall die.

In contrast thereto the righteousness of faith does not demand works at all. It does not demand that we ascend into heaven to bring Christ down, for down He is come. Nor does it demand that we descend, as though to bring Him up from the dead, since from the dead He is risen. In penning these words the Apostle evidently had in his mind the words of Moses as recorded in Deuteronomy xxx. 11-14. Read that passage and see. You will notice that verse 8 of our chapter, as to the form of it, is suggested by verse 14. The word of the Gospel is sent by God to us. Received by us in faith, it becomes the word of faith to us, entering our hearts and coming out of our mouths.

Of old God brought His commandment very near to Israel that they might do it. He has brought His word even nearer to us in Christ. It is now not a word of what we ought to do, but of what Christ has done, and of what He Himself has done in raising Christ from the dead. On our part the word only demands that we believe with the heart that God has raised Him from the dead, and that we confess Him as Lord with our mouths. When heart and mouth thus go together there is of course reality. Real subjection to Jesus as Lord carries with it salvation.

Notice the distinction that is drawn in verse 10 between righteousness and salvation. The faith of the heart in Christ puts a man into right relations with God—the faith of the *heart*, be it noted, as distinguished from the faith of the *head*, or mere intellectual apprehension. Real conviction of sin produces a heartfelt sense of need, and consequently heartfelt trust in Christ. That heartfelt faith God sees, and He reckons the man as right with Himself. Now the man goes a step further and confesses Christ publicly, or at least openly, as his Lord. This at once puts Him outside the world system in which the Lord is refused. His links with the world thus being cut, he steps into the blessedness of salvation.

Salvation is a word of very large meaning, as we have before seen. If we confine it in our thoughts to deliverance from the hell that our sins deserve, we miss a good deal of its significance. The moment we believe we are righteous before God, but until we definitely range ourselves under the Lordship of Christ by confessing Him personally as Lord, we do not get free of enslavement to the world, nor can we expect to experience the might of His authority and power on our behalf. How much do we know—each one of us—of a life of happy freedom in subjection to the Lord, and in occupation with His interests?

It is not supposed for one instant, of course, that we are going to believe in Jesus and *not* confess Him as Lord with our mouths. That would be impossible if our faith be the faith of the heart, since it is out of the abundance of the heart that the mouth speaks. Verse 11 of our chapter makes this point very clear. The believer is *not* ashamed. This is quoted from Isaiah xxviii. 16. The same verse is quoted in the last verse of the previous chapter, and it is also quoted in 1 Peter ii. 6. The, "make haste," of Isaiah becomes, "ashamed," in Romans, and "confounded," in Peter. A good illustration this of how New Testament quotations enlarge the sense of Old Testament predictions. The one who believed Isaiah's word would never have to flee in panic-stricken haste before the avenging judgment. Neither shall we. But we have also One introduced as Lord, who fills us with confidence and in whom we glory. Who, really knowing Him, would be ashamed to confess Him?

Our salvation, then, lies in calling on the name of the Lord, as is stated so plainly in verses 12 and 13. There is richness of supply and of power in Him, and all is at the disposal of the one who calls upon Him, without any distinction. Here we have the "no difference" of grace, just as in chapter iii. we had the "no difference" of guilt. Jesus is "Lord over all" whether they call upon Him or whether they do not. But the richness of His saving power is only at the disposal of those that call upon Him.

Do we call upon Him? Without a doubt we called upon Him at the hour of our conversion, and salvation we received. But is it the habit of our hearts to call upon Him in every emergency? A daily salvation we need, and a daily salvation is for us as we call upon Him—a salvation from every spiritual danger. The Lord does not always deliver His saints from physical dangers, threatened by the world without: sometimes He permits them to suffer grievous things, as in the case of Stephen, for instance. But then see how mighty was the spiritual salvation that Stephen enjoyed, even while his persecutors were breaking his bones. He furnishes us with the finest possible illustration of spiritual salvation flowing from the Lord, who is over all.

How important then is the Gospel, in which He is presented as Lord for the submission of faith. Verses 14 and 15 emphasize this. If men are to be saved they must hear the Gospel and God must send it. With Him it all begins. God sends the preacher. The preacher delivers the message. Men hear of Christ and they believe in Him. Then they call upon the Lord and are saved.

But all begins with God. Every true preacher is sent forth by Him, and beautiful are their feet as they go. Paul quotes from Isaiah lii., where the prophet speaks of the coming days, when at last the tidings of deliverance comes to Zion by the advent of the Lord in His glory. Equally beautiful however are the feet of those who carry the tidings of His advent in grace and humiliation, and of all that was accomplished by it for our salvation.

The trouble is that all have not obeyed the Gospel, as Isaiah also indicated. Obedience is by faith. The word, "report," really occurs thrice in this passage; for verse 17 more literally rendered is, "So faith then is by a report, but the report by God's word." When the report reaches our ears, backed by the authority of God's word, we believe it. Then it is that we can say like the Queen of Sheba, "It was a true report that I heard."

The report then has gone forth. It had gone forth even in the early days when Paul wrote this epistle. The blessing however was conditioned upon the obedience of faith. Now as a nation Israel had remained unbelieving, and the warning words of the prophets were in process of being fulfilled.

In the first verse of the chapter the Apostle had expressed his fervent desire and prayer, which was for their salvation. In the closing verses he sets forth the sad facts of the situation. They were a disobedient and gainsaying people. The word, "gainsaying" means, "contradicting." They continually said, "No" to all that God proposed, and denied all that He asserted.

Yet God had borne with them in long patience, stretching out His hands in entreaty, as it were. Now the moment had come for a change in His ways. Israel had stumbled over Christ as a stumbling-stone, and were for the time being set aside.

Chapter 11

THOUGH ISRAEL, AS a nation, has been set aside for a time, they have not been cast away for ever. Some Gentiles in the conceit of their hearts thought so when Paul was writing, and not a few think so today. But God forbid that it should be so, for they are His people foreknown for a special object, and in that event His object would be defeated. The Apostle immediately cites his own case as proof. Mercy had been shown to him and he was an Israelite, a *sample* of that remnant which God was then calling, and a *pledge* of the ultimate restoration of his nation. God is still today calling a remnant just as one was preserved in the days of Elijah.

"I also am an Israelite," says Paul. In passing let us place against those words that other declaration of Paul made to an unfriendly and critical audience of his own nation, "I am verily a man which am a Jew." (Acts xxii. 3.) The two statements are worthy of note in view of the widespread propaganda of British-Israelism which rests so largely upon the assumption that "Jew" always means the two tribes, who are utterly rejected; whereas "Israel" means the ten, to whom all the blessings belong, and who are identified by them with the English-speaking peoples. If that assumption be wrong the main part of their theory collapses like a bubble. Paul punctures British-Israelism.

But let us pick up the thread of the argument. When Israel was practically apostate in the days of Ahab, God reserved to Himself no less than seven thousand who were true to Himself at heart, though only Elijah was an outstanding figure in testimony. This was the fruit of His grace, and the same grace still works. The result is "a remnant according to the election of grace" (v. 5). As a nation Israel had despised grace and sought for righteousness by law-keeping, only to miss it and to be blinded (v. 7). Bowing to grace the remnant had been saved.

Verses 8-10 show us how their stumbling and consequent blindness had been anticipated by Old Testament prophets. Verse 11 indicates one great result flowing from it: thereby salvation had been presented to the Gentiles. The succeeding verses down to 15 contemplate their ultimate national restoration, and its results are strikingly contrasted with the results of their setting aside.

43

As a result of their stumble the Gospel of grace has been sent forth among the nations and the Gentile world greatly enriched. It has meant "the reconciling of the world;" that is, the world which was left alone and in the dark, while God was concentrating all His dealings upon Israel, has now come up for favourable consideration in the light of the Gospel. The reconciliation spoken of here is not, as in chapter v., something vital and eternal, the fruit of the death of Christ, but something provisional and dispensational, the fruit of Israel's stumble.

Today Israel is fallen and diminished and broken, and lo! all this has worked out in favour of the Gentiles. What then will be the result of "the receiving of them," of "their fulness?"—that is, of God once more taking them back into favour? A further great accession of blessing in the earth, so great as to be likened to "life from the dead." The main point of the passage, however, is that Israel having been set aside from the exclusive place they once held, the Gentiles are now being visited in blessing, whilst at the same time God is still preserving an election from amongst Israel according to His grace.

This is confirmed and amplified, in verses 16-24, by an illustration concerning an olive tree and grafting. No doubt the olive is specially chosen for the illustration, inasmuch as being the source of oil it is figurative of spiritual fatness, or blessing. Israel once had this place of blessing in the earth in connection with Abraham their ancestor. They forfeited it, as we have seen, and now Gentiles have come into it; as we read, "That the blessing of Abraham might come on the Gentiles through Jesus Christ." (Gal. iii. 14.)

This transference is pictured as the breaking off of natural branches from the olive tree, and the grafting in of branches from a wild olive, so that these formerly wild branches now partake of the fatness of the good olive, drawing their supplies from its root. The grafting process suggested is "contrary to nature," as verse 24 points out. It is nothing new however to discover that the processes of grace work on opposite lines to the processes of nature.

It is important for us Gentiles to realize what has happened, and the way in which it has happened. Israel has lost their old position through unbelief, and we hold our new position by faith. So let us beware! If Gentiles do not abide in faith what can they expect but that they too in turn shall be broken off? The grafted-in branches from the wild olive cannot expect better treatment than the original branches of the tree. Again bear in mind that the point here is not the spiritual blessing of individual believers, but the dispensational change in God's ways, which has put rebellious Israel under His governmental displeasure and brought Gentiles into a place of favour and opportunity in connection with the Gospel.

God's dealings in this matter illustrate the two sides of His character—goodness and severity—as verse 22 makes plain. The severity of God is tremendously discounted, if not denied, in many religious circles today. It exists nevertheless, and those who discount or deny it will have to face it in due season. The natural branches—poor scattered Israel—are going to be grafted in again, and the high-minded Gentile branches broken off. The times of the Gentiles are running to their end.

With verse 25 we drop the figure of the olive tree and resume the main theme of the chapter. The apostle very plainly predicts Israel's blindness is only going to last until the fulness of the Gentiles is come in. Then their eyes will be opened, and Israel as a whole will be saved. This will happen when once more the Lord Jesus returns. The blindness is only "in part," since all along God has been calling out an election from amongst them. When Jesus comes again "all Israel" will be saved: that is, Israel as a whole, or nationally. It does not mean that every individual Israelite will be, for the Scriptures show that many amongst them will worship anti-christ and perish.

"The fulness of the Gentiles" refers to God's present work of calling out an election from amongst the Gentile nations also. When that work is complete and the whole "fulness" or "complement" secured, the end will come. God's present purposes of grace to the nations will be secured, and then He will proceed to secure His purposes in regard to Israel; for He never repents, or changes His mind, regarding His gifts or His calling. Only He will secure those purposes, not on the ground of man's merit but of His mercy.

The rendering of verse 31 in the New Translation is, "So these also have now not believed in your mercy, in order that they also may be objects of mercy." The Jews nationally rejected the Gospel just because it was mercy, sent specially to the Gentiles (Acts xxii. 21, 22, exemplifies this), and eventually they will be profoundly humbled and receive blessing on the same ground as the Gentile dog.

As Paul concluded his survey of God's dispensational dealings and ways, as He saw mercy ultimately flowing out even to his own countryman, once so hardened and self-righteous, his soul was filled with adoration. He burst out in the doxology with which the chapter closes. We may call it the doxology of the *wisdom* of God, just as that at the end of Ephesians iii. is the doxology of His *love*, and that in 1 Timothy i. the doxology of His *grace*. The apostle glorifies that wisdom which lies behind all His ways, carrying everything finally to a glorious consummation, wherein is jointly achieved His own glory and the blessing of His creatures.

CHAPTER 12

THUS CHAPTER XI. ends very much as chapter viii. ended. In both we have the purpose of God and His electing mercy. Small wonder then that chapter xii. opens with an appeal based upon the mercies of God. In this way we commence the horatory and practical section of the epistle. There is only one thing to do in response to the abounding compassion which has reached us in the Gospel—we present our bodies to God as a sacrifice livingly devoted to Him. This is reasonable, or intelligent, service on our part, and acceptable to Him.

In verse 13 of chapter vi. the Apostle had indicated that the way of deliverance from the service of sin was to yield ourselves unto God, and our members as instruments of righteousness unto God. We were to have the thing done, definitely and for ever, as a settled thing. The exhortation here is very similar. Have we each of us had a moment in our histories when, conscious of the abounding mercies of God, perhaps overwhelmed with them, we have definitely presented our bodies as something livingly devoted to Him? Once each of us held his body as the vehicle wherein his own will would be expressed. Once we each said in effect, "I am the captain of my body and it shall serve my pleasures." Have we now surrendered it to Another, that it may serve His will and be used for His service and glory? We perform no really intelligent service for Him until we do this. We cannot be intelligent in the Gospel without seeing that such a course is the only proper response.

This will of course involve what is enjoined upon us in verse 2. Nonconformity to this world—or age—will mark us, inasmuch as we shall necessarily be conformed to the will of God. But God has His own way of bringing this about. Sometimes we see *conformed* Christians—sadly conformed to this age, and their bodies continually bearing witness to the fact. Sometimes too we see *reformed* Christians, trying with a good deal of laborious effort to imitate Christ and do as He would do. What is set before us here is the *transformed* Christian, the transformation proceeding from the mind within to the body without.

Our verse does not speak of what God has done, or is doing, for us. It speaks of what we are to do. The responsibility is put upon us. We are not to be fashioned according to this age: we are to be transformed. Both these things, the negative and the positive, are to be worked out day by day. The renewing of our minds, and the transformation effected thereby, are not things accomplished in a moment once and for all, but something to be maintained and increased all through life.

Since the divine instructions to us are that we be transformed by the renewing of our minds, we may well enquire how we may get our minds renewed. The answer is, by getting them formed according to God's thoughts and forsaking our own. And how shall this be? By soaking them in God's Word, which conveys to us God's thoughts. As we read and study the Word in prayerful dependence on the enlightening of the Spirit of God, our very thinking faculties, as well as our way of thinking, become renewed.

Here then is opened up before us the true way of Christian saintliness. We are not set to laboriously fulfil a code of morals, or even to copy the life of Christ. We are brought into contact with that which alters our whole way of *thinking*, and which consequently transforms our whole way of *living*. Thus it is that we may prove the will of God for ourselves, and discover it to be good, acceptable and perfect. What is good before God will be good to us, since our minds will have been brought into conformity to His.

The very first point where our conformity to the thoughts of God—and consequent non-conformity to the thoughts of the world—will be manifested, is in connection with self-esteem. Naturally each of us thinks no end of himself, for we have not learned to take our true measure before God. The more our minds are renewed the more we see ourselves as God sees us, and know that it is the measure of our *faith* that counts with Him. Faith brings God into our lives, and hence the measure of faith determines our spiritual calibre. We once heard a Christian remark of another, with gravity and a tinge of sadness, "Well, if we could buy that good brother at the price *we put upon him*, and sell him again at the price *he places upon himself*, we should make *a huge profit!*" God help us to learn how to think with great sobriety as to ourselves, realizing that not intellect, not social status, not money resources, not natural gifts but faith is the determining factor.

The fact is, of course, that the greatest and weightiest of us is but a tiny part of one far greater whole. This is emphasized in verses 4 and 5, where for the first time, as far as this epistle is concerned, it is intimated that though saved individually we are not to remain isolated individuals but are brought into a unity—the church of God. We are one body in Christ, each being a member of that one body. The practical outcome of this fact is that we each have our different functions, just like the members of our natural bodies have, and no one of us can absorb all the functions to himself, nor anything like all of them.

In verses 6-15 we get the practical working out of this. Each has his own gift according to the grace bestowed, so each is to recognize the part he is to play in the scheme. Each too is to take care that what he does, he does in the right way and spirit. The one who prophesies, for instance, is only to do so according to his faith. His knowledge may run beyond his faith but let him take care not to speak beyond his faith. This, if observed, would cut out a lot of unprofitable talking in the gatherings of God's people. So too he that gives is to give with simplicity. He that shows mercy with cheerfulness, so that he does not do a kind act in an unkind way. And so on. The details of these verses hardly need remarks of ours, save that we may point out that "Not slothful in business," is rather, "As to diligent zealousness, not slothful." It has no reference to the keenness with which we pursue our secular callings.

The closing verses of the chapter give more general instructions as to what becomes us according to God's mind. Lowliness of mind; openness and honesty; a peaceable spirit; absence of the almost universal spirit of retaliation and vengeance; love, so active as to "retaliate" by kindnesses, and so overcome evil with good; these are pleasing to God, and pleasing to us in so far as our minds are transformed into conformity to His. The figure of "heaping coals of fire" on the head of one's enemy is doubtless suggested by Psalm cxl. 10. The Psalmist prayed for it in keeping with the age of law in which he lived. Our verse shows us the Christian way of doing it.

We may say then that this twelfth chapter gives us the good and acceptable and perfect will of God for us in many of its details. Many of the features mentioned are by no means beloved by the men of the world. Some would please them well enough so long as they get the benefit of them—they will, for instance, quite like the honesty which would lead the Christian to be a prompt payer of accounts, and the absence of vengeance when they perchance take some unrighteous advantage of him. It is only the believer with his mind renewed who can see the beauty of them *all*.

And it is only the believer, whose renewed mind is working out a transformation in his life, that will begin to really practise them.

<h3 style="text-align:center">CHAPTER 13</h3>

THE EARLIER EXHORTATIONS of chapter xii. had to do with our behaviour in the Christian circle. Then from verse 14 to the end we were instructed how to behave in relation to the men and women of the world; it being plainly assumed that we shall find a good deal of hostility in that quarter. As we open chapter xiii., we are instructed how to act in regard to the governments and authorities of this world. A very important point this for the early Christians, who were frequently undergoing persecution from the authorities; and for us, whose lot is cast in an age when authority is treated with scant respect.

The Christian's attitude is to be, in one word—subjection. We are to avoid "resisting the power," that is setting ourselves in opposition to it. The reason given for this must be carefully noted: the "powers that be" are a divine institution, and to set oneself in opposition is to oppose the God, whom they are intended to represent, and to merit judgment. In these verses (1-7) authorities are viewed in their proper character according to the divine intention, rather than as they often are in actual practice.

At once, therefore, we may call out as to the sad travesty of authority so frequently seen. But we must remember that, when these words were penned, Nero had just about ascended the imperial throne in Rome, and the man who wrote the words was soon to suffer grievous things at the hands of the religious authorities in Jerusalem. Read Acts xxiii. 5, and xxvi. 25, noting in these instances how effectively Paul practised what here he teaches us. Only one thing exempts us from the subjection here demanded, and that is when subjection to authorities would involve us in disobedience to God. Then we must be obedient to the highest Authority. As Peter said, "We ought to obey God rather than man" (Acts v. 29).

If we merely think of government as it exists in the world today we must certainly be confused. In all directions there are overturnings, with power passing into the hands of strange people. Under the slogan of "Liberty" worse tyrannies and atrocities take place than those enacted under the despots of older times. But if we look away to God and His Word, all becomes simple. We are not set in the world to make governments or to alter governments, but to seek the interests of our Lord, while yielding all proper honour and subjection to governments, whatever they may be. The instructions apply to such matters as tribute and custom, as verse 7 shows. We are to pay all that is due in the way of rates, and custom, as well as income tax. What the authorities may do with our money, when they get it, is their matter, not ours. In the mercy of God we are relieved of that heavy responsibility.

Verse 8 extends the thought, of rendering what is due, far beyond governments to all men. The Christian is to be free of all debt, except the debt of love. *That* he can never fully pay. The object of infinite love himself, his attitude is to be love in this unloving world. In so doing he fulfils the law though he is not put under it, as we saw so clearly in chapter vi.

All the foregoing is confirmed and fortified by what we get in the closing verses of the chapter. We should be characterized by this subjection and love, because we are left in the world during the period of its night, in order that we may display the graces of the Lord Jesus Christ while we wait for the coming day. It is very easy to forget this and to settle down into a state of drowsy insensibility like the world. Hence the call to awake. The hour of our final salvation draws nearer!

We are certainly in the darkness. Do we not feel it? But the works of darkness we are to cast off, like filthy old clouts, and we are to put on "the armour of light." We are to be enveloped in the light which belongs to the day, to which we belong. The believer is to be shining and luminous in the midst of the darkness, and the very light we wear will prove itself to be *armour*. The shining Christian is by his shining protected and preserved. In one word, we are to put on the character of the Lord Himself, instead of catering for the desires of the flesh.

With what power should these words come to us! And with what urgency! If the night was far spent and the day at hand when Paul wrote, how much more so today. It is indeed high time to awake out of sleep and array ourselves in our shining armour. Only we must always remember that the "putting on," whether of verse 12 or 14, is not the assuming of something wholly external to ourselves, but rather putting on something from within, rather as a bird puts on its feathers. We saw this in principle, when considering verse 2 of chapter xii.

ROMANS

CHAPTER 14

CHAPTER XIV. IS entirely occupied with a matter that gave rise to very difficult problems in the early years of the church's history. The Jewish converts carried with them pretty naturally their views and feelings about matters of eating and drinking, about the observance of days, and customs, and the like. Their thoughts were partly based on the law of God, and partly on the tradition of the elders, but at any rate their feelings were very strong. The Gentile converts had no such feelings, and were inclined to regard it all as so much obstinate stupidity on the part of their Jewish brethren. Here was a cause of endless friction. The whole question is raised here, and settled with that admirable simplicity which characterizes Divine wisdom.

We must not let our interest flag at this point. We must not say—These questions do not exist today. The whole thing is of purely academic interest. We can dismiss it.

Not so. It is rather of very live and pressing importance. Though the exact questions that agitated and divided first-century Christians may have largely faded away, there are many others of an analogous nature taking their place, and much distress and harm is caused today when the instructions of this chapter are not observed. We will not go through the chapter verse by verse, but summarize it, by observing that there are in it three principles established, and three exhortations given; one connected with each principle.

The first is stated in verse 4. We may call it *the principle of Christian liberty*. In these matters that have to do with personal behaviour and conscientious service to the Lord, we are set free from the lordship of our brethren, by being set under the over-lordship of Christ. We may be right or wrong in our judgment, but the thing of prime importance is that we each, with a single eye for our Master, do what we believe to be pleasing to Him. The exhortation which hinges upon this is, "Let every man be fully persuaded in his own mind."

God intends us to be exercised as to such matters, each for himself. Were there a definite command in Scripture there need not be the exercise. Then, simple obedience is the only course pleasing to God. But these other matters, how many they are. Should I go here or there? Should I partake of this or that? May I enjoy this pleasurable recreation or not? Ought we to carry out this service or this ordinance in this way or that way? What acrimonious and harmful controversies have raged around such questions. And the answer is so simple. Let the wrangling cease! Hands off each other! Each man to his own knees, in the presence of his own Master, that he may get, as far as in him lies, the knowledge of his Master's will.

Having settled in the Master's presence what we believe He would have us do, let us do it in the simplicity of faith. Only it must be *faith*, and not self-will. And we must not go beyond or lag behind our faith. To do this is to bring condemnation (not, damnation) into our consciences, as the last two verses of the chapter tell us.

Some will say, "But this principle of liberty is sure to be abused." No doubt: but note how it is guarded by what we have in verses 10-12. Here is enforced *the principle of individual responsibility to God.* I may not lord it over my brother, and if I attempt to do so he need not pay much attention to me; but let him remember the judgment seat of Christ. Christ has died and risen again that He might establish His rights in both spheres, that of the dead and that of the living. All our movements then, dying or living, must be in relation to Him. But in giving account to Him we shall be rendering account to GOD. This is a tremendous fact, calculated to move every one of our hearts, and make us very careful in what we do or allow.

The exhortation in connection with this confronts us in verse 13. "Let us no longer therefore judge one another," this is the negative side of it; and the positive is, "but judge ye this rather, not to put a stumbling-block or a fall-trap before his brother" (N. Trans.). We are to keep our eyes on the judgment seat for ourselves, and as regards our brethren see to it that we do not provoke them to a fall. Lower down in the chapter this is worked out in a very practical way. Verses 15, 20, 21, for instance. Strong language is used. The Apostle speaks of destroying "him . . . for whom Christ died." He says, "destroy not the work of God."

God's sovereign work cannot be annihilated, and the true sheep of Christ shall never perish; but both one and the other can be wrecked in a practical way. The case supposed here is that of some Gentile Christian, spiritually robust and unfettered by prejudice, flaunting his liberty before the eyes of his Jewish brother, who, though still strong as to the law, is weak in the faith of the Gospel. Thereby the weak brother is tempted into doing things with which afterwards he bitterly reproaches himself, settling down perhaps under a spiritual cloud until his dying day.

You and I may be working mischief like that, if we do not take care. So let us look out, and keep our eyes on the judgment seat.

In saying this we have practically anticipated the third great principle of the chapter. It is that of *Christian brotherhood,* or *fraternity,* we may say. Verse 15 clearly states it. "Thy brother . . . for whom Christ died." If Christ died for that weak brother of ours—troublesome and awkward fellow, though he may sometimes be—then he must be very dear to Christ. Shall he not be dear to us? And let us not forget that you and I may sometimes prove ourselves troublesome and awkward fellows in his eyes. Then may God give *him* grace, as formerly to us, to view *us* as those for whom Christ died.

Based upon this principle comes the exhortation of verse 19. Being brethren we are to pursue the things that make for peace and edification. We are to be keen to build up, not to knock down. We are to aim at peace not at strife. If tempted to transgress, let us ask ourselves Moses' question, "Sirs, ye are brethren; why do you wrong one to another?"

It is possible for us to get things so astray in our thoughts that when we see a feeble brother we say, "See, here is a weak one! Let us give him a push and see if he will fall over." He does fall, poor fellow. Then we say, "We always thought he would. Now you see he is no good, and we are well rid of him." And when we stand before the judgment seat of Christ who died for him, what is going to be said to *us*? If we could hear it now, it would set our ears a-tingling. There is loss to be received as well as reward at that judgment seat!

Once more let us emphasize the fact that all these instructions relate to matters of individual life and conduct and service, and must not be stretched to include vital truth of God and to condone indifference as to that. Verse 17 lifts our thoughts onto a higher plane. God has established His authority and rule in the hearts of His saints, and this is not concerned with details as to eating and drinking, but with the features of a moral and spiritual order which are well pleasing to Him. That we should be living lives of practical righteousness and peace, and of holy joy, in the power of the Spirit of God, is to His glory. We are brought under His sway, and His Spirit is given to us, to this end.

As brought into that kingdom the principles that are to prevail amongst us are, Liberty, *Responsibility*, Fraternity—as we have seen—the responsibility being *God-ward*. At the close of the seventeenth century the great cry in France became, "Liberty, *Equality*, Fraternity"—the equality being *manward*. What tragedies followed! Very soon a situation developed which was the total negation of all three words! Let us see to it that we observe our three words, which work in the direction of righteousness, peace and joy.

CHAPTER 15

THE FIRST PARAGRAPH of chapter xv. sums up and completes this subject. The sum of the instruction is that those saints who are strong in the faith ought to bear the infirmities of their weaker brethren. Instead of pleasing themselves they are to aim at what will be for the spiritual good of the other. The attitude of mind which says, "I have a right to do this, and I am going to do it, no matter what anybody thinks!" is not the mind of Christ. It is exactly what Christ did not do!

"Christ pleased not Himself." The prophet testified this, and the Gospels bear witness to it. He was the only One on earth who had an absolute right to please Himself, yet He lived absolutely at God's disposal and identified with Him; so completely so that, if any wished to reproach God, they naturally heaped their reproaches on the head of Jesus. He is our great Example. We need to ponder Him, as made known to us in the Scriptures, and as we do, the patience and comfort necessary, if we are to follow Him, become ours.

So then, we are to manifest the grace of Christ in our dealings the one with the other: we are to be "like-minded . . . according to Christ Jesus." For this we need not only the Scriptures to direct us, but the very power of God Himself, who is the God of patience and consolation. Thus strengthened we shall be able to glorify Him together. Instead of the mind and mouth of the weak being filled with criticisms of the strong, and the mind and mouth of the strong being filled with contempt of the weak (see, xiv. 2), the minds and mouths of all are to be filled with the praise of God, even the Father of our Lord Jesus Christ. This presents a perfectly lovely picture: does it not?

Well, then, in spite of such differences as may exist, we are to receive one another in the happy enjoyment of Christian fellowship, so that the lovely picture may be realized, to the glory of God.

Having dealt with matters of practical life and behaviour, from verse 8 the Apostle gives us a little summary of his earlier teaching as to the relations of the Lord Jesus with both Jews and Gentiles. He *did* come as the Servant of all God's purposes in regard to His ancient people; so that the promises made aforetime to the fathers have been confirmed, though as yet they have not been all fulfilled. Then as regards the Gentiles, He came as God's Messenger of mercy to them, so that ultimately they too might glorify God. This showing of mercy to Gentiles, though perhaps quite unexpected by the Jews, was no new thought on God's part, for it had been indicated in Old Testament Scripture. Moses, David and Isaiah had all borne testimony to it, as verses 9-12 show us.

The believers in Rome were mainly Gentiles, hence there is a special force in the Apostle's desire in verse 13. They had been without God and without hope in the world—as the Gentile believers in Ephesus were reminded—and now God, who is the God of hope, is to fill them with such joy and peace that they abound in hope. This is a most desirable, a most glorious result, which is achieved as the fruit of faith in the Gospel; for it is, "in believing," and also, "through the power of the Holy Ghost." Believing the Gospel, the Holy Spirit is received, and peace, hope and joy follow, as the fifth chapter of our epistle taught us.

Many there are who earnestly desire peace and joy, but they think to arrive at them in working, in resolving, in praying or in feeling, but none of these things lead to the desired end. It is only *in believing*. Faith, and faith alone, puts the soul into touch with God. And only by the Spirit are our hearts filled with all joy and peace and hope, which are the proper fruits of the Gospel. It is very fitting that the Apostle should desire these things for those to whom he wrote, seeing that this epistle unfolds the Gospel which produces them.

In verse 14 Paul expresses his confidence in the believers in Rome, and from that point he turns to write of more personal matters, both as regards them and as regards himself.

First, he deals with his own service to the Lord and unbosoms to them his intentions as well as referring to what he had already accomplished. This occupies all the remaining verses of chapter xv.

Paul's ministry has especial reference to Gentiles, and in verse 16 he speaks of it in a very remarkable way. He ministered the Gospel amongst them as a sacrificial service, so that he considers those who were converted as being offered up to God for His acceptance in the sanctification and fragrance imparted by the Holy Spirit, who had been conferred upon them as believers. In this perhaps he alludes to the sanctification of the Levites, as recorded in Numbers viii. 1-19. It is expressly said there, "And Aaron shall offer the Levites before the Lord for an offering of the children of Israel, that they may execute the service of the Lord."

This shows us the spirit in which the Apostle carried on his gospel service. The apostle Peter speaks of Christians as royal priests who show forth the virtues of the One who has called them, and what we find here is in keeping with that. Paul acted in priestly fashion even in his gospel labours, and the fruit of them was seen in Gentile converts offered to God for His service as a band of spiritual Levites. In all this therefore he could boast, but his boasting was "through Jesus Christ," or, "in Christ Jesus"; for it was all referrable to Him as the great Master-worker.

These thoughts lead to a brief survey of his labours already accomplished. First, as to their great scope and extent, "from Jerusalem, and in a circuit round to Illyricum." Illyricum lay to the north west of Macedonia, so we can see what a vast district he had fully covered, considering the difficulties of transport in his day. Second, as to their peculiar character of pure and unadulterated evangelization. He was the pioneer of the Gospel in a supreme sense. He addressed himself to the Gentiles in a way that no other apostle did, and he went into strange cities that no other had visited. In this he was helping to the fulfilment of Scripture, as verse 21 shows.

Just because this was the special character of his service he had been hindered from coming to Rome. Christians had already gravitated to it as the metropolis of the world of that day, and thus the Gospel already had a footing there. Yet we can see Paul's missionary heart looking beyond Rome to distant Spain, and contemplating a journey thitherward some day, with a call at Rome on the way. For the moment he had before him a visit to Jerusalem in order to carry thither the contribution for the poor saints, made by the believers in Macedonia and Achaia.

We find an allusion to this collection for the saints in 1 Corinthians xvi. 1-4, and again at much greater length in 2 Corinthians viii. and ix. If those passages be read we can at once see why the Apostle here places Macedonia before Achaia. The Philippians were poor as compared with the Corinthians yet they were far more liberal. They talked less and gave more. The Acts of the Apostles furnishes us with a twofold explanation of what gave rise to the need. There was a famine in those days (xi. 27-30), and also the believers in Jerusalem had been in a special way impoverished by the "Christian communism" they practised at the beginning (ii. 44, 45). Their impoverishment however furnished the occasion for the cementing of practical bonds of Christian fellowship between Gentile and Jew.

There was a strong tendency in those days for Jew and Gentile to fall apart, and this tendency was increased by the scheming of Judaising teachers from Jerusalem. Hence Paul evidently considered this collection a very important matter and insisted on being the bearer of the bounty himself. He was quite aware of the danger he ran, and verse 30 and 31 of our chapter show that he had some premonitions of coming trouble. Whether he was really right in going to Jerusalem has been a much discussed question. We need not attempt to answer it here, but we shall do well to note that the prayer, in which he asked the Roman saints to join with him, was answered, though not in just the way he hoped. He was delivered, but not as a free man. He was delivered from his persecutors by his imprisonment at the hands of the representatives of Caesar.

So also did he finally come amongst the Roman Christians with joy, being refreshed among them, as Acts xxviii. 15, witnesses. Another proof this of how God answers our prayers, but in the way that is according to His will, and not according to our thoughts and wishes. We may also be sure that Paul came amongst them in fulness of blessing. Philippians i. 12, 13, is proof of this, as also Philemon 10. Peace was what the Apostle desired, peace in which both the saints of God and the work of God might flourish; hence the chapter closes with the desire that the God of peace might be with them.

We shall do well to notice the three ways in which God is characterized in this chapter. "The God of patience and consolation" in verse 5. "The God of hope" in verse 13. "The God of peace" in verse 33. Having noted them we shall do well to meditate upon them. What God is at any time He is always, and what He is for any of His people He is for all and for each. Therefore He is all this for you and for me.

CHAPTER 16

IN CHAPTER XVI. we get the closing salutations. Phebe seems to have been the bearer of the epistle, and Paul works in this word of commendation concerning her so that the saints at Rome might freely and without question receive her. She had succoured many and even Paul himself in the course of her service at Cenchrea. The word, "servant" is really, "deaconess."

From verse 3 to verse 15 we have a long list of names of those in Rome to whom salutations were sent. At the head of the list come two names that we are familiar with, Priscilla and Aquila. It is evident that they head the list designedly, for of no others are such words of high commendation spoken. They had laid down their lives on Paul's behalf, though in God's mercy their lives had been preserved to them. This is the limit of human love according to the Lord's words in John xv. 13. It is also what every Christian *ought* to do if the occasion arises, according to 1 John iii. 16; because we are here not only to display human kindness but, as those who partake of the Divine nature, to display divine love.

The Apostle shows a wonderful discrimination in his salutations. This one is a kinsman: that one a helper: the other is chosen in the Lord. Again, these are beloved, and that one is well-beloved, and these are of note among the apostles. Some have laboured and others have laboured much. In the largeness of his spiritual affections he had a definite link with each. But evidently Priscilla and Aquila outshone all as the exponents of a love which was divine, and that gave them the first place over the heads of many more gifted than themselves.

That love of divine quality, which gives itself even unto death, stands alone in its value. This was exemplified in the days of David—see, 2 Samuel xxiii. 13-17. It is made plain in the solemn words of our Lord, recorded in Revelation ii. 4. We have no doubt but that it will be most fully manifested in that day when we all stand before the judgment seat of Christ. So let us take it to heart now.

> *"Love never faileth," love is pure gold;*
> *Love is what Jesus came to unfold;*
> *Make us more loving, Master, we pray,*
> *Help us remember, love is Thy way."*

Verses 17-20 follow, giving us a picture which is the very reverse of all this. There were those in the earliest days, as also today, who served not the Lord but their own selfish desires. Such produce divisions and are to be avoided. Their words may be beautiful—smoother than butter—but they are contrary to the doctrine. This is the test. Not, can they speak pleasant things; but, do they speak according to that which we have received from God? The prime mover in all error is Satan, and when he is bruised under the feet of the saints by the God of Peace there will be peace indeed.

There follows the salutations of a band of labourers who were with Paul as he wrote; and again it seems in verse 24 as if he is closing his letter, as previously in verse 20, and at the end of chapter xv. Once more, however, a word is added. It appears that at this point according to his custom Paul took the pen from the hand of his amanuensis to write with his own hand. His closing words are of deep importance.

The Apostle Paul had a twofold ministry, as he unfolds in Colossians i. 23-29. To both ministries he alludes very briefly in these closing verses. The Gospel, which he calls "my Gospel" he had unfolded very fully in this epistle. The "mystery" he had not mentioned at all, though it had been revealed to him and other of the prophets, and had been promulgated in prophetic writings. He would have the believers at Rome know that important as it was that they should be established according to the Gospel he had just unfolded, it was equally important that they should be established according to the mystery, of which it was not his purpose to write at that time.

If important for the Romans, then for us also. God is able to establish us in both. Are we concerned about both? If not we ought to be. Because the church, as an outward, visible, professing body, is in a broken condition we are not exempted from concerning ourselves about the mystery, but rather it is the more necessary for us. The mystery concerns the Gentiles, hence it is made known to all nations, and made known for the obedience of faith: made known, not merely to be understood but to be *obeyed.*

Never more than today was there a crying need for really established Christians. God alone can establish us, and we are only fully established if established in both. No man can stand securely if only standing on one leg. The Gospel and the Mystery are like two legs whereon we may securely stand. Let us aim at standing on *both.*

1 CORINTHIANS

INTRODUCTION

WE NOW ENTER upon the epistle which above all others deals with matters concerning the local assembly, and the order which by Divine appointment should be observed in it. The church, or assembly, of God in Corinth was a large one, as we gather from Acts xviii. 10. It had within it some very unsatisfactory elements, as is not unusual in such a case, and these elements were introducing ways and habits and even doctrines, of a sort which were common enough in the Corinthian world, but which were absolutely foreign to the nature and spirit of the assembly of God. Partly perhaps it was due to the ignorance of the Corinthian saints, for they had written a letter of enquiry to the Apostle Paul, who had brought the Gospel to them, as to certain matters, as is indicated in verse 1 of chapter vii. Still Paul not only answered their questions but also brings home to them in most vigorous language their grievous errors both in behaviour and doctrine. This he did not in annoyance or anger or sarcasm, but, "out of much affliction and anguish of heart . . . with many tears" (2 Cor. ii. 4). Hence the powerful effect which his letter produced, as evidenced in 2 Corinthians vii. 8-11.

CHAPTER 1

HAVING TO WRITE in this corrective strain Paul very naturally emphasizes at the outset the apostolic place of authority which he held from God; and further, he associates with himself one of themselves. Sosthenes came from Corinth (see, Acts xviii. 17), and apparently was converted after the beating he got from the Greeks as chief ruler of the synagogue, having supplanted Crispus, who was converted somewhat earlier.

Two important facts confront us in the second verse. First, that only those who were sanctified in Christ, who were saints by the call of God, and who called upon Jesus as Lord, composed the church of God at Corinth. Second, that though the epistle was written primarily to the assembly at Corinth, yet secondarily ALL who called upon Christ as Lord were in view, no matter where they might be located. The same Lord was "both theirs and ours," and hence all saints were under a common Authority.

We do well to note with care the first fact, for the word, *church*, is used with a variety of meanings today. We may get an idea of its true meaning according to Scripture from this verse. None but true believers are saints, sanctified in Christ. It is on the other hand a fact that some may professedly call on the name of Jesus Christ our Lord without being true believers, and this accounts for passages in this epistle where Paul takes them up on the ground of their profession and says things which implies that some among them *might* NOT be real. Still, speaking generally, if a man professes faith he must be accepted as real, until proved to be otherwise.

58

1 CORINTHIANS

We do well also to observe and digest the second fact, with its significance, and the consequences that flow from it. It quite definitely shows that though each assembly has its own local conditions, and state, and responsibilities, yet it cannot be dissociated from the whole—from the church of God in its universal aspect. The order which this epistle enjoins upon the Corinthians is equally enjoined upon all saints everywhere. The discipline which was to be effected at Corinth, while affecting Corinth *immediately*, had its bearing *ultimately* upon the whole church. The recognition of this fact will preserve us from the mistake of treating each assembly as though it were an independent and autonomous unit—from laying such stress upon the local assemblies as to overshadow the fact of the unity of the whole church of God.

Paul's desire for the Corinthians was that grace and peace might be ministered to them. There was evidently a good deal of discord in their midst, which would have been eliminated had a larger measure of grace been amongst them. Yet the grace of God had been ministered to them in Christ, as verse 4 states, and that moved him to thanksgiving. Moreover, from the grace of God had sprung all the gifts that they possessed, while waiting for the coming of the Lord. The God who had called them to the fellowship of His Son is faithful as well as gracious, and consequently he was confident that they would be confirmed without blame to the end.

Notice how repeatedly the Lord Jesus Christ is named in the first nine verses, and how everything is attributed to, and referred to, Him. It is His Name, His grace, His testimony, His coming, His day, His fellowship. All this reinforces, and is intended to reinforce, the strong remonstrance of the Apostle which opens in verse 10. There were divisions, or parties, among them, leading to contention and strife. These parties struck a blow at the fact that they had been called to the fellowship of the One who is God's Son and our Lord.

When David was at Adullam, in the time of his rejection, men flocked to his standard and he became captain over them. They entered his fellowship, for he was the central figure. Had he been smitten the fellowship would have ceased to be. We are called into the fellowship of One who also is in rejection, yet is infinitely greater than David. The One who is Captain over us is God's Son. The fellowship to which we belong is dominated by Him, without a rival.

In the light of this, how great is the evil of party-making or party spirit, even though honoured names be attached to the parties, or even the very name of Christ be adopted as a party label. From verse 6 of chapter iv., we gather that the Corinthians were actually forming their parties round gifted and able men in their own assembly, and that the Apostle avoided the mention of their names by inserting his own with Apollos and Peter. Thus he maintained the delicate courtesy which is characteristic of Christianity, and at the same time heightened the effect of his argument. Paul was their spiritual father, but even to say, "I am of Paul" is not admissible.

Divisions—i.e., schisms or parties—always lead to contentions. God's desire is that we should be united in one mind and judgment. Though at a distance, tidings of the sad state of the Corinthians had reached Paul's ears, and he dealt faithfully with them. At the same time he plainly stated whence his information came. The house of Chloe could not lay information against them and yet remain anonymous, saying, "Don't let anyone know that we told you!" So also Paul himself avoided all vague and indefinite charges. He was quite explicit and definite in his statement, as indicated by the words, "Now this I say . . . " If such safeguards were always observed when charges must be brought, it would be well.

The questions of verse 13 are very much to the point. Christ is one. He only has been crucified for us. To His name alone have we been baptized. Paul was thankful that though so long at Corinth he had not baptized any of them, save two or three. In the commission given to the twelve (Matt. xxviii. and Mark xvi.) baptism had a prominent place. In his commission from Christ all the stress had been laid upon the preaching of the Gospel, and not upon baptism. It is possible of course that baptism was playing a part in these divisions and contentions at Corinth. Be that as it may, verse 17 makes it very clear that not baptism but the Gospel of the cross of Christ is the thing of all importance. And moreover, the cross must be preached in a way that does not nullify its meaning and power.

This brings us to verses 18 to 24, a great passage wherein the real force and bearing of the cross of Christ is revealed to us: the cross, that is, as passing the sentence of condemnation upon man, and of destruction upon his wisdom; while at the same time it brings in the power and wisdom of God for the salvation of those who believe. The cross of Christ is the point at which in supreme measure the world took upon itself to join issue with God. It put the Son of God to death, a death of extremest contempt and shame. God accepted the challenge, and in result the cross also became the supreme proof of the folly of human wisdom, of the disqualification and repudiation by God of even the greatest and wisest of men. Because of this, Paul was sent to preach the Gospel in a way that gave no quarter to human wisdom.

Because of this, also, the cross stands as "the great divide" amongst men whenever it is faithfully preached. On the one side of it stand "them that perish," on the other "us which are saved." To which class any individual belongs may be discerned by observing that individual's attitude toward the preaching of the cross. To the one it is but foolishness, for they adhere to the world and its wisdom. To the other it is the power of God, and that unto salvation. God saves by the foolishness of the preaching. The point of this remark in verse 21 is not that preaching appears a foolish *method*—as compared with working, for instance—but that the actual message preached—*the word of the cross*—is foolishness according to human notions, but is wisdom and power according to God.

1 CORINTHIANS

The world has its wisdom. When the Son of God arrived within its reach and scrutiny the world tested Him according to the accepted standards of its wisdom, denounced Him as acting by the power of the prince of the demons, and crucified Him. The wisdom of the world did not enable men to recognize God when they saw Him; the rather, they mistook Him for the devil. If that is the ripest fruit of the wisdom of the world then it is utterly worthless in the things of God, and condemned of God. And this is the case whether we look at Jew or Gentile.

Both Jew and Greek had their idiosyncracies. The one required signs, as the fruit of God's frequent miraculous interventions in their past history: only the sign had to be of a certain order to satisfy them. The other almost worshipped the human intellect, and wanted nothing that did not agree with current philosophic notions. To both Christ crucified was an offence. The Jew awaited the Christ, only He must be a splendid Being, and sensational according to their anticipations. The Greek would have welcomed a new philosopher to carry their speculations to a triumphant climax. Both were outraged by Christ crucified. Such a Christ was a hopeless stumbling-block to the Jew, and He appeared ridiculous beyond words to the Greek. *But there is no other Christ than the Christ who was crucified.*

And, through grace, *no other Christ is desired by us.* But then, we are amongst the "us which are saved." We are called of God, whether once we were Jews or Gentiles, and we can see that Christ really is both the power and the wisdom of God. He will bring to nothing all the mighty schemes of men in consummate wisdom and most decisive power and also establish all that God has purposed. At the same time His wisdom and power have wrought for our salvation. From the human standpoint the cross may be the foolishness and the weakness of God, but it is at the same time both wiser and stronger than men.

Now let us review these twenty-five verses that we may not miss the drift of the Apostle's argument in all this. The Corinthians were magnifying men—Christian men doubtless, and possibly very good ones at that—into leaders of parties in the assembly of God. This in effect struck a blow at the supreme and pre-eminent position of Christ; and it indicated that man, his powers, his wisdom, his gifts, had far too large a place in their thoughts. This in its turn indicated that they had but feebly realized the significance of the cross of Christ, which puts God's sentence of condemnation on man and his wisdom. Hence the Apostle's preaching of the cross, and hence his repudiation of mere human wisdom in the way he preached it.

The need for the preaching of the cross, in Pauline fashion, is not less in this twentieth century than it was in the first. Probably it is greater, inasmuch as never more than today was stress being laid upon the greatness and glory and wisdom of man. Never have men, even professing Christians sometimes, felt so pleased with their powers. Yet never has their lack of true wisdom been more manifest. The cross puts all into its real place. It makes everything of the Christ who suffered there. It makes nothing of man who put Him thereon. And that is right.

Have we learned and inwardly digested the meaning of the cross? Many millions in Christendom have turned it into an elegant symbol to be placed upon buildings devoted to religion, or even to be worn on the bosom, made in gold and studded with precious stones. Be it ours to have it engraved in "fleshly tables of the heart," in such fashion that we see through and eschew the tinsel glory of man, and seek ever and only the glory of Christ: that we are delivered from making much of any man, even the best of men, and above all from making much of ourselves. For us let it be Christ first, Christ last, Christ all the way through—Christ the power of God and the wisdom of God.

Having unfolded the significance of the cross of Christ, the Apostle proceeds to show that its meaning had been corroborated by the effects it had produced. He appealed to the Corinthians to consider their own calling, for *by the preaching of the cross* they had been called. But few among them had been reckoned amongst the wise or mighty or noble of this world. The very opposite, for these were all too prone to stumble at such a message. The rather God had chosen the foolish, the weak, the base, the despised, and even things which are not.

In each case the Apostle speaks of them doubtless according to that which they were according to human reckoning, and it was astounding that God should choose and use such as these for the confounding and bringing to nought of much that looked to them so wise and honourable. At the same time these words could no doubt be applied to that which the Corinthians really were in their unconverted days, and then the wonder is that they should have become what they now were, as the fruit of the Divine choice and workmanship. But whichever way we look at it the significance is the same. The practical effects of God's choice, and of His call by the preaching of the cross, were such as put no honour upon man. No flesh could glory in His presence. All glorying must be in the Lord.

The abundant reasons why we as believers may glory in the Lord are given us in verse 30. We are "in Christ Jesus," partakers of His life and sharing in His place and acceptance. And we are *that* "of God," and not in any way of man. God Himself is the source of all this grace which has reached us. It is true of course that we *are* "of God," as is clearly stated in 1 John iv. 4, and it is as "in Christ Jesus" that we are of God. But that is, we believe, hardly the point in the verse before us, but rather that all is of God and not of man whether we consider what we *are* in Christ, or what we *have* in Christ.

The second "of" in the verse is more literally "from." The Christ who was crucified is made unto us these things from God. Wisdom naturally comes first, inasmuch as it is the point under discussion. We need it, for sin has plunged us into ignorance and folly. But then sin has equally plunged us into guilt and condemnation; hence we need righteousness.

1 CORINTHIANS

And into contamination and corruption; whence our need of sanctification. And into bondage and slavery; so that we need redemption. Redemption comes last, inasmuch as it is a term which includes the final thing, the redemption of our bodies at the coming of the Lord.

Thus the cross excludes *in principle* all glorying in man. God's work in connection with the preaching of the cross also excludes it *in practice*. We have only the Lord in whom to glory, if we glory at all.

CHAPTER 2

WHEN PAUL WAS commissioned to preach the Gospel he was instructed to do so in a way that would endorse the message he preached. This he stated in verse 17 of chapter i. Had he as a matter of fact done as he was told? He had. And in the opening verses of chapter ii. he reminds the Corinthians of the spirit that had marked him in his approach to them, and the character of his preaching. Verse 1 gives us the style of his preaching. Verse 2 the Subject of his message. Verse 3 the spirit that characterized him. Verse 4 reverts to the style of his preaching, but adding where his positive power lay. Verse 5 shows us the end he had in view.

As to style, he was no orator well versed in the arts of moving men by excellent or enticing speech. All that he eschewed, relying only upon the Spirit of God and His power.

For theme he had Christ and His cross only. Emphasize in your mind the two words, "among you." He knew the tendencies of the Corinthians, with their great ideas as to philosophy and the human intellect. He would not meet them on their ground and be enticed into philosophic discussions of their choosing. He determined that among them he would know nothing but Christ crucified. Paul started his career with Christ glorified, yet he knew well that except they believed on, and laid hold of, Christ crucified, nothing of a divine sort, would be done. The truth of a crucified Christ was that which laid in the dust all their pride and glory; and until man comes down into the dust he cannot begin with God.

And Paul's own spirit was in keeping with this. He did not arrive in their midst with a great flourish of trumpets, announcing himself as "Palestine's most powerful Preacher," or something of that sort, as is customary in this twentieth century. The very reverse. Weakness, fear, trembling, are the things he alludes to. He was acutely conscious that the flesh was still in him, that he might easily be seduced from single-eyed fidelity to his Master, and betrayed into something which was not of God. He knew the mighty power of the devil, entrenched in Corinthian hearts. Hence his fear and trembling. And hence again the room for the demonstrated power of the Spirit of God, and the casting down of the devil's strongholds in human hearts. Would to God that there was more room made for the working of that power today!

Then we might see more of converts who really have their faith standing not in the wisdom of men but in the power of God.

Up to the end of this fifth verse the Apostle has mentioned human wisdom eight times, in every case to utterly discredit it. From this some might imagine that wisdom of every kind is to be discounted. Others again might suppose that the Christian faith only appeals to the feelings and emotions, and hence has in it nothing worthy of the attention of a thinking man.

So, in verse 6, Paul reminds the Corinthians that the faith abounds in wisdom, only it is the wisdom of God, and not of the great ones of the earth. Moreover it is wisdom of a character that only appeals to "the perfect," to those who have graduated, or are full-grown. We may be believers, but as long as we are in any uncertainty as to how we stand before God, as long as we are in the throes of self-occupation over questions of deliverance from the power of sin, we have neither heart nor leisure to learn the wisdom of God as expressed in His counsels and purposes, which were once a secret but now are made known.

The word, *world*, in verse 6 is really, *age*. In another scripture Satan is spoken of as "the god of this age." The god of this age uses the princes of this age to propound the wisdom of this age, while blinding their minds so that they have no knowledge of God's wisdom which was ordained before all the ages. When the Lord of glory was here he so blinded their minds that they crucified Him.

This really is a tremendous indictment! The supreme Lord of glory was condemned to a death of supreme degradation and shame, and that not so much by the ignorant rabble as by the princes of this age. The very superscription on His cross was written in letters of Greek and Latin and Hebrew. The Greeks were incontestably the intellectual princes of the age. The Romans were the princes in matters of military prowess and the arts of government. The Hebrews were princes without a rival in matters of religion. Yet all were involved in the crucifixion of the Lord of glory. All thereby revealed their complete ignorance of God and all brought themselves beneath His judgment.

The princes of this age "come to nought." Very humiliating this! Not only is "the understanding of the prudent" coming to "nothing," (i. 19.) but the princes of this age themselves come to nothing. The final result, the sum total, of all the clever doings is *NOTHING*. The clever men themselves come to *NOTHING*. In contrast with this we are told by the Apostle John that "he that doeth the will of God *abideth* for ever" and again we have the Lord's words to His disciples that, "your fruit should *remain*." The believer, and the believer *only*, has power to engage in that which will abide to eternity. Let us consider this very attentively, and may our lives be governed by our meditations!

It is a marvellous thought that the wisdom of God, once hidden, but now made known, was *"ordained"* before the ages unto our glory. Not only were we ourselves chosen in Christ before the foundation of the world, but God's wisdom had our glory in view before the ages began, and all was then ordained. And what God ordains never fails of consummation when God's hour is reached. Our glory then is certain, and is connected with, and subsidiary to, Christ's glory. Christ's glory is the supreme thing, but our glory is as certain as His, and equally ordained of God.

That which has been ordained, according to verse 7, has also been "*prepared*" (verse 9), and the things prepared are altogether beyond man's reach, either by eye, ear or heart. We apprehend many things by using our eyes—that is, by *observation*. Many others we apprehend by using our ears, listening to what is handed down to us—that is, by *tradition*. Other things we apprehend by the heart instinctively—that is, by *intuition*. We apprehend the things of God in none of these ways; but by *revelation*, as verse 10 shows.

The things prepared have been *revealed* by the Spirit. The "us" of that verse is primarily the apostles and prophets to whom the truth was first made known. The truth has reached the general body of saints through them, as we shall see in a moment. But in verse 11 we are made to think of the competency of the Spirit to reveal, since He is the Spirit of God. Only the human spirit can really know human things. Just so, only the Spirit of God knows the things of God and is competent to make them known.

But believers have received the Spirit of God as verse 12 states. Thus it is that we have competency to apprehend the things of God. No research, no experiment, no learning, no intellectual powers, can give us that competency; only the Spirit of God.

Let us take this very much to heart, for we live in an age marked by research and experiment and intellectual activity and it is commonly supposed that the human mind is capable of dealing with the things of God just as it deals with the things of man. IT IS NOT. Hence the fearful spiritual blunders perpetrated by otherwise learned men. Highly qualified are they in human things: yet pitiably blind and ignorant of the Divine.

Are we all keen to know the things of God? We certainly should be. We have a personal interest in them. The things "ordained," "prepared," and "revealed" have been "*given* to us of God." Are we possessing ourselves, in spiritual understanding and enjoyment, of our possessions?

We may be, since the things revealed to God's holy apostles and prophets have been *communicated* to us in divinely ordered words. This verse 13 tells us. The words "comparing spiritual things with spiritual," may be rendered "communicating spiritual [things] by spiritual [means]" (N. Tr.). Here the apostle definitely claims inspiration, and *verbal* inspiration at that, for his spoken utterances. Even more so then, if that were possible, for his written utterances. The inspiration claimed definitely relates to "words." If we have not got in the Scriptures (as originally written) *God's thoughts* clothed in *God-chosen words*, we have no inspiration of any real value at all.

65

The last link in this wonderful chain is "discerned." If we today do not discern God's things through God's word it will not avail us much that they have been ordained, prepared, revealed, given and communicated. They may be ours: *are* ours, if indeed we are Christians; but for practical blessing today, we must discern them. And the discerning on our part is by the same Spirit, by whom they were revealed and communicated.

For discerning, we need the right spiritual condition. The "natural man," i.e., man in his natural or unconverted condition, does not discern them at all. The "spiritual," i.e., the converted man, not only indwelt but also governed and characterized by the Spirit of God, alone can take them in. Possessing the Spirit we have the mind of Christ. Governed by the Spirit the eyes of our hearts are opened to understand.

The word "judgeth," occurring twice in verse 15, is just the word "discerneth," as the margin of a reference bible shows. Read *discerneth* and the sense is clearer. It is only the spiritual believer who has spiritual eyesight to see all things clearly.

Long ago someone was complaining: "I can't see it. I want more light!" It was said in reply, "It is not more light you want; it is windows!" That was doubtless true. If we allowed the Spirit of God to clean up the windows of our souls we should soon see clearly.

<h3 style="text-align:center">CHAPTER 3</h3>

IN THE OPENING verses of chapter iii, the Apostle brings the Corinthians face to face with their true condition in very plain words. Enriched as they were "in all utterance, and in all knowledge," they may have imagined themselves to be worthy of high commendation. In point of fact they came under definite censure. They were not spiritual but carnal.

They were not *natural*, for "the natural man" is man in his unconverted condition. Nor were they *spiritual*, for the spiritual man is man enlightened and controlled by the Spirit of God. They were *carnal*, for the carnal man, as spoken of in this passage, is man, who though possessing the Spirit, is controlled not by the Spirit but by the flesh. Being carnal, Paul had hitherto fed them with milk not meat; that is, he had only instructed them in the elementary things of the faith, and had not said much to them of that hidden wisdom of God, to which he alluded in chapter ii.

The Corinthians however might resent Paul's charge against them and wish to rebut it. So Paul proves his point by again referring to their divisions under party leaders, which generated envyings and strifes. In all this they were walking according to man and not according to the Spirit of God.

If the Apostle Paul wrote to us today, what would he say? What *could* he say, but the same thing with greatly added emphasis? The division of true saints into, or among, the many parties or sects could hardly go further than it has gone. We too might wish to rebut the charge.

We might say—But are we not earnest? Have we not much light? Do we not expound Scripture correctly? The reply would come to us—While some say, I am of A—, and a few, I am of B—, while many say, I am of X—, and a multitude say, I am of Z—, *are ye not carnal?*

In so saying we are not unmindful of the fact that there are to be found some who are spiritually minded. There were some amongst the Corinthians, as a later chapter reveals. But this we do say, that they who *really* are spiritual will be the last people on earth who desire to stand out as exceptions, prominent and distinguished. They know that this would be the very way to help on the evil here denounced, for they would promptly find themselves made into leaders of parties! NO. Their spirituality will rather express itself in humility of mind, and that confession which makes the sin of all the people of God their own. They will pray in the spirit of Ezra ix. Ezra said, "OUR iniquities are increased over our head, and OUR trespass is grown up into the heavens," though personally he had had very little share in all the wickedness, but rather was marked by a very exceptional piety.

The same humble spirit marks Paul here. He promptly disclaims for himself any place of importance, and for Apollos also. Evidently he had full confidence in Apollos, that in this matter he was wholly like-minded with himself, and therefore he could freely use his name. Whilst his omission here of the name of Cephas (Peter), is a witness to his own delicacy of feeling; since there had once been a serious issue between himself and Peter, as Galatians ii. bears witness.

Neither Paul nor Apollos were anything more than servants by whom God had been pleased to work. God was the great Workman. In this passage (verses 5 to 11) the Corinthians are viewed in a twofold way, as God's husbandry, and as God's building. Paul and Apollos were but "God's fellow-workmen." That is the force of the first clause of verse 9. They were not *competing* workmen, much less were they *antagonistic* workmen. They were *fellow*-workmen, and both belonged to God.

Each however had his own distinctive work. In the husbandry, Paul planted and Apollos followed to water the young plants: in the building, Paul was the wise architect who laid the foundation, and Apollos built upon it. Their labours were diverse, but their object was one. This is emphasized in verses 7 and 8. Paul and Apollos in themselves were nothing, yet they worked each in his appointed sphere. And both were *one* as to their object and aim, though each should finally be rewarded according to their own labour. Thus among His servants does God maintain both unity and diversity, and there is to be no pitting of one against another.

So much for Paul and Apollos. But they were not the only labourers who had taken part in the work at Corinth. So at the end of verse 10 the application of the figure is widened out to embrace "every man," that is, every man who had put his hand to the work at Corinth. It applies of course equally to any man who puts his hand to any work of God, anywhere, and at any time. It applies therefore to us today.

The foundation had been well and irrevocably laid by Paul when he first visited Corinth and stayed for a year and a half. It had been the right foundation—Jesus Christ. The question now was as to his successors. Not so much *how* they built as *what* they built in. Was it substance precious in nature, and capable of standing the fire? Or was it common in substance, and easily consumed? The day is coming when the fire test will be applied. Everything will be made manifest. The true character of all our work will be revealed. Not merely how much we have done, but "of what sort" it is. How searching is the thought that, "THE DAY shall declare it."

When *that* day sheds its light upon us and applies its test, it may leave our work standing. If so, we shall receive reward. God grant it may be so for each of us!

On the other hand, our work may be consumed and fall in ruins, yet we ourselves be saved, "so as through fire." When the three Hebrews passed through the fire, as recorded in Daniel iii, they and their clothes were wholly untouched: only their bonds were consumed. What loss for us if we come through the fire naked, stripped of all that with which we had clothed ourselves as the fruit of our labours here.

But further, there was evidently a doubt in the Apostle's mind whether all those who had wrought at Corinth were truly converted men. Hence the solemn warning of verses 16 and 17. Work may be done which is positively destructive in its effect upon the building. This raises a further important question. What is the *nature* of this building, which is God's?

The Apostle asks the Corinthians if they did not know that as God's building they had the character of His temple? In them as His temple God dwelt by His Spirit. This gave to them collectively a very sacred character. To do work which would "defile," or "corrupt," or "destroy," God's temple was terribly serious. If in the coming day any man's work is found to be of that destructive character, God will destroy him.

Apparently some who were going about in those days and doing, as Paul feared, this destructive work, were men who had a good deal of the wisdom of this world, and posed therefore amongst the saints, as very superior persons. This would account for the pungent words that fill verses 18 to 20. The wisdom of this world is foolishness with God. So let no man deceive himself on this point. And if the destructive workers still go about, deceived themselves, and deceiving others, let *us* not be deceived by them.

What woe and destruction must await the destructive critics, the semi-infidel modernistic teachers, of Christendom! Inflated by the wisdom of this world, they take it upon themselves to deny and contradict the wisdom of God. They may imagine that they only have to expect the opposition of unlearned and old-fashioned Christians. They forget the day that shall declare God's judgment—THE DAY!

Let us not glory in men. Some of those in whom the Corintians had been glorying may have been men of quite undesirable type. But let us not glory in the best of men. On the one hand, no man is worth it, as chapter i. showed us. On the other hand, as emphasized here, grace has given us a place which should put us far above glorying in a mere man. "All things" are ours. All things? That is rather a staggering statement. Is it really *all things*? Well, look at the wide sweep of verse 22. The best of saints on the one hand, and the world on the other. Life on the one hand and death on the other. Things present on the one hand and things to come on the other. All are ours.

How are they ours? Verse 23 answers that. They are ours because we are Christ's, and Christ is God's. All things are God's. No one can dispute that, and there we begin. But then God has His Christ, who is the Heir of all things. And, most wonderful to say, the Christ proposes to practically possess Himself of His mighty possessions by putting His saints into possession. Even in Daniel vii. this is hinted at. The "Ancient of Days" takes the supreme throne. When He does, "One like the Son of Man" appears, and to Him there was given "dominion and glory and a kingdom." But that is not the end of the story, for we further read, "the time came that the saints possessed the kingdom." Read that chapter before proceeding further.

So all things *are* ours, and we must never forget it. The remembrance of it will lift us above the world with its false attractions, above the wisdom of this world, above glorying in man, in even the best of saints.

CHAPTER 4

THE MEN OF THIS WORLD, and—sad to say—especially modernistic preachers, are often remarkably like "Muckrake" of Bunyan's great allegory. They have no eye for the things of heaven. They boast a purely earthly religion, which aims at producing a little more order amongst the sticks and stones and refuse of the floor. But Paul and Apollos? Who and what are they? May we not glory in them? They are but servants and stewards. And the fourth chapter opens with a reminder of this, and with the statement that the essential virtue of a steward is faithfulness. This again raises the thought of THE DAY, which is to declare all things, as the 13th verse of the previous chapter told us.

In verse 3 the words, "man's judgment," should read "man's day," and thus the connection and contrast is made plain. In the light of "*the day*," Paul was not overmuch troubled or concerned about the judgment of "*man's day*," or even of the Corinthians themselves. Had they been in a spiritual condition he would doubtless have listened patiently to any criticism of himself which they wished to proffer. But they were carnal and consequently their judgment was of but little worth. Paul lets them know this.

Moreover Paul had a good conscience. The opening of verse 4 has been translated, "For I am conscious of nothing in myself; but I am not justified by this." How good it would be if we could each speak thus: if we were each so true to what we have learned of the mind of God that we are not conscious of anything amiss. Yet even a Paul had to admit that this did not justify him, for he is to be judged not by *what he knew*, but by the Lord and *what He knows*. So have we all; and there is a vast difference between the standard erected by our consciousness and that erected by the omniscience of the Lord.

What does the Lord know? Let verse 5 tell us—one of the most searching verses in the Bible. When the Lord comes He will usher in the day, and the beams of its light will have X-ray properties. This verse is written, not in view of the enormous evils of the world without, but of the actions that take place within the Christian circle.

Oh! what painful episodes—in their uncountable thousands—have taken place amongst the saints of God. Many of them more or less private in nature; some of them public and ecclesiastical. We may form our judgments and even become violent partizans; and all the while there may be dark corners hidden from our eyes in which *hidden things* are secreted. There may be secret motives in hearts, altogether veiled from us. All is coming out in the light of the day. The final court of appeal lies in the presence of the Lord. His verdict may irrevocably upset all the verdicts of the courts below. So, if we feel ourselves wronged, let us have patience. If inclined to take some drastic action, let us take great care. Search well the dark corners lest there be some hidden things which should see the light. Search your own heart lest a wrong motive lurk there. Think twice and thrice before launching the thunderbolt, especially if it be an ecclesiastical one which may affect many.

The last clause of verse 5 is rather, "then shall each have praise from God." That is to say, the point is not that every man is going to be praised, but that each who *is* praised will have his praise *from GOD*, and not from some few of his fellow-creatures. The Corinthians had their party leaders. They praised this one extravagantly, and these they condemned; and *vice versa*. It was all worthless. God give us grace to avoid this kind of thing. The only praise worth having is praise from God.

Verse 6 shows us that the real party leaders at Corinth were other than Paul or Apollos, probably gifted local leaders, or even visiting brethren of Judaising tendencies, to whom he alludes more plainly in his second epistle. Paul avoided the use of their names, but he wanted all to learn the lesson, not to be puffed up for one as against another. No one has any ground for boasting, however shining their gift, for all that they have they have received from God.

Now this glorying in man is of the spirit of the world. And if the world creeps in at one point, it will soon creep in at another. So it had at Corinth. They were full and rich, and reigning like kings, having a real "good time," while their Lord was still rejected, and the apostles of the Lord were sharing His rejection. There is a tinge of holy sarcasm in that word, "I would to God ye did reign, that we also [Paul and his companions] might reign with you." The saints will reign when Christ reigns, and the apostles will not be missing from their thrones.

What a picture of the apostles, as they were then, do verses 9 to 13 present! Comment is not needed. We only need to let the picture be engraved on our minds. Paul painted the picture not to shame us but to warn us. But without a doubt we shall be both warned and shamed. He was a spiritual father to the Corinthians and not merely an instructor, for he had been used to their conversion. We, too, as Gentiles, have been converted through him, though indirectly, and he is our instructor through his inspired writings. So let us also take him as our model, and imitate his faith and devotedness.

The closing verses of our chapter show that some amongst the Corinthians were not only running after party leaders, and worldly in life, but they were conceited and puffed up. To such the Apostle writes very plain words. For the moment Timothy had come to remind them of what was right and becoming, but he anticipated coming shortly himself. When he came in the power of God's kingdom, of God's authority, these conceited brethren might measure themselves against it, if they so desired.

Did they desire it? How effectively it would puncture their inflated pretensions! Would it not be better to humble themselves before God, and enable Paul to visit them in a far happier spirit?

And will it not be well for us all to be searched and humbled as we close this chapter?

CHAPTER 5

As WE READ the opening verses of chapter v., we see that the Corinthians quite deserved the rod of which Paul spoke, as he closed chapter iv. There was a very grave case of immorality in their midst. Corinth was a licentious city, and the standard of morality amongst the Gentiles was deplorably low, yet even they avoided the particular sin which had been perpetrated by this professing Christian. The thing had not been done in secret. It was known on all hands.

But though it was a matter of common report the assembly at Corinth had taken no action. That was bad enough, but they aggravated their indifference by their conceit. Possibly they might have pleaded that as yet they had no instructions what to do in such a case. But this, if true, was no real excuse, for a very small measure of spiritual sensibility would have led them to mourn for the dishonour done to the Lord's name, and also to pray that God would interfere by removing the evil-doer from their midst. Instead of this they were "puffed up" with a foolish and baseless pride.

In verses 3 to 5 we see the holy vigour and decision which marked Paul, in contrast to the supine indecision of the Corinthians. They should have been gathered together in the Name of the Lord Jesus Christ, and acted in the putting away of the wicked person from among themselves, as indicated in the last verse of the chapter. They had not done so. Paul steps into the breach, judges and acts with Apostolic authority, though associating the Corinthians with his judgment and act. Such an one as this he would deliver unto Satan, for even Satan may be used for the disciplining of a guilty saint.

Apparently the utmost limit to which Satan can go is the destruction of the flesh. In the case of Job he was not allowed to go to that limit, though he grievously tormented his flesh. But if the flesh be even destroyed and death supervene, it is in order that the spirit may be saved in the coming day. This, you see, supposes that the one coming under this extremest form of discipline is after all a real believer.

But there was another fact overlooked by the Corinthians, which showed the wrong and folly of their boastful spirit. They were like a lump of dough in which a little leaven had been placed. Now leaven has well-known properties. It ferments, until the whole lump is permeated by it. Thus they could not rightly look upon this sin of one of their number as being a thing in which they were not involved. The very opposite. It was indeed the "old leaven," the very thing that had been rampant amongst them in their unconverted days, and would be very certain to spread amongst them again if unjudged. Hence they were to purge it out, by putting the wicked person away.

The effect of so doing would be to render them practically "a new lump, as ye are unleavened." They really were a new and unleavened lump, as regards their place and condition before God; and they were so to act that they might be in practice what God had made them to be in Christ. Let us all seize the underlying principle of this, for it is the principle on which God always acts in grace. The law did indeed demand that we should be what we were *not*. Grace makes us to be what is according to God, and then calls upon us to act in accordance with *what we are*. You may apply this in a multitude of ways. You are always so to act, "that ye may be ... as ye are."

The Apostle uses a figure, of course, in speaking thus of leaven. But it is a most appropriate figure. Israel's passover feast had to be eaten without leaven, and was followed by the feast of unleavened bread. Now the passover pointed forward to the death of Christ as its fulfilment, and the church during the whole time of its sojourn here is to fulfil the type of the feast of unleavened bread by eschewing all evil, and walking in sincerity and truth.

Just as Israel had to sweep all leaven out of their houses, so are you and I to sweep all evil out of our lives. And beside this there are certain cases in which assembly action is demanded by the Word of God. Such cases in the matter of moral evil are those mentioned in verse 11. The transgressor may be a "man that is called a brother." Just because he has professed conversion he has been found inside the assembly and not without it; and because he is within he comes under its judgment and has to be put away. This putting away is not just a formal and technical excommunication. It is an action of such reality that all the saints were no longer to "keep company" in any way with the offender. When dealing with the men of the world on a business basis we cannot discriminate in this way as to their moral characters: but if a professed Christian is guilty of the sins mentioned in verse 11 we are to have done with him, and not own him as a Christian at all for the time being. Time future will reveal what he really is.

This chapter shows very clearly that while an evil-doer might be dealt with, while the apostles were alive, on the basis of apostolic authority and energy, the normal way is by the action of the assembly gathered together in the name of the Lord. Its jurisdiction only extends over those who are within it. Those who are without must be left to the judgment of God which will reach them in due season.

<h2 style="text-align:center">CHAPTER 6</h2>

THERE WAS ANOTHER very grievous scandal amongst these Corinthians, to which Paul alludes in chapter vi. It was less grave perhaps than the foregoing, but apparantly it was more widespread. Some amongst them were quarrelsome, and dragging their disputes into the public law courts. Thus they launched their accusations and aired their wrongs, whether real or imaginary, before the unbelievers.

Here again spiritual instinct ought to have delivered them from such an error. It was virtually confessing that they had not one wise man in their midst with the ability to discriminate and judge in such matters. Thus they were noising abroad their own shame.

And further than this, they were proclaiming their own ignorance. Verse 2 commences with, "Do ye not know?" and five times before the chapter is finished do we find the question, "Know ye not?" Like many other carnal believers the Corinthians did not know nearly as much as they thought they did. If truth *governs* us, we *really* know it. Mere intellectual knowledge does not count.

They ought to have *really* known that "the saints shall judge the world." This fact had been stated in the Old Testament. "The Ancient of days came, and judgment was given to the saints of the Most High; and the time came that the saints possessed the kingdom" (Dan. vii. 22). Had they really known it they would not have dragged one another into heathen law courts. If we really knew it, we perhaps should avoid certain things that we do. A still more astonishing fact confronts us in verse 3: though here the change from, "the saints," to, "we," may indicate that the judging of angels is confined to the apostles.

Be that as it may, these verses open up before us a vista of extraordinary authority and responsibility, in the light of which things pertaining to this life can only be spoken of as "the smallest matters." In keeping with this estimate, is the instruction that if such questions are brought before the saints for judgment, those least esteemed in the church are to hear the case. We notice that it does not say that *all* the saints are going to judge in the coming age. Perhaps all are not, and so those least likely to be judges then are to be judges now. Such is the estimate which Scripture gives of the relative importance of the things of the coming age as compared with the things of this age.

It is quite evident, then, that if one Christian has an accusation of unrighteousness to lay against another, he must lay his case before the saints and not before the world. There is however something better than *that*, as indicated in verse 7. Better than *all* is it to meekly suffer the wrong, leaving the Lord to deal with it, and work repentance in the wrong-doer. Worst of all is it to do the wrong and defraud even the brethren.

If one called a Christian acts fraudulently, serious questions are raised in view of the fact that the unrighteous shall not inherit the kingdom of God. The first question we ask is—Is he a true Christian after all? God alone knows. We stand in doubt of him. A true believer may fall into any of the terrible evils enumerated in verses 9 and 10, but he is not *characterized* by any of them, and through repentance he is eventually restored. Those characterized by these things have no part in the kingdom of God, either here or hereafter. They are consequently clean outside the fellowship of the assembly of God.

Some of the Corinthians had been sinners of this type, but their conversion had involved three things—washing, sanctification, justification. Washing signifies that deep and fundamental work of moral renovation which is accomplished by the new birth. Sanctification is a setting apart for God, now to be for His use and pleasure. Justification is a clearance from every count that otherwise would lie against us; a judicial setting right, so that we stand in righteousness before God. All three are ours in the Name of the Lord Jesus—that is, in virtue of His sacrificial work; and by the Spirit of our God—that is, by His effective work in our hearts. We might have been inclined to connect the washing with the work of the Spirit exclusively, and the justification exclusively with the work of Christ. But it is not so stated here. The objective and the subjective go hand in hand.

We might also have been inclined to have put justification in the first place. But washing comes first here, since the point of the passage is, that the believer manifests an altogether new character. The old filthy characteristics are washed away in the new birth. And if they are manifestly not washed away, then no matter what a man may profess he cannot be accepted as a true believer, or in God's kingdom.

Verse 12 commences a fresh paragraph, and introduces another line of thought. Meats are mentioned in the next verse, and we shall have more concerning that matter in chapter viii. It was a burning question amongst the early Christians. In such matters as that Paul was not under law. Yet even so what is quite lawful may be by no means "expedient," or "profitable" (see margin). Moreover even a lawful thing may have a tendency to enslave, and we are not to allow ourselves to be brought under the power of anything, but rather hold ourselves free to be the bondslaves of our Lord and Saviour. How often one hears it said concerning a debated point—"But it is not forbidden. What is the harm of it?" And the reply has to be in the form of another question—Is it profitable? We want things which have not only the negative virtue of having no harm in them, but also the positive virtue of having profit in them.

This last paragraph of the chapter contains very important teaching as to the body of the believer. As yet our bodies are not redeemed, and consequently are the seat of various lusts, and they must be held as dead. Still we must not fall into the error of treating them lightly. Three great facts concerning them are stated in this passage.

First, they are "members of Christ." (ver. 15). Though not yet redeemed, they are going to be redeemed, and the Lord claims them as His. So really are they His that it is possible for the life of Jesus to be made manifest in our bodies. (See 2 Cor. iv. 10). They are members in which is to be displayed the life of Him who is our Head.

Second, the body of each believer is "the temple of the Holy Ghost." (ver. 19). Our old life has been judged. Sin in the flesh, which formerly dominated us, has been condemned; and now the Spirit indwells us as the energy of that new life which we have in Christ. Every believer should regard his body as a shrine wherein dwells the Holy Spirit, which he has of God. God has taken possession of his body in this way: a fact of tremendous import.

Third, we have been bought with a price, (ver. 20) body as well as soul. The price that has been paid is beyond all our computation, as we know right well. The point we might overlook is that it covers the purchase of our bodies.

Now note the implications of these facts. How can we make the members of Christ the members of an harlot? Again, how can I treat my body as if it were exclusively my own? We are not our own. We are Another's, spirit and soul and body. Hence, "glorify God in your body," is the word for us. The whole idea of the unconverted is to gratify and glorify themselves in and through their bodies. Be it ours to gratify and glorify God.

What a lofty standard is set before us in these things! We may feel that it is indeed high and that we do not attain unto it. Still we would not have it altered. A great present blessing lies here, and also a great pledge of future glory. If already our bodies are the temples of the Holy Ghost, how sure it must be that the redemption of our bodies is coming. Then the *Holy* Spirit will have a temple perfect in *holiness*. Meanwhile He promotes holiness in us, and that is for our highest blessing.

Finally, glance at verse 17. This verse flatly denies the idea that our union with Christ lies in the Incarnation, which idea lies at the root of much ritualistic error. The union lies not in flesh but in spirit. This is one of the cases where it is a question whether to begin the word spirit with a capital or not. The Spirit, who indwells us, is the Spirit of Christ; and by Him we are one spirit with the Lord. What a marvellous fact! Ponder it well.

CHAPTER 7

FROM THE FIRST verse of chapter vii. we infer that Paul sat down to write this epistle in reply to a letter of enquiry, previously received from the Corinthians. Only, when he did so there were graver and more urgent matters to be first disposed of, and these fill up chapters i. to vi. He now turns to deal with their enquiries; and we find the words, "Now concerning," repeated at the beginning of chapters viii., xii. and xvi. They had evidently written raising questions as to marriage, things offered to idols, spiritual gifts and collections.

Chapter vii. is almost entirely taken up with marriage, though in verses 17 to 24 instructions are given as to the secular callings that believers may be in, inasmuch as similar principles apply in both cases.

It looks as if the enquiries as to marriage had been occasioned by the fact that Paul, who was their spiritual father and example, had no wife himself. Most of them had been pagans, and hence their thoughts as to this great institution of God had been utterly astray and corrupted. The Apostle seized the opportunity to put things on the basis intended by God, while maintaining that there might be a few who, like to himself, could live above the claims of nature and forego marriage, because so fully claimed by the Lord and His service.

Clearly then, for the believer the normal thing is that marriage should take place, and all its duties and responsibilities be observed. It is contemplated in verse 5 that husband and wife may separate for a season, in order more fully to be at the Lord's disposal, but that is to be done mutually, and with prayer, lest the adversary should gain any advantage by it.

In verses 10 and 11 the Apostle enforces the instructions already laid down by the Lord. In verses 12 to 16 he gives further instructions in view of complications that often arise when the Gospel has reached one partner and the other is left unconverted, at least for the moment. If a Jew, male or female, contracted a matrimonial alliance with one of the surrounding nations there was nothing but defilement for both them and their children. This is made very plain in such chapters as Ezra ix., and Nehemiah xiii.

With the Gospel this is reversed, as verse 14 shows us. The sanctification and holiness spoken of is not intrinsic of course, but relative. If there be but a believing wife, God acknowledges the household as set apart for Him. The unbelieving partner may so hate the light that has come into the home that he will not stay there. But if he will stay there, and the children who do stay there—they enjoy the privileges that the light confers, it is to be hoped to their ultimate salvation.

These instructions may appear to us to be of but little interest. That is because we live under the abnormal conditions which Christendom has created. Had the church maintained its proper character, as a circle of light and blessing, surrounded by the darkness of this world, yet separate from it, we should more easily see the point of it all. Those preaching the Gospel among the heathen and seeking sympathetically to help their converts in the problems that arise, find here the guidance that they need.

In the matter of one's earthly calling, as in marriage, the path for the believer is to accept the existing situation, only bringing into it a new power, to the glory of God. We are to abide in the calling in which we were called by the Gospel, only it must be "with God." (ver. 24). If we cannot have God with us in it, then we must abandon it.

Having given these instructions to the married, Paul turns in verse 25 to "virgins" and the instructions concerning them continue to verse 38. Then the two verses that close the chapter give a brief word of guidance to widows.

It seems pretty clear that in this passage the word, "virgin" is used as covering the unmarried of either sex. The Apostle's teaching may be summarized in this: that marriage is good, as is every divine institution; it is wholly right and permissible; yet that to remain in the unmarried state is better, if it is maintained in order to be more wholly at the Lord's disposal for His interests. If such do not "attend upon the Lord without distraction," their celibacy may only cast a snare upon them.

Now let it be noted that this is the point of view maintained all through the chapter. If the married couple separate it is to be as giving themselves to fasting and prayer. If in a mixed marriage the converted partner goes on peacefully and patiently with the unconverted, it is as seeking the Lord's glory in his or her salvation. If the slave, being converted goes on humbly and contentedly with his menial occupations, it is because therein he abides with God. If the "virgin" remains unmarried, it is because he or she aims at being without worldly care, only caring for holiness and the service of the Lord. If the widow remarries, she does so "in the Lord;" which means, according to His will and direction.

See, then, how this chapter, which some might feel inclined to skip as being of no particular interest, not only contains instructions as to marriage, valuable in themselves, but also enforces the great point that for the Christian the claims of God and His service take precedence of all else. We are to recognize that, "the time is short," or, "straitened:" the word used means contracted as to space, and is only used in one other place in the New Testament, viz., Acts v. 6., in reference to Ananias being "wound up" for burial. Alas! how often we do not recognize that we are living in a straitened time, when the issue has been narrowed up by the death and resurrection of Christ, and hence we should hold all that we possess in the world with a light hand, ready to quit at a moment's notice.

Before passing on to chapter viii., let us glance more particularly at verses 6, 10, 12, 17, 25, 40. Some of the expressions used in these verses have been seized upon by those who would deny, or at least weaken, the inspiration of Scripture.

The force of verse 6 is, "I speak as permitting, not as commanding." Certain things in connection with marriage are commanded, others permitted. This is simple enough.

Verse 10 refers to some of these commands; only Paul recalls that there was nothing new about them, for the Lord Himself had so commanded, when here amongst men.

On the other hand, beginning with verse 12 the Apostle does give commands which had not previously been issued by the Lord. The time to issue them had not come until the problems that they meet had been created by the Gospel being widely preached. There is no difficulty in this, for what the Apostle commanded, and ordained in all assemblies, as stated in verse 17, was of full authority. There is no difference *as to authority* between commands coming from the lips of the Lord when on earth, and those coming from Him in heaven, through the lips or pens of His apostles.

In verse 25 Paul carefully guards the instructions that follow, lest they be used as absolute commands to the casting of a snare upon some (ver. 35). They are but his judgment, yet judgment of a very spiritual order, for, as the last words of the chapter significantly say, "I think that I also have the Spirit of God." The application of these Spirit-given instructions all depended upon the spiritual state of those who heard them. Hence Paul was inspired to issue no command but to give his judgment.

These fine distinctions are very striking, and indicative of the wisdom of God, and of the reality and scope of divine inspiration. Instead of weakening it they confirm it.

CHAPTER 8

THE OPENING WORDS of chapter viii. are really, "Now concerning," for evidently the Corinthians were perplexed as to the right course to adopt in relation to things offered to idols, and had mentioned the matter in their letter to Paul. No such problems confront us, yet we shall find the instructions laid down of much value, for our guidance in many a problem that does confront us.

Before coming to the point, however, the Apostle puts in parenthetically a word of warning. The Corinthians prided themselves upon their knowledge. Yet knowledge is a small and poor thing compared with love. Knowledge, if by itself, only puffs up, whereas love builds up. Moreover, at best all our knowledge is partial. It has strict limitations. We do not really know anything with a full and absolute knowledge. If we imagine that we do we only show thereby that we as yet know nothing as we ought to know it. Whereas if we love God we can rest assured that we are known of Him. And that is the great thing.

With verse 4 the Apostle commences his instructions. And first of all, what is the truth about the idols themselves? The truth is that they are nothing in the world. Deluded men may venerate these strange objects and treat them as gods, but we know them as but the work of men's hands, and that there is no other God but one. In thus speaking Paul was not overlooking the fact that demons and their power lay behind the idols, for he alludes to this sinister fact in verses 19 and 20 of chapter x.

Pagans may venerate many gods and lords, but to us they are nothing. We know but one God and one Lord. There is the Father, the Originator and Source of all, and we are for Him. There is the Lord Jesus, the great Administrator in the Godhead, and all things, ourselves included, are by Him. This being so we may utterly decline to recognise the idols of the heathen in any way, and so treat all meats as alike—whether offered to idols or not.

However, as verse 7 says, this knowledge is by no means the portion of all. There will always be found many in the ranks of believers who are unable to view such matters in the calm, dispassionate light of pure knowledge. They do not rise above their feelings and other subjective impressions. Once these knew that the meat had been so offered, they could not get away from the feelings engendered by it. They had "conscience of the idol" and it troubled them continually. Their conscience was weak, for it was not fortified by that clear and happy knowledge which Paul enjoyed, and being weak it was defiled. How was the situation to be met? What was the stronger believer to do?

The answer is very instructive. The Apostle firmly maintains the freedom of the stronger brother. It really is a fact that meat does not commend us to God. Our practices may differ. Some may eat and some not eat. But there is no advantage in the one, nor is there any coming short in the other. There is neither plus nor minus in the question, *as before God*.

But *as among ourselves*, in the Christian circle, there is something to be considered. Apparently some of the Corinthians, strong in their knowledge of the nothingness of idols, went as far as sitting at the meat in the precincts of the idol's temple. This was carrying their knowledge to a great length, and running the risk of becoming a stumbling-block. Some of the weaker ones might be tempted to copy them, wishing for a larger liberty, and having done so become stricken by an accusing conscience, and perish.

The perishing has nothing to do with the salvation of the soul. It means rather that the weak brother would be put out of action and destroyed as to his spiritual state, and consequently as to his testimony and service, by his weak conscience being wounded. No believer who falls under a cloud, owing to a defiled conscience, is of any use in the wars of the Lord.

Some of us might feel inclined to say, "Oh, but he is after all only a weak brother, and consequently of very little account as a servant or soldier of the Lord." If we should speak thus we should be guilty of forgetting that he is one of those "for whom Christ died," and therefore of immeasureable value to Him. This is the true light in which to view our brother. So dear is he that to sin against him is to sin against Christ.

The Apostle never forgot those words, "Saul, Saul, why persecutest thou Me?" And we must never forget them. The truth enshrined in them confronts us in a number of scriptures. Those who would strike a blow at Christ today, strike at His saints. Those who would serve Christ today, care for and serve His saints. That which is done to even the least of His brethren He will accept as done to Himself. God grant that we may not forget this. Real devotion to Christ is far more truly and effectively expressed by devoted service to His cause and people than by much outpouring of devotional and endearing language, either to Him or concerning Him.

Paul's own attitude is tersely summed up in the last verse of the chapter. Rather than be a cause of stumbling to his brother he would never eat flesh again. He would practise self-denial, and cut out of his life what was perfectly lawful, with a view to his brother's good. This is the fruit of divine love being at work. Would to God we had much more of it working in our hearts!

There is one further remark to be made as regards this chapter. Verse 6 is sometimes quoted by those who would deny the deity of the Lord Jesus. They make the point that since "there is but one God, the Father," and Jesus Christ is spoken of only as "one Lord," it must be incorrect to speak of Him also as God, even though other scriptures clearly do so.

Without a doubt, in this verse deity is attributed to the Father alone, and dominion as Lord to Jesus alone. It has however been very aptly remarked that, "The deity of Christ can no more be denied because the Father is here called 'one God,' than the dominion of the Father can be denied because the Son is called 'one Lord.'" To this we may add—or the deity and dominion of the Spirit be denied, because He is not mentioned at all.

The fact is, of course, that the Godhead is being presented in contrast with the many gods and lords of the pagan world; and in the Godhead the Son is He who has taken the place of Lord. Read the verse as limited by its context, and there is no real difficulty.

1 CORINTHIANS

Chapter 9

CHAPTER VIII CLOSES with Paul's considerate willingness to forego his undoubted rights, if thereby he might save one of his weaker brethren from a spiritual disaster. Chapter ix. opens with a very forcible assertion of his apostolic position and its privileges. The two things are entirely consistent, but he knew only too well that the adversaries of himself and of his Lord would attempt to score a point off him in this matter. They would insinuate that this gracious consideration of his was merely a piece of camouflage, intended to disguise the fact that he was no real apostle at all, but just an unaccredited upstart. The Corinthians had evidently been impressed by the pretentious claims of the adversaries, and their minds somewhat warped as a consequence. Hence Paul had to speak plainly as to his divinely-given authority.

He was indeed an apostle; and he had full liberty as to the matters just discussed. He had not been with Christ in the days of His flesh, as had the twelve, but he had seen the Lord in His glory. Moreover the Corinthians themselves were the fruit of his apostolic labours. Verse 2 delivers a crushing answer to any among them who, influenced by the adversaries, were inclined to question his apostleship. Why, they were themselves the proof of the validity of his work! To throw doubt on the reality of his work was to throw doubt on the reality of their own conversion. At the end of his second epistle he reverts to this argument, and he amplifies it. See xiii. 3-5.

Hence, if any wished to cross-examine him on the point, he had an answer that could not be gainsaid. His adversaries thought any stick good enough to beat him with. Again and again he did not eat or drink this or that out of consideration for others. He did not, like other apostles, have a wife to help him and share his travels. He and Barnabas had travelled and laboured unceasingly, without those breaks for rest which others enjoyed. And further, instead of being chargeable to others in respect of his bodily needs, he had laboured with his own hands for a living and taken nothing from anybody at Corinth. Every one of these things was seized upon in the endeavour to discredit him. As a matter of fact they were heavily to his credit; for each was within his rights. He was foregoing things that were properly his, as a man and as a servant of the Lord, because of his utter devotion to his Master's interests.

Paul was thus forced to speak of his own case. But the Holy Spirit who inspired him took occasion to lay down what is the Lord's will and pleasure as regards those whose whole time, by His call, is devoted to the Gospel, and the service of God's holy things. It is ordained that "they which preach the gospel should live of the gospel." That evidently is the normal thing. If any who thus labour have means of their own and do not need such help, or if any are found who though needing it are great enough, like Paul, to do without it, that is another matter. Only there is just this difference, that there is no virtue in the declining of help by those who have enough: the virtue is when those who have nothing forego their rights.

The principle that the Apostle lays down is supported by spiritual reasoning in verse 7. But then it was not merely the word of a man—even of a spiritual man: the law spoke in exactly the same way. The little piece of legislation, which seems so strangely interjected, in Deuteronomy xxv. 4, established the principle in connection with a humble beast of burden. Moreover it was also enforced practically in connection with the temple service and Jewish altars. Finally, it was definitely so ordained by the Lord Himself for the present moment. Matthew x. 10, and other passages in the Gospels show this. The principle then is overwhelmingly established. Let all who love the Lord be very careful not to neglect any true servant, called by Him to His service. If we do so we shall be flying in the face of His word, and consequently be great losers ourselves.

In passing, let us notice that the way in which Deuteronomy xxv. is quoted here leads us to expect that we shall find in the law, both enshrined and illustrated, many a principle of conduct which the New Testament enjoins upon us as well pleasing to God. There is nothing surprising in this for God Himself is ever the Same. We shall however find new principles of conduct in the New Testament which are not found in the Old. Just one word of caution is needful. Keep a tight rein on the imagination when thus searching the law. The dreamy mind can produce seeming analogies, which though piously intended, are nothing but fancy running riot!

The last clause of verse 10 is somewhat obscure. The New Translation runs, "and he that treads out corn, in hope of partaking of it," which makes it quite plain. Only the application is, that he who labours to share with us *spiritual* things must not be debarred from sharing in our *carnal* things—things that have to do with the needs of our flesh.

Has ever another lived during the church's history like unto Paul—entitled to so much, yet claiming so little? His mind was to suffer all things rather than be the least hindrance to the progress of the Gospel. He would rather die than fail as to this. Blessed man! No wonder he could exhort the saints saying, "Be imitators of me."

See, too, how tremendously real to him was the call of God to preach the Gospel. He knew that a "dispensation" (or an "administration") was committed to him, and it was woe to him should he be wanting in it. It might have been displeasing to him and against his will, as it was against Jonah's will to preach to Nineveh; but then necessity was laid upon him. He would have been compelled to serve through a good deal of woe, even as Jonah was. Of course it was not distasteful. He gloried *in* it, though in doing it he had nothing to glory *of*. And doing it willingly he knew that his reward was sure. It was part of his reward to be able to preach the Gospel without charge. How lovely to be able to declare the salvation which is "without money and without price," raising no questions as to money or price in return for preaching it!

But the Apostle's zeal for the Gospel carried him further even than this. He was perfectly free. He lay under obligations to no man. Yet in calculating love he made himself servant to all that he might gain "the more," or, "the most possible." He was out to win as many as possible, so, within the limits of the will of God, he adapted himself to those he sought to win. He specifies four classes, the Jews, those under law, those without law and the weak. He accommodated himself to each class as he approached them, but of course without doing anything contrary to the revealed will of God. Testimony to this is found in the short parenthesis which occur in verses 20 and 21.

The parenthesis in verse 20 does not appear in our Authorized Version. But it should be there. "As under the law (not being myself under law) that I might gain them that are under the law." In verse 21 the parenthesis is quite evident, being printed in brackets. In the New Translation it is rendered, "not as without law to God, but as legitimately subject to Christ." This signifies that when Paul approached the man under law, he observed the conventions which the law imposed, so as not to offend their susceptibilities—everything in fact, so long as it did not deny the fact that he himself was not under the law. When he approached the man without law he did so on *that* basis. Only he was always careful to let it be seen that he himself was not a lawless man but rightly subject to the Lord. It is evident then that the Apostle really studied the people that he approached, and their idiosyncracies, so that he might avoid everything which would needlessly prejudice them against the Message that he brought. He was far removed from that mistaken spirit that would say, "God can save and take care of His own elect," and as a result almost hurl the Gospel at people's heads, without much care as to the result.

Fancy the Apostle becoming as weak to the weak—talking in very simple and elementary terms for people of small intellect! No easy task that for a man of giant intellect! Yet he did it. This is the holy art which every really devoted and efficient teacher in a Sunday School has to learn. They need to become as a child to gain the children. This does not mean that they become childish. No, but they should become child-like, and study the mind of a child. And the one end in view is, *salvation.*

When we come to verse 24 we can see how the Apostle's thoughts began to expand and take in the whole spirit and character which should mark the servant of the Lord. We are viewed as athletes contending in the games, whether running or fighting. Hence we should be marked by zeal, directness of purpose, and a temperate, self-denying life in all things. The athlete, whether in the Grecian games of two thousand years ago, or in the contests today, is careful not to let his body get the mastery of him. The very opposite. He masters his body, brings it into subjection to a very strict regime, even buffets it with continual exercises. And all this to the winning

83

of a crown that quickly fades. Let us aim at the same things, only of a spiritual sort, that we may be invested in due season with a fadeless crown; for, alternatively, it is possible to ignore these things, and though a very eloquent preacher to others, to be rejected oneself.

Our chapter ends upon a very unpleasing word, "castaway," or, *rejected*, or *reprobate*. A good deal of controversy has raged around it. Many have seized upon it to prove that the true believer may yet be rejected, and lost for ever. Others realizing that other passages plainly negative this, have sought to explain it as simply signifying disapproved and rejected as to service, as to receiving a prize—disqualified, in fact.

We believe, however, that the true force of the expression is seen if we allow the word to have the full and weighty meaning which is proper to it, and read it in connection with the first twelve verses of chapter x. In our version the first word of the chapter is, "Moreover." It appears however that really the word is simply, "For." This indicated that what follows directly illustrates the point in question. "For . . . all our fathers were under the cloud . . . but with many of them God was not well pleased: for they were overthrown in the wilderness. The great mass of Israel had the externals of their holy religion, yet they totally missed its vital power, having no faith. They did not keep under their bodies but gave themselves up to their lusts, and miserably perished. From this point of view they were types of people who, though well fortified in the profession of the Christian religion, are yet not true believers and perish.

The meaning of "castaway," seems clearly fixed thus by the character of its context. But the difficulty remains—why did Paul speak of himself in this way? Why be so emphatic, "I MYSELF should be a castaway?" The answer is, we believe, that in so writing Paul had in view not only the Corinthians, whom he had just been blaming for great laxity of life, but also—and perhaps mainly—the mischief-making adversaries who had been leading them astray. These adversaries were unquestionably men who were lax self-pleasers, the very opposite of such as keep under their body, though great preachers to others. Yet Paul did not name them directly, any more than he directly named the leaders of parties earlier in the epistle. Then he transferred the matter to himself and to Apollos. Here he does not even bring Apollos into the matter, but just transfers it to himself alone. It is after all a very common figure of speech. Many a preacher has said, "When I owe a year's rent, and cannot pay a penny of it, then . . . so and so." The good man never owed any rent in his life, but to illustrate his point he transfers the matter to himself. Delicacy forbids that he should transfer it to his hearers, and suggest that they had rent which they could not pay.

Paul had no doubt about himself. In just the verse before he had said, "I therefore so run, *not as uncertainly*." But he had many grave doubts about the adversaries, and some about the Corinthians. And he made his warning the more effective by applying it to himself. The mere fact that one is a preacher guarantees nothing.

CHAPTER 10

OUTWARD PRIVILEGES AND rites also guarantee nothing, as is witnessed by the history of Israel, summarized in the opening verses of chapter x. They had things that answered to baptism and the supper of the Lord, and yet they were overthrown and destroyed. And in all this they were "ensamples," or "types," for us.

In their passage of the Sea we have a type of baptism. At that point they definitely commited themselves to the authority and leadership of Moses; just as in Christian baptism, which is in the Name of the Lord Jesus, we are definitely committed to *His* authority and leadership. Though neither cloud nor sea actually touched them, they were *under* the one and *through* the other.

Verse 3 refers to the manna: verse 4 to the rock of which they drank in Exodus xvii, and Numbers xx. Both one and the other were "spiritual," for both were supernatural: and both were types of Christ. But in spite of these peculiar privileges, which were common to all Israel, the great majority of them were overthrown in the wilderness. This sad fact is referred to again in Hebrews iii. and iv., and there it is pointed out that the root of the whole trouble was that they had no faith. Our scripture tells us that what they did have was lust, and idolatry, and fornication, and the spirit of tempting God and of murmuring. Where faith comes in these evil things go out.

Now the Spirit of God has recorded these things for our warning. The true believer is marked by confidence in God, and the more simple and absolute his confidence the better. But it is correspondingly true that he is marked by no confidence in himself, and the more deep his self-distrust the better. It is when we think that *we* stand that we are in danger of a fall. It is quite another thing when a saint has confidence that "God is able to make him stand" (Rom. xiv. 4).

And not only is God able to support us, but also He keeps a watchful eye upon us in His faithfulness, not permitting us to be tempted beyond a certain limit. The temptations that confront us are "common to man," or such as "belong to man." They are not of some superhuman sort. And again there is with them an issue, or way out. "Way of escape," might lead us to suppose that we may always expect some way by which we may escape the temptation altogether. It is not that, but that God always sees to it that there is a way through by which we may emerge unscathed at the other side. Temptation may be like a long dark tunnel, but there is always visible the light of day at the further end.

Having issued this tremendous warning, the Apostle gives it a very personal turn in verse 14. The whole of chapter viii was taken up with the matter of idols, and of meats offered to them; and now this verse brings us back to that point. That chapter asserted the liberty of the believer in regard to meats offered to idols. This verse counter-balances the matter by stressing the enormous evil of the idols themselves. Idolatry is not merely to be avoided; it is to be fled from, as an utterly abhorrent thing.

Let us in every sense of the word keep ourselves from idols.

Up to this point in the epistle the Apostle had addressed the Corinthians on the ground of their responsibility, and therefore assumed that there might be some amongst them who were unreal. At verse 15 he changes his view-point somewhat and addresses them as "wise-men." Not every true Christian could be so designated, we fear; and it is certain that no unconverted person could be. He speaks to the true members of the body of Christ, who possess His Spirit, and hence are capable ot judging concerning that which he is now going to bring before them. Verses 16 to 22 contain reasonings, the spiritual force of which should come home to us.

The simple primary meaning of the cup and the loaf, of which we partake in the Supper of the Lord, is the blood and the body of Christ. This was quite evident from the moment of the original institution, as recorded in three of the Gospels. But there was a further significance, underlying the primary meaning, which does not come to light until we reach the verses now before us: that is, the thought of "communion" or "fellowship." This holy ordinance is not merely an occasion appealing to the deepest instincts of personal and individual piety; it is an occasion of communion, springing out of the fact that we who partake of the one loaf are as much one as is the loaf of which we partake.

But let us at this point carefully distinguish things that differ. The one loaf signifies the body of Christ which was given for us in death. The fact that we believers, though many, *all partake* of that one loaf signifies that we are one body. We are one body by a Divine act—see xii. 13. Partaking all together of the one loaf does not make us one body, but it is the sign that we are one body. And to that sign Paul appeals to enforce his point.

The point he enforces is this, that communion is involved in the Supper of the Lord: not merely communion *with* one another, but the communion *of* the blood and body of the Lord. There is nothing here to foster superstition. That which we *break* is bread. That of which we *partake* is bread. Yet in drinking and in partaking we have communion *in that which the cup and the bread signify;* and shall be held responsible in regard to *that*, as is plainly stated in the next chapter, verse 27. This is exceedingly solemn truth—truth, which all too often is overlooked.

In verse 18 the Apostle shows that there was a fore-shadowing of this truth in the case of Israel, inasmuch as the priests were permitted to eat certain parts of certain offerings, and in the case of the peace offering even the offerer had certain parts to eat. Details as to this are given in Leviticus vi. and vii. If these chapters be read it will be seen that restrictions were laid upon those who eat. All defilement had to be kept far from them just because they were thereby in communion with the altar of God, and all that it signified. Had they taken liberties with their holy food and treated it unworthily, they would have come under serious consequences.

The same thing was true in principle of the idol sacrifices of the Gentile world. The idols they venerated represented demons; and these demons were but subordinate officers of Satan. By their sacrifices they entered into the communion of demons. Now such a communion as this the child of God is to flee at all costs.

Verses 16 to 20, then, set before us three communions, the Christian, the Jewish, the heathen; centred respectively in the Table of the Lord, the Altar in the midst of Israel, and the idol sacrifices of paganism; and expressed in each case by the act of eating. In this passage Israel's altar is not in question so it is merely introduced as an illustration; and left at that, (to be referred to further in Hebrews xiii. 10). The issue here lies between the communion of Christ's death and the communion of demons. These two are totally, fundamentally and continuously opposed. It is impossible to be a participator in both. "Ye cannot," says the Apostle, twice in verse 21.

And supposing someone ignores this "cannot" and is bold enough, having partaken of the Lord's table, to partake of the table of demons—what then? Then, he provokes the Lord to jealousy for the sake of His Name and glory. The Lord will not give His glory to another, and the offender will come into sharp collision with the Lord Himself, and taste the bitterness of coming under His dealing in discipline, possibly unto death. Disciplined of the Lord he will soon discover that he is not stronger than He, and come face to face with the toilsome road of repentance, which is the only way that leads to recovery.

In the mercy of God we are hardly endangered by "the fellowship of demons." But, because of that, let us not lightly dismiss this truth from our minds, for the principle of it is of much wider application. If we partake of the Lord's table it is necessary for us to set a watch lest we partake also in things that are inconsistent with it and its holiness. If we are in the communion of the blood and body of Christ, we shall find it great enough to exclude all other communions. We shall keep clear of communions that can only entangle us, and may possibly defile us. We fear that the implications of this truth are often ignored. It is all too possible to partake of the cup and of the loaf without giving much thought to the solemn obligations that are connected therewith. We can have no fellowship with evil things.

This serious matter disposed of, there remained the questions as to meats which had been offered to idols, to which the Apostle had previously referred. He digressed from it at the beginning of chapter ix., and he returns to it in verse 23 of our chapter. The pagan world was so full of

87

1 CORINTHIANS

idols that most of the animals, whose carcases were offered for sale in their markets, had been killed in connection with idol sacrifices and ceremonies. Supposing the Christian bought his food in the "shambles," or "markets," and if he was eating in the house of someone who did not believe, and hence had no feelings on these points, what was he to do?

In this connection Paul makes the statement twice over, "All things are lawful." That is he sets us in a place of liberty. Yet he reminds us that by no means everything is either "expedient," (that is, "profitable") or "edifying;" and moreover that we are not merely to consider what is good for ourselves, but what is good for others. The two-fold test that he mentions is capable of a thousand applications. Again and again situations arise as to which we have not only to raise the question, Is it lawful? but also, Is there profit in it? and, Does it tend to building up? And further we have to consider the profit and the building up of *all*. If we ordered our lives by that standard we should be cutting out a good many things of a doubtful and unprofitable nature.

We may well thank God for the liberty which is ordained in this passage. It would have been an intolerable burden to the early Christians if they had been responsible to track out the history of every bit of meat they bought in the markets, or consumed in the house of some acquaintance. For us today, living under conditions which are highly complicated and artificial, it would be ten times worse. It is evidently God's will for His people that they accept the conditions in which their lot is cast, and pursue a simple path through, without inquisitively looking for sources of trouble, whether meat be in question or any other matter.

If, on the other hand, without any special inquisition, one becomes aware of defilement, as in the case supposed in verse 28, then it is to be carefully avoided. In so saying the Apostle reasserts what he had stated at the end of chapter viii.

This leads up to the very comprehensive instruction of verse 31, a statement which covers the whole of our lives. In all things we are to seek the glory of God: just as the next verse adds that we are to avoid giving offence to man. Indeed, taking this passage as a whole we may observe five valuable points which offer us guidance as to whether any course may, or may not, be according to the will of God. That which is according to His will (1) is lawful, (2) is expedient or profitable, (3) is to the edifying or building up of oneself or others, (4) is to the glory of God, (5) gives no occasion of stumbling to any. Often the question is asked, How may I get guidance? Well, here is some guidance of a very sure and definite sort. Are we always so willing to be guided when we get the guidance?

Verse 32 classifies mankind under three heads. Notice how distinctly "the church of God" stands out from both Jew and Gentile. The Old Testament classified men under two heads, Israel and the Gentiles. The Church, a body called out from both Jews and Gentiles, only appears in the New Testament. Though we have thus been called out from the mass of mankind we are to consider men, seeking their highest good, even their salvation. This was Paul's way even as it was the way of Christ. And we are to be imitators of Paul. Verse 1 of chapter xi. should be treated as the last verse of chapter x.

CHAPTER 11

THE FRESH PARAGRAPH begins with verse 2, which stands in very direct contrast with verse 17. The Apostle had referred to the institution of the Lord's Supper in chapter x., as we have seen; and there had been grave disorders in connection with it, demanding very heavy censure. However there were certain matters as to which he could praise them. So first he utters a word of praise. Certain "ordinances," or "directions," had been given to them, and they had remembered Paul and observed them. So even in this we see the Apostle exemplifying what he had just been saying. He sought the profit of the Corinthians by praising them before he blamed them, and in this he followed Christ, for it is exactly His way, as exemplified in His messages to the seven churches in Revelation ii. and iii.

But even here there was something as to which the Corinthians were ignorant. It seems that they observed directions given as to the behaviour of men and of women in connection with prayer and prophecy, without understanding the truth that governed those directions. That the man should engage in these spiritual exercises with uncovered head, and the woman with covered head, was not a mere whim, an arbitrary order. On the contrary it was in accord with the Divine order, established in connection with Christ. Three headships are mentioned in verse 3.

The highest of these springs from the fact that in becoming Man, that He might assume the office of Mediator, the Lord Jesus took the place of subjection. Isaiah had prophesied the coming of Jehovah's Servant, who would have the ear of the learner, and never swerve from His direction: that is to say, Jehovah would be His Head and Director in all things. This was perfectly fulfilled in Christ; and the fact that He is now risen and glorified has not altered the position. He is still the Servant of the will of God (though never less than God Himself) and the pleasure of Jehovah is to prosper in His hand to eternity. So the Head of Christ is God.

But then Christ is the Head of the man, as distinguished from the woman. A certain order was established in creation since "Adam was first formed, then Eve." That order is stated also in verses 8 and 9 of our chapter. She shared in his place and his distinctions, and even in the days of innocence headship was vested in Adam. Sin did not alter that headship, neither has the coming in of God's grace in Christ. So Christ is the Head of man, and of every man. And the head of the woman is the man.

Every member of the human body is directed from the head. So the figure is very simple and expressive. It is a matter, in one word, of *direction*. The woman is to accept direction from the man. The man is to accept direction from Christ. And Christ accepts direction from God, and does so perfectly. For the rest, it is done very imperfectly. The great mass of menfolk do not recognize Christ at all; and at the present time there is a great uprising of womenfolk against the direction and leadership of men, and that—significantly enough—especially in Christendom. Still none of these things alter that which is the divine ideal and order.

Now if any believer, man or woman, has to do with God and His things, whether it be in praying (i.e., addressing oneself to Him), or in prophesying (i.e., speaking forth words from Him), there is to be the observance of these directions as to the uncovering or covering of the head, as a sign that God's order is recognized and obeyed. Verses 14 and 15 further show that it is in keeping with this that the man has short and the woman long hair.

There is no contradiction between verse 5 of our chapter and verse 34 of chapter xiv., for the simple reason that there speaking in the assembly is in question, whereas in our chapter the assembly does not come into view until verse 17 is reached. Only then do we begin to consider things that may happen when we "come together." The praying or prophesying contemplated in verse 5 is not in connection with the formal assemblies of God's saints.

It was when the Apostle turned to deal with things that were transpiring in connection with their assemblies that he found himself bound to blame them. They came together to no profit but the reverse. In the first chapter he had alluded to these divisions or schisms in their midst, and it was when they came together that they were so painfully manifest. They still came together in one place. Things had not reached such a pass that they refused to meet any longer as one, and met in different buildings. Yet there were internal splits or fissures in the assembly, with all their disastrous effects.

Tidings of this had reached Paul's ears and he tells them plainly that he partly believed it, for he knew their carnal state. The word "heresies," in verse 19 means, "sects," or "schools of opinion;" and they are mentioned in Galatians v. 20, amongst the terrible "works of the flesh." If saints are found in a fleshly condition, heresies crop up as sure as they are alive. Hence, says the Apostle to the fleshly Corinthians, "there *must* be heresies among *you*." These heresies may have the effect of making manifest those foolishly "approved" by men: they will certainly reveal those who refuse this party making, and hence are "approved" of God.

What must be the judgment of the Spirit of God as to us today, in view of the way in which schools of opinion are flourishing in the church of God?

It is quite clear from the 20th verse that the Corinthian saints, though very numerous, were still meeting together in one building. They came together "in the church," as verse eighteen puts it: but those words have no reference to a building of any kind, but rather to the fact that they came together "in assembly;" that is in their church or assembly character. And when they did so these sects, or parties became painfully manifest, and also their proceedings were very disorderly; so disorderly in fact that the apostle refuses to recognize their feasts, which they called, "the Lord's supper," as being truly the supper of the Lord at all. They are not he says, *the Lord's Supper*, but *each one* taking *his own* supper.

There is, we believe, a double contrast here. First, between "the Lord's" and "his own." They treated the matter as if they were the masters of it and hence could arrange it as they pleased and generally do as they liked. This led to outrageous disorder at Corinth—some getting nothing, and others getting so much of the wine as to be drunken. Similar gross disorder may be avoided today, but have not many assumed that they are masters of the situation when this holy ordinance is in question, and so felt themselves perfectly free to alter it to taste?—free to turn it into a mass, or a sacrifice, free to have it ornate, or choral, free to confine its ministration to a priestly caste and have it so frequently as to be almost continuous, free to have it only once in several months, or to abolish it altogether.

But there is also the contrast between the Lord's supper which is a matter of *fellowship*, as chapter x. has just unfolded, and "every one" (or "each one") taking his own supper: that is, making it a purely *individual* matter. Even supposing that saints come together and observe the ordinance quite faultlessly, as regards all its externals, and yet treat it as a *purely personal privilege*, eliminating from it in their mind the thought that we do it as one body, they have missed the mark. It is not *each one acting and eating for himself*: it is rather *all acting together*.

Now the only remedy for disorder in connection with the Lord's supper—even in apostolic days, be it noted—was to go back to the original institution in its spirit, its significance, its orderly simplicity. Paul did not argue on the subject. In verses 23 to 27, he simply reverts to what had been instituted by the Lord Himself. And he did so, not as having received authentic information from the other apostles who had been present, but as having received the ordinance directly from the Lord, by divinely-given revelation. This revelation confirms the account already given by the inspired evangelists, and clarifies its meaning. Much that passes as an "orderly" and "beautiful" celebration or observance of this institution is simply *disorder* in the divine estimation. Any "order", however ornate or beautiful to human eyes, which is not *the divine order*, is *disorder* in the Divine eyes.

God has been pleased to give us four accounts of the institution of the Lord's supper, and the fourth through Paul has its own peculiar importance, inasmuch as it makes it quite clear that it is to be observed by Gentile believers as much as by Jewish, and also that it is to continue "till He come." The materials used are of the simplest—the bread, the cup— everyday sights in the homes of those days. The significance of the materials was very profound—"My body," "the new testament in my blood." And the whole spirit of the ordinance is "remembrance." We are to remember Him in the circumstances in which once He was, *in death*, though we know Him as the One now glorified in heaven.

The supper of the Lord then begins with remembrance of Him in death. Much will flow out of this remembrance and we cannot fail to be conscious of *blessing* (it is, "the cup of blessing") and consequently *bless God* in return. But we must penetrate beneath the symbols to that which they symbolize. We must discern the body and blood of Christ; and discerning this, we shall be preserved from treating these holy things in an unholy or unworthy manner, as the Corinthians had been doing. The Lord did not hold them guiltless, and they were eating and drinking judgment (see, margin) to themselves. They were guilty in respect of dishonour done not merely to a loaf and a cup, but to the body and blood of Christ, symbolized by the loaf and the cup. This is the plain force of verses 27 and 29.

What then should we do? When the Lord smote Uzzah in judgment because he treated the Ark of God as though it had been an ordinary object (see 2 Sam. vi.) David was displeased and left the Ark severely alone for a time. This was a mistake, which afterwards he rectified by honouring the Ark, and treating it as had been commanded by God. Paul's instructions to the Corinthians, in verses 28 to 30, exactly agree with this. God had interfered in judgment amongst them, many were weak and sickly and some had been removed by death. But this should not make them refuse to observe the Lord's supper further. The rather it should make them examine themselves and partake in a spirit of self-judgment. There had been *abuse*, but the remedy for this was not *disuse* but rather a careful *use*, in obedience to the design of God.

The closing verses of the chapter give us an example of God's chastening by way of retribution. They were being disciplined because of wrong committed. God chastens His children that they may not be judged with the world. And if only we judged ourselves we should be preserved from the evil and hence not need the hand of God upon us. Let us mark that! How excellent is the holy art of *self-judgment;* and how little practised. Let us cultivate it more and more. By it we should be preserved from innumerable errors. The Corinthians evidently neglected it and much was wrong with them. The Apostle had corrected the most glaring of their errors when they partook of the Lord's supper. There were others, but these could wait until he visited them in person: so he closes the chapter by saying, "the rest will I set in order when I come."

CHAPTER 12

THE CORINTHIANS CAME together in assembly not only to partake of the Lord's supper but also for the exercise of spiritual gifts, especially that of prophecy. In those days there were found prophets who were enabled by the Holy Spirit to give inspired utterances in the assembly. In this way God gave authoritative instruction and guidance while as yet the New Testament scriptures were in the making, and so not freely in the hands of believers as they are today. There was however a great danger in connection with this.

When God raised up prophets in Israel's history, Satan promptly confused the issue by raising up many false ones. In the days of Ahab there were 850 false to one true! The adversary followed the same tactics in the early days of the church and introduced into the public assemblies of saints men who gave inspired utterances truly, but inspired not by the Holy Spirit but by demons. Hence the test laid down in verse 3 of chapter xii. The confession of Jesus as LORD is the test. Many testimonies could be adduced, proving that this test always is effective. It infallibly works. In modern spiritist seances demons will often utter sentiments which are apparently high class and beautiful, but they will never acknowledge Jesus as Lord.

Moreover, in the pagan world it was supposed that each demon had a special line of things in which he operated: one was the spirit of healing, another the spirit of prophecy or divination, and so on. The Apostle instructs the Corinthians therefore, in verses 4 to 11, that all the gifts of a divine sort which may be manifested in the church, proceed from one and the self-same Spirit—the Holy Spirit of God. The Spirit is one: the manifestations of His power and working are many. Whether it be the Spirit (verse 4) or the Lord (verse 5) or God (verse 6) diversity proceeding from unity is the feature. Gifts are connected with the Spirit: administrations with the Lord: operations with God.

Now the gifts or manifestations of the Spirit are expressed through men in the assembly of God. No one man possesses all. Occasionally one may possess many. More usually he possesses but one. But whether one or many what is possessed by each one is intended not for the sole benefit of the possessor but for the profit of all. The better rendering of verse 7 is "But to each the manifestation of the Spirit is given for profit." (N. Tr.) The Corinthians were evidently acting rather like children; assuming that the spiritual gift conferred was something like a new toy, to be used and enjoyed for their personal pleasure and distinction. It was not; but rather a gift conferred on one member for the benefit of the whole body.

Hence, having ennumerated the different gifts, and again emphasized that all proceed from the same Holy Spirit, being bestowed at His sovereign will and discretion, the apostle passes in verse 12 to the one body, for the benefit of which all is given. The human body is used as an illustration. It has many members and yet is an organic unity. Then he adds, "so also is the Christ"—the definite article, "the," is in the Greek original.

This is a remarkable expression. It is not Christ personally; but rather that the one body—the church—being the body of Christ, His name can be called upon it.

The church then, as Christ's body, is an organic unity, just as the human body is. It has been formed by an act of God in the energy of the one Spirit. It is important that we should remember this, since by this fact its integrity is guaranteed. It cannot be violated or destroyed by man or by Satanic power, though the visible manifestation of it during its sojourn on earth may be, and has been, marred. The thing itself, divinely formed, abides, and will be perfectly displayed in glory.

The action of the Spirit in forming the one body is described as a "baptism." In baptism a man is submerged and figuratively buried. The one body was formed, and we are brought into it, on this basis; namely, that we as natural men, as children of Adam, with all our personal peculiarities and angularities, have been submerged in the one Spirit. Hence all our natural distinctions have disappeared in the one body. There was no greater national distinction than Jew and Gentile; no clearer social cleavage than bond and free. But these distinctions and cleavages, and all others like them, are gone in the one body. In the light of this how foolish and sinful were the parties and schools and cleavages among the Corinthians: how puerile their strivings for personal distinctions and profit! And how foolish and sinful and puerile are similar things which disfigure Christians today!

Let us take it to heart. We have forgotten the real force and meaning of that baptism by which we have found our place in the one body. Thank God, I am in the one body, but I am there on the basis of having my old "*I*" submerged. And you are there as having your old "*I*" submerged. And every other member of the body is there as having the old "*I*" submerged. And there is no other way of being in the one body but by having the old "*I*" submerged. If we all were really in the truth of this, what a change would come over the outward aspect of all things, amongst the saints of God.

But not only have we all been baptised in one Spirit into one body, but we each severally and for ourselves have been made to "drink into (or, of) one Spirit." This seems to be an allusion to John vii. 37-39. Each member of the body has personally received or imbibed of the one Spirit, so that He characterizes and governs each. Unity is thus produced in this two-fold way. Each has been submerged *in* the Spirit: and the Spirit is *in* each by a personal imbibing.

Verses 12 and 13 then, give us what has been brought to pass by God Himself in the energy of His Spirit, and consequently human failure does not enter into the matter. It is the ideal thing, but it is not, because of that, idealistic and unreal. It is not just a beautiful idea to be left in the airy region of mere ideas. No, it is an actual existing fact by Divine act; and faith perceives it and acts accordingly. If we do not perceive it we cannot act accordingly.

Let us then have faith to perceive what has been brought to pass by the Spirit's act, and what we have received by drinking of one Spirit; and may our whole life in relation to Christ Himself and our fellow members be influenced thereby.

If verse 13 teaches that all true believers have been baptized into one body, the next verse again emphasizes the corresponding truth that the body is composed of many members. The *unity* which God has established in the one body must not be confounded with *uniformity*. Uniformity is largely stamped upon man's work, especially in this our day, but not upon God's work. Man invents machines which turn out articles by the thousand or the million exactly uniform in all respects. In God's handiwork we see the utmost diversity in unity—unity in the most marvellous diversity.

In verses 14 to 26, the human body is taken as an illustration of this, and the point is worked out with great fulness of detail. The Apostle evidently felt it to be most important that the matter should be clearly understood. And why so important?

The answer to this is, we judge, that he knew the inveterate tendency of human hearts. It is so natural, even to believers, to love a little party all intent upon the same thing; in which all can settle down amiably and comfortably and without friction to enjoy themselves, in connection with that upon which all are intent. Then of course others, whose thoughts or activities or functions are so widely different, can be dispensed with; and the schism or division, of which verse 25 speaks, supervenes.

The illustration of this point, given in verse 21, is very striking. The eye is the organ of sight, the hand the organ of work. Some believers are "seers" marked by intelligence and spiritual insight. They revel in an understanding of the things of God. They give themselves to study and contemplation, and probably have very little time for active work. Other believers are very active workers: they put their hand to many a hard task in the interests of their Lord. Indeed they work so hard that their danger is lest their labour becomes uninstructed, and hence astray from the will of the Lord. Now the danger is that the "eye" may say to the "hand" I have no need of thee. It is not suggested that the "hand" may say this to the "eye". Practical experience proves that it is usually the intellectual, far-seeing brother who is tempted to speak thus to the brother who is far less intelligent but a far harder worker, rather than *vice versa*.

Again, the head and feet are placed in contrast. Not only seeing, but hearing, smelling and tasting are confined to the head. Only one of the five senses is distributed over the body. If the head is to exercise its functions it needs quietude and repose. But the feet are instruments of motion. The head wishes for what is still and stationary that it may be enabled to observe and hear and think, but the feet are all for that activity and movement that will disturb it. The head may be strongly tempted to say to the feet, I have no need of you!

In the human body every member is necessary, for God has tempered it together. He has given more abundant honour to those parts which might be esteemed without honour, and given abundant comeliness to what might appear uncomely. The Medical science seems to be accumulating proofs of this, by showing how obscure glands, which formerly no one thought much of, are really of great importance, exercising such a control that if they cease functioning the body dies. So it is in the body of Christ, and hence the members are to have the same care and interest in one another. If one is affected, either for good or ill, all are affected.

Observe that all through the illustration the human body is contemplated as the work of God. Verse 18 states it, and again verse 24 mentions it, and thereby schism is excluded. Again in verse 21 it does not say that the eye *should* not say to the hand, I have no need of thee, but that it *cannot*. In just the same way the one body of Christ is viewed as the fruit of God's work. It is what God has established; God's work which can never be undone by man.

Observe on the other hand that though it is God's work it is not because of that an idealistic thing, removed from the sphere of present and practical life, without any bearing upon the church in its present condition. The very opposite, for the Apostle at once proceeds to give just that present application.

That application begins in verse 27. The definite article "the," is not in the Greek, and is better omitted even though it produces clumsy English. He did not say, "Ye are *the* body of Christ," for that would have indicated to these saints at Corinth that they were the whole thing, and might have led to the further supposition that they were merely the one body in Corinth. Then there might be the one body in Ephesus, and so on, until the contradictory and inconsistent idea of there being many "one bodies" might have been reached. He said, "Ye are body of Christ," that is, they were of the body of Christ and bore the "body of Christ" character in Corinth, each of them being a member in particular.

They were members, then, of Christ's body, and from that he turns, in the next verse, to speak of how God had set some of these members in the "church," or "assembly." We do well to differentiate in our thoughts between the body of Christ, formed by Divine act, and the assembly as found in this world, whether locally at Corinth, or in its totality. But while we differentiate we must not divorce the two, since the action of the members takes place in the assembly, and their action is to be governed and regulated by the truth just set forth as to the body.

The "gifts" or "manifestations" of the Spirit, which were granted to some of the members, are detailed in verse 28. The order of them is to be noted. Apostles come first, diversities of tongues come last. The Corinthians, who were carnal, set great store by the more spectacular gifts, as do many carnally minded believers today. To speak in an unknown tongue was to them evidently the most desirable thing of all. Their estimate was however a mistaken one. The gifts are divided according to the sovereign

1 CORINTHIANS

will of the Spirit. No one gift was given to everybody. As a rule each individual had one distinguishing gift.

Seven questions are found in verses 29 and 30. They are asked but not answered because the answer is obvious. Uniformly the answer is, No. Notice the sixth question, since there are those who insist that no one has properly received the Holy Ghost if they do not speak with tongues. But, "do all speak with tongues?" The answer is, No. Yet they had all been "made to drink into one Spirit."

What then is to be our attitude in regard to the various gifts? We are to desire earnestly the better, or greater, gifts; that is, such as prophesying, or teaching, as is evident from the opening verses of chapter xiv. These are better because they are for wider and more general profit, and the gifts are given to each for the profit of all. And there is a way of more surpassing excellence by which this end may be reached. This way is the way of "charity" or *divine love*, as unfolded in chapter xiii. The Apostle turns aside for a moment from the main line of his theme to stress the surpassing excellence of that love which is the very nature of God himself.

Chapter 13

CHAPTER XIII. HAS become famous. Its extraordinary power is acknowledged not only by Christians but by a multitude of others. Foremost men acclaim it as marvellous, one of the literary wonders of the world, without perhaps at all appreciating the real drift of its teaching. What is it that it really says? The opening verse of chapter viii. has told us that it is love that edifies. This chapter expands that fact and shows us in the first place that the most shining gifts, if without love, are of no value; and in the second place that love is the force, even when gifts are present, that really accomplishes everything.

The first three verses contemplate gifts which may be possessed and exercised without love. If they are, the sum total of all that they effect and produce is, Nothing. Speaking with tongues is mentioned first, as that was the particular gift that was becoming rather a snare to the Corinthians. But that is followed by prophecy, which later is eulogised by the Apostle as first in importance; and that by knowledge and faith, and by the practical benevolence that nowadays goes by the name of "charity"; and that again by self-sacrifice of a very remarkable kind. What tremendous assertions are these which Paul makes!

A brother rises in the assembly and speaks words of peculiar sweetness and thrill, though quite unintelligible to us. We discover that he has actually made a Divine communication in a language of heaven, which angels use. How marvellous! How we should gaze at him! Yes. But if he has done this without love he might as well have brought an old brass pan into the meeting and hit it with a poker, for the good he has done, as regards the Lord's interests in the assembly.

And here comes another who has astonishing knowledge and understanding. He not only penetrates to the heart of Divine things, but he can communicate to others what he knows by reason of his prophetic gift. Also he has faith of an almost miraculous power. Yet he has not love! We are not told that he is like a clanging piece of brass, for it is possible that we may gain some help and understanding from what he says, and some inspiration from his remarkable faith. What we are told is, that he himself is nothing. If unspiritual ourselves we might imagine him to be a giant. Really he is less than a pigmy. He is *nothing*.

And supposing a third appears, who resolves, "I shall dole out all my goods in food," (N. Trans.) and is prepared to give his body to be burned! Why, we should feel inclined to exclaim, What a reward he will have in the coming day! But alas, he has not love. Then it will profit him *nothing*. The absence of love has rendered valueless the whole thing. In the light of these facts, negative though they are in their bearing, of what surpassing value is love!

Now we are to contemplate more closely the features that characterize love. First comes a very positive feature. It suffers long (or, has *long patience*) and is *kind*. Could anything surpass the long patience and kindness of God's dealings with rebellious man? No. Well, God is love. And in the measure in which we manifest the divine nature, we shall manifest long patience and kindness towards men generally, as well as towards our brethren.

This one positive feature is followed by negative features. Love is marked by the total absence of certain hideous deformities of character and behaviour, which are perfectly natural to us as men in the flesh. Paul strings them together. Here they are: (1) Envy of others: (2) Vaunting oneself, or vainglory, or as it has been translated, being "insolent and rash:" (3) Being puffed up or inflated with one's own importance: (4) Unseemly behaviour which follows hard on the heels of an inflated mind: (5) Self-seeking: (6) Touchiness, easily taking offence and provoked to anger: (7) Thinking evil, that is, quick to impute evil to others: (8) Rejoicing in iniquity, that is, glad to be able to point out inquity in others, and to denounce it. The string that runs right through these eight things is, *love of self*.

Alas! alas! how often are these features discernible in ourselves, and yet we are saints of God. It is all too easy for us to be like ships stranded on the dirty mud flats of self-love. What can lift us off? Nothing but a mighty inflow of the tide of Divine love. When saints forget themselves in the uplift of that tide most wonderful transformations are effected.

Verse 6, which mentions the eighth negative feature also introduces us to the second positive feature that is mentioned. Love *rejoices*, for it is indeed a joyous thing, but its joy is in or with the truth. Love and truth go hand in hand, and truth is joyous and full of gladness for our hearts.

Further positive features follow. Four are mentioned in verse 7. Love bears, or *covers*, all things. It never condones unrighteousness of course, yet it never finds its pleasure in publishing other people's misdeeds. It rather *believes* all that it can discover of the truth; it *hopes* that all that may be lacking will be supplied in due course; it *endures* meanwhile every deficiency that may exist. It is evident that the expression, "all things," four times repeated, must be understood as limited by its context. For instance, he who believes "all things," in an unlimited way, would simply be landed into a morass of uncertainties and deceptions.

The seventh positive characteristic of love is that it *never fails*. This is at once seen if we look at it as seen in all its fulness in God Himself. If Divine love had failed, every region, that ever had been touched by sin, would have been lying in the hopeless blackness of everlasting night. In the presence of sin's great catastrophe Divine love did not waver or fail. It designed rather the way of righteousness whereby the situation should be much more than retrieved; men blessed and the Divine Name triumphantly vindicated. True, it may appear for a time to fail. But God has a long outlook and plans by milleniums rather than days. Love always wins in the end. And so it does when Divine love works in and through feeble saints such as ourselves. It may appear to be defeated a hundred times over, but it is not: in the end it wins, it does not fail.

Now this cannot be said of even the greatest of gifts. Prophecies may fail, in the sense of being done away with, having served their purpose (the word "fail" is not the same as "faileth" which occurs just before). Tongues shall cease; they will not be needed in a coming day. Knowledge even shall "vanish away," (same word as translated "fail" in connection with prophecies). What this vanishing away means is shown in the next few verses. Our knowledge and prophesying—even that of a Paul—is in part. Presently in regard to both knowledge and prophecy, perfection will be reached and, when it is, all that is partial will fail and vanish away; just as the moon fails and vanishes away in the light of the sun.

The Apostle further illustrates this point by his own childhood. When a child he spoke, thought, reasoned, as a child. When manhood was reached he was done with what belonged to childhood's days. The application of this illustration is in verse 21. The contrast lies between now and then; between our present condition, limited as we are by flesh and blood, though we are indwelt by the Holy Ghost, and the heavenly condition into which we shall enter when we are in the likeness of Christ, even as to our bodies. *Now* it is seeing as through a glass obscurely: *then* knowing according as we have been known.

Spiritual gifts are indeed wonderful things, but we are apt to overestimate them. Wonderful as they are, they are but partial, even the greatest of them. Take note of this ye gifted men! Your knowledge and your prophesyings, even when in the full energy of the Spirit, are but partial. They are not the full and complete thing. If you do not remember

99

this you might become arrogant in your knowledge. If you do remember it you will be humble.

We are very thankful for the knowledge and the prophecies, yet we know that all of it will vanish away in the blaze of that perfect light into which we are going. There are things that abide, and the greatest of them is LOVE.

Sometimes we sing,
"When faith and hope shall cease,
And love abide alone."

That may be true, but it is not what is stated here. On the contrary, it says, "Now *abideth* faith, hope, charity, these three." The contrast is between the most shining gifts which *pass* and the *abiding* characteristics of Divine life in the saints. The more we approximate to what is carnal, the more likely we are to be dazzled by mere gifts. The more we approximate to the spiritual, the more we appreciate faith, hope, and love. And the more we shall see that love is the greatest of all.

It will be found ultimately that the greatest saint is not he of the most striking gift, but he or she that most truly dwells in love, for, "he that dwelleth in love dwelleth in God, and God in him." (1 John iv. 16).

No gift counts for much except it is controlled and energized by love. LOVE is indeed the more excellent way.

CHAPTER 14

CHAPTER XIII. BEING a parenthesis, showing the surpassing excellence of divine love, the first verse of chapter xiv. is connected with the last verse of chapter xii. Love is to be pursued as the thing of all importance, for where it is, spiritual gifts may safely be desired. Where love reigns, they will be desired not for personal advancement or distinction, but for the profit and blessing of all. Hence the gift of prophecy is given the first place. It is amongst the best gifts which may be coveted earnestly.

The Apostle at once proceeds to contrast the gift of prophecy with the gift of tongues, which evidently had great attractions in the estimation of the Corinthian believers, being so obviously supernatural in its origin. He does not cast any doubt upon this particular spiritual manifestation. The "tongues" to which he alluded, were the genuine manifestation of the power of the Holy Spirit, and *under the control of the speaker*. The Apostle spoke with tongues himself in larger measure than any of the Corinthians, but he did so in a controlled and restrained way. Verses 6, 15, 18, and 19 show this. The point is, that even when the gift of tongues is at its best, it is of less profit than the gift of prophecy.

When the Corinthian saints came together in assembly before the Lord, He was to be their Director in all things, and all their activities were to be in the energy of the Spirit of God. This chapter furnishes us with many directions from the Lord—directions of a general character, which are binding at all times. Whether on a given occasion this or that brother should take *any* audible part, and if they should, *what* part, is a matter which must be settled in reference to the Lord's will when the occasion comes. But when they *do* take part, they must do so in subjection to the general instructions given by the Lord in this chapter, acting as men of a sound mind enlightened by the word of the Lord. It may be remembered how Paul speaks to Timothy of God having given us the spirit "of power, and of love, and of a sound mind." This is exemplified in the chapter before us. Chapter xii. shows us the Spirit of power in the assembly; chapter xiii. the spirit of love; chapter xiv. the spirit of a sound mind.

Spiritual activities in the assembly may be Godward or manward. Activities Godward are mentioned in verses 14 to 17—praying, singing, giving of thanks. But in the main the chapter is concerned with what is manward—prophecy, tongues, doctrine, interpretation. These gifts are to be exercised for the benefit of others, and the test the Apostle applies is that of general edification. If the exercise of the gift edifies it is of profit. If it does not edify it is to no profit.

According to verse 3 the end to be attained is threefold. The simple meaning of edification is building up. The foundation is laid when the Gospel is received; but upon the foundation an immense deal has to be built up, so that edification may rightly continue throughout a long Christian life. Exhortation, or encouragement, follows. We pass through a hostile world, subject to all kinds of adverse influences. Hence we continually need what will stir us up to spiritual vigour. Then thirdly, comfort, or consolation is a continuous need in the assembly; for there are always those present who are face to face with sorrow and trouble and disappointment, and who need that which will lift them above their sorrows. We might summarize this threefold end as, *building up, stirring up*, and *lifting up*. Prophecy leads to the attainment of these three things.

Prophecy is not only the foretelling of future events. It includes the forth-telling of God's mind and message. In the apostolic days, before the written New Testament Scriptures were in circulation, there was prophecy of an inspired sort, such as is claimed by the Apostle Paul for himself and others in chapter ii. of our epistle, verse 13. We have not that today, nor do we need it, having the inspired Scriptures in our hands. Prophecy of an uninspired sort we may still have, for we may still find men gifted of God to open up to us, from the inspired Scriptures, the mind of God and His message for any given moment; and when we find it we do well to be very thankful for it. Such ministry of the Word of God does indeed build up, and stir up, and lift up.

As to the gift of tongues; its exercise is not forbidden, but it is definitely and strictly regulated in this chapter. The regulations laid down are of much importance. They make it certain that this gift if present, and exercised, shall be used for profit. Further, we have no hesitation in saying that when and where the gift is claimed, and yet those exercising it systematically ignore these divinely given regulations, a doubt is at once raised in any sound mind as to the genuineness of the alleged gift.

Even apart from this, however, these regulations are full of profit for us, for what is laid down must obviously apply in other directions also. For an instance of what we mean take verses 6 to 9. The immediate point of these verses is that mere vocal sounds are of no value. What is uttered by the voice must have some meaning to those who listen. It must be *intelligible*. Is that only of importance in connection with the gift of tongues? By no means. It applies universally. In our meetings it will not be enough that the speaker talks in English, for he may be enticed into a display of his learning by using hosts of long words of uncommon use, which leave the minds of his learners a complete blank as to his meaning. Or he may speak with such rapidity, or with such mystic obscurity, as to be unintelligible. In all such cases people merely "speak into the air," and there is no profit.

We might wonder at Paul writing as he does in verses 14 and 15, did we not know what sometimes takes place even in our day. It is not God's way that even the speaker himself should be ignorant of the meaning of the words he has just uttered. He is to utter words, whether in speaking to others, or in prayer, or in song, which he himself understands and which are understandable to others.

If anyone address himself to God in the assembly, whether in prayer or thanksgiving he must remember that he does so as giving expression to the desires or the praises of the assembly. He is not speaking merely on his own behalf. Consequently he must carry the assembly with him; and they, understanding and following his utterances, ratify them before God and make them their own by saying "Amen" (signifying "So be it") at the end. They cannot intelligibly and honestly say "Amen" at the end if they are quite unaware of what it is all about. Far better is it to speak but five words profitable for instruction, than ten thousand words that mean nothing to the hearers.

Take note that verse 16 supposes that each in the assembly, even the unlearned and insignificant, *do* say "Amen." They *say* it, and not merely *think* it. If our experience be any guide, a very small percentage in the assembly say "Amen" today. Test what we say in an average prayer meeting. If a brother in prayer really voices our desires let us ratify what he has uttered with a good distinct "Amen." If he has not, honesty compels us to refrain from saying it. If the earnest, fervent outpouring of our desires were ratified by all of us in the utterance of a hearty "Amen" at the close, and the wearisome parade of information, and discussion of doctrines with God, which sometimes is inflicted on us at great length as a substitute for prayer, were ended in a rather chilling silence, the offender might possibly be awakened to what he is doing. When however every prayer finishes in silence save for a few feeble "Amens," no such discrimination can be felt, and one begins to fear that all may be formalism and with little or no meaning or depth. Let us think on these things and cultivate reality.

Also we are to cultivate understanding in the things of God, while retaining a child-like spirit in other regards, as verse 20 tells us. When tongues are misused, as indicated in verse 23, it only shows a complete lack of mature sense. Children might act in that foolish way, just as they love to show off their new clothes. But the believer is to act as having the understanding of a man, not a child. The prophetic ministry of the Word of God brings the soul into the very presence of God. And the power of such ministry may be felt even by an unbeliever who happens to be present.

It is not enough that there should be prophecy. The gift must be exercised according to God's order, which is laid down in verses 29 to 33. The Corinthians were highly gifted, and the tendency in their assemblies was evidently to have a great excess of talking. Verse 26 shows this. Each was eager to exercise his gift and get it in evidence. Confusion, disorder, tumult, was the result. God was not the Author of this.

So definite instructions were laid down. Speaking in tongues was not forbidden, but it is strictly regulated in verses 27 and 28; and if no interpreter is present it is forbidden. Prophecy too is regulated. Two or three speakers in any given meeting are enough. How wise is this regulation! The Lord knows the receptive capacity of the average believer. If two speak at considerable length it is enough. If more brevity marks the speakers, three may find an opportunity. Then it is enough. Someone may ignore this ruling and insist on giving us his word, but we are wearied and end by retaining less than if we had heard only three.

Note that the others who listen are to "judge." That is, even in days when inspired utterances by direct revelation (see verse 30) were given in the assembly, those who listened were to do so with discernment. They were not to receive without testing what they heard. They were never to adopt the attitude of:—"Oh, everything that dear brother A— says *must* be right!" Such an attitude is a direct incitement to the devil to pervert the ideas of brother A— and so encompass the fall of many. It is a disaster for brother A— as well as his admirers. There is liberty for all the prophets to prophecy, though not of course on any one occasion. If on any given occasion a prophet may have something to say and yet no opportunity occurs, he must restrain himself and wait on God till the opportunity comes. He himself is to be master of his own spirit and not mastered by it.

Verses 34 and 35 deal with the silence of women in the assembly. The instruction is very plain and the word used for "speak" is the ordinary word and does not mean "chatter" as some have made out. This regulation cuts across the spirit of the age, without a doubt. But if that be a reason for ignoring Scripture, there will not be much Scripture left that is not ignored.

The Spirit of God foreknew how these regulations would be ignored or challenged. Some at Corinth evidently were inclined in that direction. Hence verses 36 and 37. The Word of God came *out* through the Lord Himself and His apostles and not through the Corinthians. It came *to* them. They might fancy themselves as spiritual people. If they really were spiritual they would prove it by discerning that these rules laid down by Paul were not just his notions, but the commandments of the Lord through him. The test of our spirituality today is just the same.

Take note that the Word of God does not come out through the church. It comes to the church. The crowning pretension of the great Romish system is that "the church"—and by that they mean the Romish authorities—is the teaching body. We need not here concern ourselves with their claim to be "the church," for it is evident from this passage that the Apostles are the fountains, whence have flowed the pure waters of the Word, and we have them today in their inspired writings—the New Testament Scriptures. The church is not "the *teaching* body" it is "the *taught* body." The Word of God comes to it, and its duty is *to bow to the Word of God*.

CHAPTER 15

THE OPENING WORDS of chapter xv. appear at first sight rather extraordinary. Why, we may ask, should the Apostle declare the Gospel to people who had already received it?

There was, we believe a little wholesome irony in his words, as also there had been in verses 37 and 38 of the previous chapter. As we have noticed several times previously the Corinthians had inflated ideas of themselves, their gifts and accomplishments, so the Spirit of God confronted them with realities. The intellectualism they affected was leading them to deny, or at least question, the resurrection from the dead—a fundamental truth of the Gospel. Paul had to begin declaring the Gospel to them all over again.

The Gospel saves us *if* we "keep in memory" or "hold fast" its message. If we do not hold fast the Word it does not save. Some people do not like the "If," but it is there nevertheless. It is easy to say, "I believe," and as result be numbered amongst the believers. Yet time tests us. The real believer always holds fast; the unreal does not. With that proviso we can say to all who take the place of Christians, "The Gospel has saved you, and in it you *stand*." Consequently he who tampers with, and disturbs, the truth of the Gospel is cutting away the ground from beneath his own feet.

Now the Gospel brings us tidings of facts. First, the fact of Christ's death for our sins, as the Scriptures had foretold—Isaiah liii. 5 and 8, for instance. Second the two facts of His burial and resurrection, which are grouped together, as according to the Scriptures—Isaiah liii. 9 and 10, for instance.

There was no question as to the first and second of these facts: they were publicly known. The third was not publicly known, but it was the prominent theme of apostolic preaching as recorded in the Acts. It was the third that was being called in question here, and hence Paul reminds them of the overwhelming witness of its truth that existed. He cites six different occasions on which He was seen in resurrection, ending with his own case when He was not only risen, but also in glory. Paul's list is by no means exhaustive, for he does not cite any of the occasions on which He appeared to the believing women.

However, he himself came at the end of a long line of witnesses, and this reminded him of the fact that when the other apostles were having a sight of their risen Lord, he was an opponent and a persecutor, at least in heart. The thought of this humbled him, and made him feel unworthy to be numbered amongst the apostles. At the same time it filled his heart with a sense of the grace of God—grace which not only had called him, but also led him into a life of labour for his Lord more abundant than all the rest.

Still as regards their testimony there was no difference. Whether the twelve or himself, they had all equally preached the Gospel of the risen Christ. The Corinthians had heard no other Gospel from their lips than this. Upon the risen Christ they had believed.

Now the whole truth as to resurrection hinges upon the resurrection of Christ, as verse 12 indicates. How can resurrection be denied, if Christ be risen?

However the Apostle proceeds to argue the whole matter out in orderly fashion. First he contemplates the assumption that after all there is no resurrection, and shows what the logical results would be. This occupies verses 13 to 19. Quite obviously if there be no resurrection then Christ is not risen. And if Christ be not risen, what then?

Then a whole sequence of results must necessarily ensue. Paul's preaching then was vain, for he must be convicted of preaching not a fact but a myth. Their faith was equally vain, for they had believed a myth. This explains the remark at the end of verse 2. The "believing in vain," there spoken of, does not refer to faith of an inferior or defective kind but to faith, be it ever so vigorous, which rests in an unworthy or false object.

Then further, it would mean that the apostles were not true men but false witnesses, and that the Corinthians themselves, in spite of their faith in that witness, were yet in their sins. It would mean that those believers—some of them Corinthians—who had already died, had not entered into bliss but perished. Indeed it would narrow down any benefit or hope to be derived from Christ to things within the confines of this life. What a tragedy! Every bright hope of an eternity of glory extinguished in the night of death from which there is no awaking. All that Christ can give us is whittled down to a kindly example, which, if followed, would somewhat improve our short lives in this world.

There is no exaggeration in the statement that if that is all, "we are of all men most miserable." Of course we are! Every Christian, worth the name, has deliberately turned his back on the sinful pleasures of the world. So he is in the position of denying himself what he might have, the pleasure that comes from gratifying his lusts, in view of a future, which after all does not exist. In that case we are indeed like the dog in the fable who dropped the piece of meat in clutching at its shadow. The out-and-out worldling at least has the pleasures of sin, whereas we should draw a blank in both worlds.

In verse 20 the Apostle turns from this negative line of reasoning to a positive argument. He starts now from the glorious fact that after all Christ is risen from the dead, and risen as the Firstfruits of the sleeping saints. The saints are the afterfruits of the same order as Himself. This important truth is expounded fully in the later part of the chapter; it is implied here in the use of the word, "firstfruits." No one would present you with a potato as the firstfruits of the wheat harvest, or even a plum as the firstfruits of the apple crop. They would be incongruent. But there is nothing incongruent here. Though Christ is God yet He became Man, and as the risen Man He is the firstfruits of them that have died in faith. His resurrection must involve the resurrection of all that are His.

This point is of such importance that the flow of the argument is interrupted for a moment, and it is enlarged upon in verses 21 to 23. Death was introduced by man, and so now resurrection also is by Man. Adam brought death in, and all who are in him, that is, of his race, are under the death sentence. Christ has brought in resurrection, and all who are in Him, of His race, are to be "made alive," or "quickened." This quickening is special to those who are Christ's. Though the unjust will be raised their resurrection will not involve quickening. The saints are going to enter into what is properly "life." How complete and glorious has been God's answer to man's sin!

But in resurrection an order is to be observed: "each in his own rank." (N. Tr.) as verse 23 puts it. Christ rose from amongst the dead first, and is pre-eminent. Afterward, at His coming, all who are His are also to rise from amongst the dead, leaving the unsaved dead in their graves. And, "then cometh the end," when the unsaved dead will be raised, though this is not explicitly stated here, but implied in verse 26. If Revelation xx. 11—xxi. 4, be read, it will be seen that death is destroyed when the wicked dead have been raised.

What is plainly stated in our passage is that the end which is to be reached in virtue of resurrection is the complete subjugation of every adverse power, so that all may be in subjection to God, who is to be all in all. This brings us to the eternal state, which is also alluded to in 2 Peter iii. 13, and is described at greater length in Revelation xxi. 1 - 5. The millennial kingdom will serve the purpose for which it is designed. There will be found in it the perfection of government, and it will not end until the last

1 CORINTHIANS

enemy has been brought to nothing.

When that point is reached the whole work of redemption and new creation will have reached finality, and the Son will deliver up the kingdom to the Father. In becoming Man the Son took the subject place, and that place He retains to all eternity: a clear proof that He has taken up Manhood for ever. Subjection, be it remembered, does not necessarily imply inferiority. The Son was no whit inferior to the Father when here on earth, nor will He be in eternity. In the eternal state God is to be everything, and in everything; but of course the Spirit is God, and the Son is God, equally with the Father. The Son however retains His place in Manhood, the Head and the Sustainer of the new creation universe, which exists as the fruit of His work; this guarantees that it shall never be encroached upon by evil, but remain in its original splendour for ever.

Before passing on, just notice this contrast: that whereas the denial of resurrection worked out to its logical result leaves us in our sins and in hopeless misery, the fact of resurrection, accomplished in Christ, lands us into the eternal state of glory.

Verses 20-28 are somewhat parenthetical in nature, and hence verse 29 picks up the thread from verse 19 and reads on quite naturally, though its meaning is perhaps rather obscure. We believe that "for" in this verse indicates "in the place of." A large percentage of the dead amongst the early Christians had fallen as martyrs, and so Paul views the newer converts as stepping by baptism into the place of the fallen, to become themselves targets for the adversary. Very courageous; but of course foolish and futile if there is no resurrection of the dead.

This interpretation of verse 29 is confirmed by verse 30. Why should the Apostle and his associates expose themselves to the adversary, if there were no resurrection? And in asking this he was not indulging in a mere figure of speech. It was a hard fact, and a daily fact with him. Not long before he had gone through the terrific riot in the Ephesian theatre, as recorded in Acts xix., when men fought against him like wild beasts, and every day his life was in danger. What an absurd man he was to live a life like this! Apart from the fact of resurrection one had better adopt the motto of the godless world, "Let us eat and drink; for tomorrow we die." In this way once more do we reach the logical result of discarding the truth of resurrection. Not only are we left the most miserable of all men, but we are left with nothing better than the gratification of our animal appetites.

Having reached this point the Apostle appeals very pointedly to the Corinthians. They were being deceived, and all evil teachings have a reaction in the sphere of morals. If we think wrong we cannot act right. This throws light on the immorality amongst them, denounced in chapters v. and vi. Questioning the resurrection of the body, they had the more easily fallen into sins involving the abuse of the body. They needed to awake to what was right and gain the knowledge of God.

1 CORINTHIANS

But the Corinthians, though having so little knowledge of God and righteousness, were an intellectual, reasoning people; so two questions that were sure to spring to their lips, are anticipated in verse 35. The first raises the question, *How?* the second, the question, *What?* The answers to these questions occupy practically the rest of the chapter. The second question—being more definite perhaps—is answered first.

Intellectualism proves itself again and again to be a great snare for believers. Having begun with faith some are inclined to continue on the basis of mere intellect, unaware that the things of God (as chapter ii. has told us) are so deep as to entirely submerge the greatest human intellect. Nothing baffles human thought more than resurrection, as may be discovered if one listens for a little to the pronouncements of "Liberal Theologians." We cannot fail to know what the Liberal Theologians think of God, for they are sufficiently vociferous. Here we see what God thinks of the Liberal Theologians. He dismisses them with one word— "Fool!" That one word is as much inspired of God as is John iii. 16.

Still Paul was writing to saints, even though they had got tainted with that peculiar folly which is so fully developed in the Liberal Theologians of today. So having plainly indicated to them their foolishness, he proceeds to answer the question.

Nature itself furnishes us with a striking analogy on the point, an analogy used previously by our Lord Himself. When He said, "Except a corn of wheat fall into the ground and die, it abideth alone: but if it die, it bringeth forth much fruit," He indicated His own death and resurrection.

Here the same analogy is used but with a different application. A seed is sown in the earth, yet, though its identity is preserved, it comes up with a vastly different body. The acorn is buried, but the oak springs up. Every seed has what we may call its own special resurrection body in which it comes forth. The bearing of this on the point before us is plain. The dead body of that saint is laid in the grave: in the resurrection it will come up vastly different, yet with its identity preserved.

Again nature teaches us that this presents no difficulty to God, for He is of infinite resource. Look at the variety seen in creation. These are different orders of flesh—men, beasts, fishes, birds: and within those orders there are again vast differences of body. Again, there are bodies of a heavenly order—as to which at present we know so little—and bodies of an earthly order, which we know well. It is very probably true that no two stars are in all respects the same.

This conducts us to the marvellous declaration of verses 42-44. The body that is sown in the grave is characterized by corruption, dishonour, weakness, soulishness,—if we may be allowed to coin that word, for the word, "natural" is more literally "soulish," something fitted for the animal soul rather than the spirit. It is raised in incorruption, glory, power, and a spiritual body rather than a soulish one. The identity is preserved, as witnessed by the words, four times repeated, "It is sown . . . it is raised." Nevertheless the condition in which it is found is of a different order entirely. This answers the question, "With what body do they come?"

The first question of verse 32, "How are the dead raised up?" gets a very full answer in verses 45 to 54. In this question the force of "How" seems to be "In what condition?" rather than, "In what way?" or "By what means?" Otherwise there would be no conclusive answer to the question in the chapter. Moreover, if God did condescend to explain in what way or by what process He will raise the dead, we should be no wiser, for the explanation would be utterly beyond us. As it is, we have an answer. In a nutshell it is this—we shall be raised in the image of the heavenly Christ.

In order to understand it we must consider the contrast between the two Adams, the first and the last. The first was made a living soul, as Genesis ii. tells us. The last is of another order entirely. Though as truly Adam (i.e. Man) as the first, He is a life-giving Spirit. The one, then, is "natural" or "soulish": the Other, spiritual. We might have expected that the Spiritual would take precedence of the soulish as to time. But it is not so, as verse 46 points out. The first Adam was constituted a living soul by the Divine in-breathing. Consequently he was "soulish," and he possessed a "natural" or "soulish" body (verse 44) which was "earthy." He has reproduced himself in abundance; but all who spring from him are earthy also, as being of his order (verse 48).

The last Adam stands in sharp contrast to the first. Though truly Man, being a life-giving Spirit He is God. He is the "Lord from Heaven." He is not only Man, however—the "Second Man" as stated in verse 47—He is Adam, i.e. He is the Progenitor and Head of a race. And He is the *last* Adam, for He is never to be succeeded by another head. In Him God has reached perfection and finality. God be praised for this! We are amongst the heavenly ones who are of His order.

Let it be emphasized in our minds that He is not only "last Adam," but also "the second Man." This latter expression shows that between Adam and Christ no man is counted. Cain was not the second man. He was only Adam reproduced in the first generation. So were all men—only Adam reproduced in their various generations. But when Christ was born, He was *not* Adam reproduced. By the "virgin birth," under the action of the Holy Ghost, the entail was broken, a new and original Man appeared worthy of being called "the second Man." He, in His turn becoming the Head of a new race, He stands forth as "the last Adam."

Now we all started as children of the earthy Adam, bearing his image. Brought to Christ, we have become subjects of the Divine workmanship, and find ourselves transferred from the earthy to the heavenly. That transference however has not so far touched our bodies, for we still bear the image of the earthy, and consequently our bodies decay and are subject to death and the grave. In resurrection we are to bear "the image of the heavenly." We are to be conformed to the image of God's Son, not only as to our characters, but as to our very bodies. Most glorious fact! How are the dead raised up? In a condition of perfection and glory such as that!

Do not let us overlook the fact that, though we must wait for the realization of this perfection, we have not to wait in order to be under the headship of the last Adam, to be linked up with the second Man. The end of verse 48 does not say, "such are they also that *shall be* heavenly"—but "that *are* heavenly." We *ARE* heavenly. Is not that wonderful! Does it seem too wonderful? Are we inclined to shrink from it? Do we feel that its implications are very sweeping and make demands upon us which we cannot face? Well, let us beware of paring down the truth to suit our low walk. Behaviour which is low, and carnal, and earthly, and worldly, does not befit those who *are* heavenly.

With verse 50 the Apostle passes on to speak of the great moment when the change from things earthy to things heavenly shall reach our bodies. We are going to inherit the kingdom on its heavenly side and find ourselves in a scene of absolute incorruptibility. We cannot enter there in our present "flesh and blood" condition, to which corruption is attached.

"Behold I show you a mystery," he says. These words indicate that he is going to announce something hitherto unrevealed. That there would be a resurrection of the dead, that the Lord was coming, they knew. They had not hitherto known that when the Lord came He would raise the dead saints in a condition of glorious incorruptibility and change the living saints into a like condition. It seems that saints of Old Testament days conceived of resurrection as being a raising up of the dead to a glorified life on earth. It is certain that they had no knowledge as yet of the resurrection *out from among* the dead, which believers are to enjoy at the coming of the Lord. Until the truth of the heavenly calling of saints, of the calling out of the church, came to light, the moment had not come for the full truth as to resurrection to be made known. This orderly progress of doctrine can be noted all through the New Testament.

Now it is plainly revealed. We shall not all "sleep" (i.e. die) but we shall all be changed, whether alive or dead at the moment when the Lord comes *for* His saints. The change will involve the swallowing up of all that is mortal or corruptible about us, in life and in victory. We shall "all be changed," you notice, "in a moment, in the twinkling of an eye"—not in many, or at least several, different moments, as would be the case if by a partial rapture, or series of partial raptures, the church is destined to enter into its glory.

The mighty change will be wrought instantaneously by the power of God, at the "last trump." In verse 29 believers were considered as soldiers stepping into the ranks by baptism to take the places of their fallen comrades. In verse 52 we see them all—whether in the ranks still, or fallen out of them by death—put, in one moment at the last trump, beyond death and corruption. Their warfare will be over. They will never need another trumpet blast for ever!

As regards ourselves, the saying of Isaiah xxv. 8 will be fulfilled when we are changed bodily into a condition of immortality and incorruptibility. This illustrates what we have just said. The Old Testament has in view the victorious resurrection power of God exercised on earth. Our Scripture brings to light a greater fulness of meaning, lying dormant in the verse until the Gospel day was reached. When the saints reach the image of the heavenly, death will be swallowed up in a victory that none can deny. Our Scripture, you notice, does not speak of the "rapture," the catching up of the saints. For that we must turn to 1 Thessalonians iv.

The sense of how great the victory of that day will be, moves the Apostle to an outburst of exultation. He flings a triumphant challenge to death and "the grave"—or more strictly *"hades."* The fact is, the victory is already ours. It has been won in the resurrection of Christ which has been so fully established in this chapter. The resurrection of saints is merely the outworking of *that* victory, and we can treat it as being as good as done. The victory is ours today—thanks be to God!

With what tremendous force does the closing exhortation of the chapter come! *"Therefore—."* Behind that word lies all the weight of the glorious truth established in the earlier 57 verses of the chapter. Having entertained doubts as to the truth of resurrection they must have become unsteady, easily moved, slack, and inclined to subscribe to the motto, "Let us eat and drink for tomorrow we die."

Resurrection however is a glorious certainty. Christ is risen, and we, being of His heavenly order, are to join Him in His heavenly likeness. These things being so, THEREFORE an unmoveable stability becomes us. Instead of fooling away our time eating and drinking, we are to abound in the work of the Lord, knowing that nothing really done for Him shall be lost. All shall be found again as fruit in the resurrection world.

Are we living in the light of that resurrection world? We may recite the creed correctly, and have resurrection as a prominent item in it; but if our souls really have it full in view, we shall be diligent and untiring workers in the service of the Lord, as He may be pleased to direct us.

CHAPTER 16

THE LAST DIRECTION of the Apostle in this epistle concerns the special collection being made at that time for poor saints in Judæa. Today in many religious circles money is so often the *first* topic. Here it is the *last.* Still it comes in, and instructions of abiding value are given. In verse 2 *systematic* giving is advocated as opposed to haphazard. *Proportionate*

1 CORINTHIANS

giving is also what God expects—in proportion to the prosperity which God Himself may have given. In Jewish days God fixed the proportion at one tenth. He has not fixed any proportion for us who are under grace; but depend upon it we shall hear something pretty serious at the judgment seat if we fall below the standard set by the law. If all believers practised giving which is both proportionate and systematic, there would be no money problem in connection with the work of the Lord. The chapter division perhaps leads us to miss the connection between xv. 58, and xvi. 2.

The closing messages of a personal sort begin after this, and verses 5—12 are illuminating if compared with the history of Acts xviii. 24—xx. 6. Paul wrote from Ephesus while in the midst of a great work with many adversaries, whose opposition culminated in the great riot in the theatre. Apollos had preceded Paul at Ephesus, and then after being further instructed in the way of the Lord through Aquila and Priscilla, he visited Achaia, where Corinth was situated. Paul had come to Ephesus while Apollos was at Corinth, but by this time Apollos had passed on from Corinth. Meanwhile Paul contemplated passing through Macedonia and visiting Corinth on the way. This visit to Macedonia was accomplished, as Acts xx. records, though his second epistle shows that his visit to Corinth was delayed. He had begged Apollos to pay them another visit, but without avail.

Observe from this that if God raises up a servant he is responsible only to the Lord who commissions him, and not even to an Apostle. Paul assumed no jurisdiction over Apollos. The fact that he begged him *to go* shows that he entertained no feelings of jealousy towards this fresh man of gift who had suddenly appeared. The fact that Apollos felt he should *not* go to Corinth at this juncture probably indicates that he on his part had no wish to push himself forward lest he should fan the flames of that partisanship and rivalry which would say, "I am of Apollos."

The Corinthians had been unwatchful. They had been vacillating as to the faith of the Gospel. They had behaved more like weak children than strong men. Hence the graphic exhortations of verse 13. We must keep those exhortations connected with verse 14, or we may go astray. All our things are to be done "with charity," or "in love." Otherwise our manliness and our strength will degenerate into something fleshly and almost brutal. Christian manliness and strength exercised *in love* is according to God and very powerful.

Verse 15 gives an interesting side-light on service. The household of Stephanus had "addicted themselves to the ministry of the saints," or, "devoted themselves to the saints for service." They laid themselves out to serve the saints realizing that thus they would be serving Christ in His members on earth. There might be a lot that was commonplace and humdrum in such work, but it was rendered to Christ. Such service is not very common, we fear. It receives mention and commendation in verse 16. It exemplifies, we judge, what is meant by "helps," mentioned amongst the gifts in chapter xii. 28.

The three closing verses are a blending of solemnity and grace. The Corinthians were prominent as to gift but deficient as to love. Hence verse 22. Many of us are like the Corinthians. Let us take it to heart that it is love that counts. Not to love the Lord Jesus means a curse at His coming, when all profession will be tested. Maran-atha is not Greek but Aramaic, signifying "The Lord is coming."

For those who do love the Lord there is a full supply of grace from Him, and the outflow of love from those who are His, as seen in the affectionate closing salutation of the Apostle Paul.

2 CORINTHIANS

Introduction

THE SECOND EPISTLE to the Corinthians was evidently written not very long after the first. In the closing chapter of the first, Paul intimates that he wrote from Ephesus, where an effectual door of service had been opened to him of the Lord, and where adversaries abounded. In the opening chapter of the second he alludes to the great riot in the Ephesian theatre which closed his service of over two years in that great city; and later in the epistle he indicates some of his subsequent movements. It may be well to trace these at the outset as they throw light on some of the remarks he makes.

Before the riot occurred the purpose of the Apostle was to pass through Macedonia and Achaia on his way to Jerusalem, and later to go to Rome. Acts xix. 12, proves this, and there is confirmation of the first part of the plan in 1 Corinthians xvi. 5, and in verses 15 and 16 of our chapter. However he had been diverted from what he had planned. First of all the riot led to a hurried departure for Macedonia. He got as far as Troas, where again the Lord opened a door before him (see ii. 12, 13). As yet he was too disturbed in mind about the Corinthians, and the possible effect on them of his first epistle, so instead of passing by them into Macedonia (i. 16) he sailed for Macedonia direct. When he got into Macedonia things were even more disquieting, but presently he was cheered by Titus with good tidings as regards the Corinthians. This gave him great relief and prompted the second epistle which we are now to consider.

CHAPTER 1

DURING THE STAY at Ephesus, Timothy had been sent in advance into Macedonia (Acts xix. 22), which accounts probably for the omission of his name at the beginning of the first epistle. By the time the second was written both Paul and Timothy were in Macedonia, and hence his name appears.

The opening salutation given, the Apostle at once gives expression to the thankfulness and comfort and encouragement that filled his heart. He traces it all back to God, the Father of our Lord Jesus Christ, who is the Father of mercies and the God of all comfort. Comfort had been poured into the heart of Paul, and he returned it Godward in the form of blessing or thanksgiving.

This however was not the end of it, for it also flowed outward for the help of others. Having been through heavy tribulation and received abundant comfort from God, he turned it to account and traded with it for the comfort of those similarly suffering. This is, without a doubt, an important principle in the ways of God. Whatever spiritual favour we receive from God, whether comfort, or joy, or warning, or instruction, or anything else, we are not to treat it as though it were entirely personal to ourselves,

114

but rather as something granted us to be shared with others. We are never to forget the oneness of the saints of God. Indeed, we believe that we really never possess things in their fulness until we do begin to pass them on to others. A Christian poet has said,

> For we must share if we would keep
> That good thing from above;
> Ceasing to give, we cease to have;
> Such is the law of love.

The poet's word is undoubtedly true. If we do not use what we have, we ultimately lose it. Again and again, does the Lord pass His servants through trying circumstances in order that they may learn valuable lessons and obtain the needed grace; and having done so, that thus qualified in an experimental way, they may become more efficient in helping others.

Another important principle comes to light in verse 5. God suits and proportions the consolation to the sufferings. If the sufferings are slight the consolation is slight. If the sufferings abound, the consolations abound. The sufferings, be it noted, are "*of* Christ." That is, they are not only endured for His sake, but they are of the same character as those which He endured because of His absolute identification with God and His interests. Such sufferings, the sufferings of Christ in His people, are always followed or accompanied by consolation, which is ministered *through* Christ.

In verses 3 to 7, one word occurs (in various forms) no less than ten times. It is translated six times by comfort, and four times by consolation. It indicates a "cheering and supporting influence," and in Darby's New Translation is rendered consistently by "encourage" or "encouragement." A slightly different form of the word is applied to the Holy Spirit by our Lord, and in John xiv., xv., xvi., is translated "Comforter." In the same verses the tribulation, the trouble, the afflictions, the suffering, are only mentioned seven times: so that even in these verses the encouragement over-abounds in comparison with the sufferings. Without a doubt, herein lay the supernatural fortitude of the martyrs. Called of God to face unusual suffering, they were carried through it on a wave of unusual encouragement. The cheering and supporting influence abounded in their cases.

There is very little persecution from the world today in the English-speaking regions. For a century and a half great quietude and toleration has prevailed without; and it has synchronized with a period of disintegration and doctrinal laxity within. The sufferings that characterize the saints are mainly of the order spoken of in the first epistle, "many are weak and sickly among you," or else troubles connected with trying circumstances, and the like. The sufferings of which Paul speaks in these verses are very largely unknown by us. The encouragement of which he speaks is also very largely unknown. The saint overflowing with encouragement in the midst of severe persecution is a sight but rarely seen. This we say to our shame, and our loss as well.

In verses 6 and 7 the Apostle links the Corinthians with himself in a very beautiful way. Carnal though they had been and feeble as to many things, they yet had partaken in sufferings akin to those of the Apostle, and this fact in itself might yield them encouragement. Then in addition it was certain that in due season they would partake also of the encouragement.

This leads Paul to allude plainly to the special tribulation he had suffered in Ephesus, the capital of Asia. In Acts xix, the occasion is called, "no small stir," but his words in verse 8 reveal to us that it was even more critical and full of danger than we should deduce from Luke's account of it. Death evidently stared him in the face. Later in the epistle he recounts his experiences as a servant of the Lord, and speaks of being "in deaths oft." This was one of the times when he was in death.

The riotous mob in Ephesus put upon him the sentence of death, and did their best to execute it. The Apostle met the situation with the "sentence of death" in himself. Thereby he was brought to nothing as to any hope or trust in himself, or in any powers that he possessed. He was shut up to God and His power. The God whom he trusted is the God who raises the dead, and who therefore would undo all that the mob might have done, had they been permitted to do their worst.

God however had intervened and held them in check. Paul and his friends had been delivered on that day, and were still being delivered. The Apostle did not contemplate the danger ceasing. The rather he knew that it would continue throughout his course. So he anticipated that he yet would be delivered, and that the Corinthians would have the privilege of helping to this end with their prayers. Then indeed God's gracious answers would call forth a larger volume of thanksgiving. If many had joined in the request, many would join in the giving of thanks.

What gave him such boldness in requesting the prayers of the Corinthians was that he had a good conscience as to his whole manner of life. The simplicity and sincerity which are of God had marked him, and the wisdom which is of the flesh had been ruled out. This was true as to his general attitude in the world, but especially true as regards his course amongst the saints. He knew that in thus boasting he was only stating what the Corinthians themselves recognized right well. There had been those amongst the Corinthians who had aimed at defaming him, and at prejudicing them against him. The effect of this had by now been partly removed, for, as he says in verse 14, "Ye have acknowledged in part that we are your rejoicing." That is, they had acknowledged in part that he was their boasting, even as they were his, in the day of the Lord Jesus. They were thus in considerable measure in happy accord.

In this delicate way does he allude to the great improvement that had come over the feelings of the Corinthians towards himself since the dispatch of his first epistle. But let us take to heart the fact that he based his request for prayer upon the simplicity and godly sincerity of his life. We hear Christians pretty frequently asking prayer from one and another. Sometimes we ask for prayer ourselves. But can we always ask for it upon this basis? We fear not; and possibly this accounts for a good deal of prayer and intercession being unanswered. For our lives, and all the secret motives governing them, are perfectly open to the eye of God.

Even before, when writing the first epistle, Paul had confidence that the relations between himself and them, though for the moment imperilled would be of this happy order. Because of this he had proposed to visit them previously, even before he took his journey into Macedonia. However things had been ordered otherwise, and the projected visit had not taken place. Here let us pause a moment. Even an apostle, you see, had plans disarranged and upset; and was led of God to record that fact for us in Scripture. The change, as we shall see presently, though not exactly ordered of God was overruled of God for ultimate blessing. Guidance may reach the servant in many ways; and if he misses direct guidance he may yet find even his mistakes overruled for blessing. Our concern should be to maintain that simplicity and godly sincerity of which verse 12 speaks.

Now those who were opponents used even this change of plans as a ground of attack. They insinuated that it indicated that Paul was a man of lightness, and shallowness of purpose: that he had no depth of character: that he would say one thing today and another thing tomorrow. The Apostle knew this and therefore he asked the question of verse 17. Was he a man swayed merely by fleshly impulse, so as to be pulled easily in this direction or that—saying yes today, and no tomorrow?

He answered this question by an appeal to his preaching when first, together with Sylvanus and Timotheus, he came amongst them. There had been nothing indefinite or contradictory about that. When he says, "Our word toward you was not yea and nay," he alludes apparently to the *manner* of his preaching. Then in the following verse he mentions the great *theme* of his preaching—Jesus Christ, the Son of God. In Him everything has been firmly established for God. In Him is eternal stability.

Having such a theme, Paul's preaching was marked by a rock-like definiteness and certainty. The same definiteness and certainty should mark all the preaching of the Word today. Modernistic preachers, in the very nature of things, can only preach ideas—ideas based upon the latest pronouncements of speculative science, which are for ever changing. Their word most emphatically is, "*yea and nay.*" The statements of today, strongly *affirmed*, will be *negatived* before very many years have passed, just as the statements of not many years ago are negatived today.

We need not be unduly perturbed by the modernists. Their little day will soon be over, their vacillating pronouncements silenced. Let us be careful to preach the unchanging Christ in an unchanging way.

There is a very definite contrast between the "yea and nay," of verse 19, and the "yea and . . Amen," of the following verse. The former indicates that which is vacillating and contradictory: the latter that which is definitely affirmed, and then unswervingly confirmed in due season.

Man is fickle. With him it is frequently yes on one occasion and no the next. Moreover man is contradictory when it is a question of God and His will. Again and again does he break down, and consequently negative all that God desires for him. His reply to God's will is uniformly "Nay." The opposite of this is found in Christ, for "in Him was, yea." He said "Yes" to every purpose and desire of God.

And not only was the yea found in Him but the Amen also. He not only assents to all the will of God, expressed in His promises, but He proceeds to carry all out, and bring all to full and final completion. In Him the thing is done, and shall be done, until a great Amen can be put to all God's pleasure, so that God is glorified. And further, He obtains a people who become His servants for the carrying out of the Divine will: so that the two words, "by us," can be added at the end of verse 10. What glorious stability and security is here! What confidence, what repose garrisons the heart that rests in Christ!

The Son of God, preached by Paul among the Corinthians, bore this wonderful character. Hence the solidity and certainty of his preaching. Hence also the stability which characterized Paul himself, and which is properly the character of every true Christian. We have been established in Christ. And it is God who has done it. What man does, he may very likely undo at some subsequent period. What God does, He does for ever.

We are thus firmly established in Christ—the Christ in whom is established all the counsel of God—by an act of God. Let us lay hold of this fact, for it lifts the whole thing on to a plane immeasurably above man. We have received too, the anointing of the Spirit equally by an act of God.

Bear in mind that the significance of "Christ" is "the Anointed One." So verse 21 shows us that we are anointed as those who are established in the Anointed One. The Anointing reaches us as those who are connected with Him. When Aaron was anointed the "precious ointment" that was poured upon his head ran down even "to the skirts of his garments" (Psa. cxxxiii. 2). Which thing was a type or allegory; for the grace and power of our exalted Head has been carried down to us His members by the anointing of the Spirit. Thus it is—and only thus—that the promises of God can be carried into effect to the glory of God "by us." It is Christ Himself who will bring to perfect fruition the promises of God in the coming day; but He will do it *by us*. That is, He will carry things out in detail through His saints, who are His anointed members. If only our hearts lay hold of this, we shall be very much lifted above this present evil world.

But the Spirit of God is not only the Anointing: He is also the Seal and the Earnest. As the Anointing He connects us with Christ. As the Seal He marks us off as being wholly for God. We are the Divine possession and marked as such, just as the farmer, who purchases sheep, at once puts a mark upon them that they may be identified as his. In the book of Revelation we read how the coming "beasts" will cause all to "receive a mark" (xiii. 16). Those who do receive that mark will have to face the fierce wrath of God, as the next chapter shows; and chapter vii., of the same book reveals to us that God anticipates the wicked action of the beasts by putting "the seal of the living God" on His own.

God "hath also sealed us," and we may well rejoice in this blessed fact. But do we always bear in mind its serious implications? We cannot carry two marks, if the one mark, that has been placed upon us, is God's mark. He is a jealous God. The mark that is upon us is exclusive. If we attempt to carry also the world's mark—to say nothing of the devil's mark—we shall provoke Him to jealousy, and lay up much discipline and sorrow for ourselves. Take great care, O young Christian! for the world is ever seeking to put its unholy marks upon you, as though you belonged to it. You do not belong to it, you belong to God; so be careful not to wear the seals and badges it wishes to put upon you.

Then again, the Holy Spirit is the Earnest in our hearts. If, as the Anointing, we view Him in connection with Christ; and as the Seal, more in connection with God the Father, the Earnest indicates what He is in Himself. Presently, when the promises of God reach their fulfilment, we shall be in the full flood-tide energy of the Spirit of God. But today He is the Earnest of all this in our hearts. "In our *hearts*," notice: not merely in our bodies, or in our minds. Our bodies are indeed His temple. Our minds may happily be suffused with His light. But in the deepest affections of our hearts we have the earnest—the pledge and foretaste of the glory that is coming. By the Holy Ghost given to us, we may realize anticipatively something of all the good that shall be ours, when the promises of God are brought to fruition to His glory, and by us.

In these three verses (20-22) we have been conducted to a wonderful climax of blessedness; and it all springs out of the seemingly small matter of the Apostle being obliged to make it plain that he was not a man of light mind, promising things that he had no real intention of performing. He did not merely defend himself. He improved the occasion to some purpose.

Having done so, he returns in verse 23 to the more personal matter out of which it all sprang. Another thing had most evidently weighed with him, and helped to divert him for the moment from another visit to Corinth. He had no wish to come amongst them, only to find himself bound to act in severity by reason of sin and grave disorder still being found in their midst. Hence he had waited until he had news of the effect of the earlier epistle he had written to them. He hoped for better things. It was not that he assumed dominion over their faith, but rather that he was just a "helper," or "fellow-worker," to the end that they might be delivered and rejoice.

The chapter closes with the words, "by faith ye stand." This is a fact that we ought very much to lay to heart. If he had assumed dominion over their faith in any matter, their faith in that respect would have ceased to be. He would have merely ordered them to do certain things (quite right things, doubtless) and they would have done them, not as the fruit of the exercise of faith, but mechanically. There would then have been no faith in their actions, but just the mechanical action as a kind of outward shell. And then one day they would have scandalized everyone by collapsing; just as a hut in the tropics collapses suddenly, when all the insides of the supporting posts have been eaten away by the white ants.

There are plenty of Christian folk today who would much like to live their lives on somebody else's faith. They would like to be told what to do. Let somebody else have the exercise, and solve the problem, and issue orders as to what is the correct thing! They will be good and obedient and do as they are told. But it does not work, save disastrously. It is by faith we stand, not by somebody else's faith. By somebody else's faith we fall. And further, it is not good for the somebody else. Such forceful individuals begin to love having dominion over the faith of their brethren, and so becoming little popes. Consequently it ends disastrously for them.

CHAPTER 2

THE APOSTLE HAD made up his mind that he would postpone his visit until it could be made under happier circumstances: and now, as he wrote this second letter, the heaviness was passing and brighter things coming into view. His first letter had made them sorry, as he intended it should, and their sorrow now made him glad, as verse 2 of chapter ii. shows. It had been sent ahead on its mission so that when he did come amongst them it might be with confidence established, and with joy.

In verse 4 we get a very touching and valuable glimpse of the manner and spirit of Paul's writing. Reading his earlier epistle we can discern its powerful and trenchant style: we can notice how calculated it was to humble them with its touches of holy irony. We should hardly have known however that he wrote it "out of much affliction and anguish of heart . . . with many tears," had he not told us this. But so it was. Foolish and carnal though they were, yet he loved them with a tender affection. Consequently the inspired Word of God flowed to them through the human channel of a loving and afflicted heart, and was mightily effective. Would to God that we were followers of Paul in this, and learned the holy art through him! How much more effective we should be.

What a deluge of controversial writings has flowed through the church's history! What polemics have been indulged in! And how little, comparatively speaking, has been accomplished by them. We venture to believe that if only one tenth had been written, but that tenth had been produced by men of God, writing with much affliction and anguish of heart, and with many tears, because of that which made the writing needful, ten times as much would have been accomplished for the glory of God.

After all, love lies as the rock-bottom foundation of everything. Not cleverness, not ability, not sarcasm, not anger, but LOVE is God's way of blessing.

"Out in the darkness, shadowed by sin,
Souls are in bondage, souls we would win.
How can we win them? How show the way?
'Love never faileth,' Love is the way.

'Love never faileth,' Love is pure gold;
Love is what Jesus came to unfold,
Make us more loving, Master, we pray,
Help us remember, Love is Thy way."

It might have seemed harsh of Paul to call the evil-doer at Corinth, "that wicked person," and to instruct that he be put away from their midst. But his loving heart caused his eyes to shed tears as he penned the words. Paul's words and tears were effective and the punishment was inflicted, as verse 6 states; and inflicted not by Paul merely, or by one or two of the more spiritual at Corinth, but by the whole mass of the saints. Thus the man was made to feel that they all abhorred and disowned his sin. His conscience was reached. He was brought to repentance.

This, of course, is the end that discipline is designed to reach. Erring believers are not disciplined merely for the sake of punishment, but that they may be brought to repentance and so restored, both in their souls, and to their place of fellowship amongst God's people. This happy end was reached in the case of the offender at Corinth.

How unfrequently is it reached today! All too often the putting away is done in a hard judicial spirit. The anguish of heart, the tears are absent, and the offender becomes more occupied with the harsh manner of his brethren than with his own delinquencies. Hence his repentance is a long way off—to his loss and theirs.

The action taken at Corinth was so effective that the man was brought himself into much affliction and anguish of heart. Indeed the danger now was that the Corinthian assembly would in their zeal against his sin, overlook his sorrow, and not forgive him administratively by restoring him to his place in their midst. Now, therefore, Paul has to write to them urging them to do this, and thus confirm their love towards him. It was possible otherwise that he might be overwhelmed with overmuch sorrow. Sorrow for sin is good; yet there is a point where it may become excessive and harmful—a point where sorrow should cease and the joy of forgiveness be known. The joy of the Lord, and not sorrow for sin, is our strength.

121

Verse 10 shows that if the assembly at Corinth forgave the man, their forgiveness carried with it Paul's. And again, that if Paul forgave any, by reason of his apostolic authority, he did so for their sakes, and as acting on behalf of Christ. The forgiveness spoken of in this verse may be termed administrative forgiveness. It is the forgiveness of which the Lord spoke in such scriptures as Matthew xvi. 19, where it is apostolic; Matthew xviii. 18, where it is vested in the assembly; John xx. 23, where it is confirmed to the apostolic company by the Lord in His risen condition. In 1 Corinthians v. we have a case in which the powers of "binding" or "retaining" were exercised. In our chapter we have an example of "loosing" or "remitting."

Paul wrote thus, not merely for the sake of the sorrowing brother, but for the sake of all, lest Satan should get an advantage over all of them. Note it well! The very devil himself in some cases likes to see believers righteous overmuch, at the expense of "the meekness and gentleness of Christ." The Apostle could add, "for we are not ignorant of his devices." Alas, that so often we cannot truthfully say that! We *are* ignorant of his devices, and though our intentions are good we fall into traps that he sets.

What wisdom we need to hold the balance evenly, in practical matters, between the claims of righteousness and love. How necessary to remember that all discipline is inflicted in righteousness, whether by God Himself or by men, in order that repentance may be produced: and that when it is produced love claims the right to hold sway. Let us not continue to smite in discipline a repentant soul, lest we come under Divinely inflicted discipline ourselves.

One remarkable feature about this epistle is the way in which historical details as to Paul's movements and experiences form a kind of framework, in the midst of which is set the unfolding of much important truth, which is introduced rather in the form of digressions—often lengthy ones. The epistle opened with his sufferings and trouble in Asia, and the consequent change in his plans, and this led to the important digression of verses 19-22 of chapter i. Then he picks up the thread as to his subsequent movements, only to digress further in chapter ii., as to the forgiveness of the repentant offender.

At verse 12 he again reverts to his movements. This brief visit to Troas must be distinguished from that recorded in Acts xx. 6. It apparently came between the departure from Ephesus and the arrival in Macedonia, as recorded in Acts xx. 1. Though an open door was set before him by the Lord he was unable to avail himself of it, owing to his great anxiety for news of the Corinthians. In this case his pastoral solicitude prevailed against his evangelistic fervour. If the servant is not at rest in his spirit he cannot effectively serve the Lord.

The apostle was evidently conscious that this was failure on his part. Yet looking back he was equally conscious that God had overruled it to the glory of Christ; and this led him to an outburst of thanksgiving to God. It also led him once more to digress from his account of his experiences, and we do not come back to them until chapter vii. 5, is reached. The long digression which starts with verse 14 of our chapter, contains the main teaching of the epistle.

As regards his service, one thing he knew: he really and truly set forth Christ. Many there were who dared to manipulate the Word of God to serve their own ends. He, on the other hand, spoke with all sincerity as of God, and as in the sight of God, and as representing Christ. Moreover Christ was his great theme. Hence God led him in triumph in Christ.

The language the Apostle uses seems to be based upon the custom of according a triumph to victorious generals, when sweet odours were burned, and some of the captives, who helped to augment the triumph, were appointed to die, and some to live. The triumph was Christ's; but Paul had a share in it as spreading abroad the sweet odour of Christ wherever he went—an odour so infinitely fragrant to God. This was so whether he were in Troas or whether in Macedonia.

He preached Christ as the One who died and rose again, whether men believed and were saved, or whether they believed not and perished. If they believed not and were perishing, then the tidings of the *death* of Christ simply meant *death* for them. If He died *for* sins, and they refused Him, they certainly must die *in* their sins. If some believed, then tidings of His *life* in resurrection brought the odour of *life* for them. Because He lived they should live also.

How solemn then is the effect of a true preaching of Christ! What eternal issues hang upon it! This is so, whether the lips that utter it be Paul's in the first century or ours in the twentieth. No wonder the question is raised, "Who is sufficient for these things?" It is raised, but, not answered immediately. It is answered however in verse 5 of the next chapter. The whole thing being of God there is no sufficiency but of God. Would that every servant of God always bore this in mind! What deep-toned earnestness it would produce in us: what dependence upon the power of God. How careful we should be not to adulterate the message, and not to carry out the work just as we like, or as we think best; but to serve according to the Word of God.

CHAPTER 3

PAUL HAD JUST spoken of the way in which he preached the Word, but this did not mean that he wished to commend himself to the Corinthians, or that he needed others to commend him. The fact was that they themselves were his "letter of commendation," being so evidently, in spite of their sad faults, the fruit of a genuine work of God through him. He speaks of them as an epistle in two ways. First as written in his own heart. In so saying, we believe he wished them to realize how deeply they were engraved, as it were, on his affections. They little realized the intensity of his love in Christ for them. But then they were an epistle of Christ in a more objective sense, and of this verse 3 speaks.

They were "the epistle of Christ" in a double sense, inasmuch as that which is written is, in one word, Christ; and also it is Christ Himself who is the great and effective Writer. True, He writes by the hand of His servant, and so we find the words, "ministered by us." Paul was *only* the minister, still he *was* the minister, and this sufficiently commended him.

Next we have a double contrast. The thoughts of the Apostle went back to the former ministry of the law through Moses. Then the Divine commandments were engraved on tables of stone, and apparently made the more visible by some kind of ink. Now it is not ink but the Spirit of the living God: not tables of stone but the tables of the heart. That was *dead;* this was *living.* The Gospel had indeed been to the Corinthians a savour of life unto life.

In this verse the work of God in the hearts of the Corinthians is viewed as being equally the fruit of the operation of Christ and of the Spirit of the living God. Christ and the Spirit are very closely linked together thus all through this remarkable passage, as we shall see.

This work of Christ and of the Spirit had been carried out through Paul. He had been the minister. Every servant of God who preaches the Gospel is in that position. Yet Paul had that place in a very special sense. He had no more sufficiency for it than we have, yet he had very specially been made "able" or a "competent" minister of the New Covenant, which had found its basis and foundation in the death and resurrection of Christ. The New Covenant, of which Jeremiah prophesied is of course to be formally established in the future with the house of Israel and the house of Judah, but the basis of it has already been laid, and the Gospel preached today is of a new covenant order. The blessings promised in the New Covenant are found in it, as well as blessings that go beyond anything that the New Covenant contemplates.

Again in verse 6 the living character of the Gospel ministry is emphasized, whereas the law brought in death. We get the expression "the letter" twice in verse 6, and the same word (in a slightly different form) occurs in verse 7, where it is translated, "written." The New Translation renders it, "the ministry of death, in letters, graven in stones," which shows that in this passage the term, "letter," refers to the law. The law kills. Its ministry is unto death. The Spirit quickens.

What we have just pointed out is worth notice, for some have sought to deduce from this Scripture that the letter of Scripture kills! Under cover of this idea they feel free to disregard the letter of Scripture in favour of what they are pleased to declare is its spirit. What Scripture *says* is waved aside in order to introduce what it is *supposed* to mean. And if other passages be quoted which definitely contradict the alleged meaning, that matters not, for those other passages can be waved aside as also being but the letter which kills. Such people kill the letter because, they say, the letter kills. But it is all a mistake. There is no such idea in this verse.

We have been pointing out the digressions of this epistle. We now have to note that there is a big parenthesis in the midst of this lengthy digression, covering from verse 7 to verse 16 inclusive. Within this parenthesis the very striking contrast between the ministry of the Law and the New Covenant is developed, and the point is particularly made that the glory connected with the latter far outshines the glory connected with the former.

First, the law was but a ministry of death: the Gospel is a ministry of the life-giving Spirit. Yet there was a glory connected with the law: a glory so great that the children of Israel could not behold it, nor could they look at the reflection of it as seen in the face of Moses. That glory was to be done away, for presently it faded from the face of Moses, and the time came when the signs of the divine presence left Sinai's crest. So our verse states that the law system "began with glory," (N. Tr.) not merely that it "was glorious." It began, but it did not continue. Now comes the question, "How shall not rather the ministry of the Spirit subsist in glory?" (N. Tr.). The glory of the law began, but soon it was quenched in the ministry of death to all who came under it. When the ministry of the quickening Spirit comes in, it abides in glory.

Again the law was a ministry of condemnation, whereas the Gospel is a ministry of righteousness. That demanded righteousness from man, and, because he had none of it, utterly condemned him. This brings righteousness, and ministers it to man by means of faith. Without a question a ministry which confers righteousness, and thus enables sinful man to stand in the presence of God, greatly exceeds in glory a ministry which merely demands righteousness where it is non-existent, and as a result condemns.

There is a further contrast in verse 11. The law system and its glory is "done away" or "annulled" in Christ; whereas the glory introduced by Him abides. There has been introduced by the Lord Jesus that which remains to eternity; and the glory of that is so surpassing that it completely eclipses any glory that once existed in connection with the law, as verse 10 points out.

This then was the wonderful character of that ministry with which the Apostle was entrusted; and the character of it influenced the manner of its presentation. That which the Gospel ministry presents is not yet brought into full display, but it will be in due season. Hence he speaks here of having a *hope*, and *such* a hope. Having it, he was able to confront men with "great plainness of speech" or "boldness," and also with great openness and absence of reserve. There had to be reserve in connection with the law, for men could not stand in the presence of its glory.

Moses had to put a veil on his face when he had come down from the mount, to hide the glory from the children of Israel. That which has been annulled had an "end" which they did not see. "End" signifies not the finish or termination of the law, but the purpose of God in the law; which was Christ, as Romans x. 4 tells us. The law provided man with a very thorny road for his feet, but it led to Christ; just as every other road laid down by God leads to Christ. The glory that shone in the face of Moses was really a faint reflection of Christ. But Israel could not see it. Had they seen it they would have condemned themselves and waited with eager expectancy for the advent of Christ, the Deliverer.

Alas, their minds were blinded. They used the law as though it were a kind of feather stuck in their cap, to give them a pre-eminent place among the nations; and it is as though the veil that once was upon the face of Moses had been transferred to their minds and hearts. There is of course an election of grace today from amongst Israel, nevertheless it is still true of them as a nation that they read the Old Testament with the veil on their hearts.

Still a moment is coming when the veil shall be removed. Verse 16 of our chapter is an allusion to Exodus xxxiv. 33-35. Though Moses veiled his face when he dealt with the people, when he turned to the Lord and had to do with Him he removed the veil from his face. This is a kind of allegory as to what will happen with Israel. When at last they shall turn to the Lord in sincerity and repentance the veil will be lifted from their minds, and the glory of the Christ, whom once they crucified, will burst upon them.

Verse 16 completes the parenthesis which began at verse 7. With verse 17 we pick up the thread from verse 6, where it was stated that the Spirit quickens. Here we find the Lord and the Spirit identified in a very remarkable way, the Spirit being the Spirit of the Lord, as also He is the Spirit of God. We are so accustomed to *distinguishing* between the Persons of the Godhead that we may easily fall into the error of *separating* between them. This we must not do. There is the related truth of the unity of the Godhead, and we must never lose sight of their essential *oneness*.

The Lord is the life-giving Spirit of the New Covenant, and where the Spirit of the Lord is there is liberty. *Life* and *liberty* go together, just as law and bondage are associated. The divine life is not to be hampered or entangled within legal restraints. There is no need that it should be. Legal restraints are necessary and suitable enough when the flesh or the world are in question. They are not effective, for the flesh and the world break through them and transgress. In another way the law *is* effective, for it curses and brings death in upon the transgressor. All is changed when once the Spirit has given life. Then liberty can be safely accorded, for the Spirit of the Lord holds sway.

Verse 18 brings in a third wonderful thing. In addition to life and liberty there is *transformation*. As we have it in the Authorized Version the words, "with open face," are a little vague, and would probably be read as applying to us. It is true of course that we have no veil upon us as Israel has; but the point seems to be that the glory of the Lord, upon which we gaze, has no veil upon it. There is no veil upon the face of our Lord as there was upon the face of Moses. Moreover the glory that shines in Him is not repellent as was the glory in the face of Moses, it is attractive: and not only attractive but transforming also. The more Christ in His glory is before our spiritual vision the more we gain His likeness.

This transformation is a gradual process, and not reached all at once. We are changed "from glory to glory," that is, from one degree of glory to another. It is a Divine work, "even as by the Spirit of the Lord." Here again the wording is remarkable. "Even as by [the] Lord [the] Spirit." (N. Tr.). The definite article "the" is omitted both times in the Greek. Our little plumb-line may utterly fail when let down into the depths of this statement; but at least we can see that both the Lord and the Spirit work together in this transformation process; the Lord as an Object before faith's vision, the Spirit as a power within us.

Oh, that we might be kept steady with the eye on Christ; kept as true to Him as the needle is true to the pole!

CHAPTER 4

THE NEW COVENANT ministry entrusted to the Apostle Paul is unfolded to us in chapter iii. As we open chapter iv., our thoughts are directed to the things that characterized him as the minister of it. And first of all he was marked by good courage. Since God had entrusted him with the ministry, He gave with it suitable mercy. So, whatever the opposition or difficulty he did not faint. The same thing holds good for us. The Lord never calls us to ministry of any kind without the needed mercy being available. "Ministry" of course is just "Service;" the kind of thing that any of us might render, though it is a word of wide meaning and covers things that many of us might not be called to do.

The second verse emphasizes the honesty and transparency that marked Paul in his service. He descended to none of the tricks that so commonly disfigure the world's propaganda. Many a zealot, religious as well as political, will stoop to a great deal of craft and falsification in order to gain his end. The end justifies the means, to his way of thinking. Paul was very conscious that he was proclaiming the "Word of God," and this must not be falsified, but rather made manifest in all its truth. His transparent honesty in handling the truth was thus made manifest to every upright conscience.

And another thing also was gained. Things were brought to an issue in the case of those who did not receive his message. The word, "hid" which occurs twice in verse 3, is really, "veiled;" the same word (in a slightly different form) as occurs several times in the latter part of chapter ii. "If also our gospel is veiled, it is veiled in those that are lost." (N. Tr.). There was no veil on the Gospel, for Paul declared it in its purity and its clarity: but there was a veil upon the hearts and minds of the perishing who did not believe; a veil that had been dropped in their minds by the god of this world. Had Paul preached the word only partially, or in deceitful fashion, the issue would not have been so clear.

What a word is this for those of us who preach the Gospel! Are we rightly affected by the awful solemnity of preaching the Word of God? Have we renounced every "hidden thing," whether of dishonesty, craft, deceit, or anything else unworthy? Do we make manifest the truth, and only the truth? These are tremendous questions. If we do not, the unbelief of our hearers may not be attributable to *their blindness*, but to *our unfaithfulness*.

However, even when the Gospel is preached as it should be preached there are found those who do not believe; and the explanation is that the devil has blinded their eyes. The sun in the heavens has not been eclipsed, but a very dark blind has been dropped over the window of their little room. The light of the Gospel of the glory of Christ shines, but it does not shine into them. The god of this age will use anything, no matter what, so long as it blots out the Gospel: not usually material things, but rather speculative notions and teachings of men. During the past three-quarters of a century he has very effectually blinded multitudes by the revival of a favourite speculation of the pagan world before Christ—evolution. The light of the gospel of the glory of Christ does not penetrate where the evolutionary blind has been securely dropped. The blinded soul may entertain miserable notions of man as the image of a monkey—or some other elementary creature—or of a monkey as the image of man. He cannot in the nature of things know Christ as "the Image of God," though he may talk about a Christ of his own imagination. There are many imaginary Christs: Christ, as men wish He had been. There is only one real Christ, the image of God; Christ as He was and is, the Christ of the Bible.

Christ Jesus was the great theme of the Apostle's preaching, and he emphasized His position as Lord. He kept himself out of sight as a mere bondman of others. Preaching Him as Lord, he of course presented Him in His present glory at the right hand of God; and so he could speak of his message as, "the glad tidings of the glory of the Christ" (ver. 4. N. Tr.). Elsewhere He speaks of preaching, "the gospel of the grace of God" (Acts xx. 24). There are not two gospels, of course. The one Gospel of God has both the grace of God and the glory of Christ amongst its outstanding features, and so either may be presented as characterizing it. Here the glory of Christ is the prominent feature as befits the context, for he had been speaking of the passing glory of the Old Covenant which once shone in the face of Moses. We can declare that the glory of God now shines, and will for ever shine, in the face of Jesus Christ.

Verse 6 is very striking, for it clearly alludes first to God's act in creation, then to His act in Paul's own conversion, and lastly to the ministry to which he was called. Of old God said, "Let there be light," and light shone out of the darkness. That was in the material creation. But now there is a work of new creation proceeding, and something analogous takes place. Divine light—the light of the glory of God in the face of Jesus—shines into dark hearts, as it did in such a pre-eminent fashion into Paul's on the road to Damascus, producing marvellous effects. It shines in that it may shine out. It is "for the shining forth of the knowledge" (N. Tr.). In that way the believer becomes luminous himself. He begins to shine, just as the moon shines in the light of the sun, save of course that the moon is a dead body merely reflecting light from its surface without being affected itself.

The fact we are dwelling on accounts for the wonderful character of Paul's ministry. He was not a mere preacher—a mere professional evangelist—throwing off so many sermons a week. He preached more than others indeed, but his preaching was the shining out of the light that was shining within, the telling forth of things that were thus wrought into every fibre of his being. No one knew better than he that every Divine excellence shines forth in Jesus, and that He dwells in light above the brightness of the sun, for he had seen it on the road to Damascus. That which he knew was as a precious treasure deposited within him.

We have not seen Christ in His glory as Paul did, yet by faith we do see him there; so that we too can speak of having a treasure. As with Paul so with us, "we have this treasure in earthen vessels." The allusion here is to our present mortal bodies, for as to his body "the Lord God formed man of the dust of the ground" (Gen. ii. 7). As originally formed, man's body was perfect, and perfectly suited to his environment and his place in the scheme of creation. As fallen his body becomes marred, and so the earthen vessels in which the treasure is found are poor and feeble. But then that only makes more manifest the fact that the power at work is of God and not of man.

In the passage before us, extending to the early verses of chapter v., we have many allusions to the body, and it is spoken of in various ways. In verse 10 it is clearly mentioned apart from figurative language as, "our body." In verse 11 it is, "our mortal flesh." In verse 16, "our outward man." And in the next chapter, verses 1 and 4, "our earthly house of this tabernacle," and "this tabernacle." The whole passage instructs us as to the dealings of God with Paul as regards his body, and it throws great light on many an event in our own histories.

All God's dealings with us, as regards the earthen vessel of the body, have as their object the better and more adequate shining forth of the treasure which He has placed within. There is an "excellency," or "surpassingness" of power about this treasure, which was very manifest in the case of Paul. By virtue of it not only was he sustained under unparalleled afflictions, but life worked in those to whom he ministered, as verse 12 shows. Now, as we know, there is truly a surpassingness about the power of natural life which is inexplicable by us. Seeds get buried under heavy flagstones, and lo, in the days to come tender green shoots, *filled with life,* manifest surprising energy sufficient to lift the stone and push it aside. Life of a spiritual sort manifests even more surprising powers.

Now this power was operating very energetically in a frail mortal man like Paul. Had he been sent into the world to serve, clothed in a splendid body of glory, he would have been viewed as a kind of superman, and the power largely attributed to him. As it was, the surpassing power that wrought in him and through him was obviously of God.

The trouble with us so often is that we rather want to wield power as though it were connected with ourselves. We are not content to be like an earthen vessel containing a power manifestly not its own. Hence very little power, or perhaps even complete absence of power, is what marks us. This indeed is the inveterate tendency of our poor human hearts.

And it was also the tendency of Paul's heart, for he was a man of like passions to ourselves. Verses 8 to 11 clearly show this. He was continually faced with seas of trouble and difficulty. On the other hand, he was continually maintained and carried through, and made a blessing to others by the power of God.

If we examine these verses carefully we see that what he had to face came upon him in a threefold way. First, there were adverse circumstances. These are mentioned in verses 8 and 9. Trouble, perplexity, persecution, castings down, all these came upon him. Verily he was "a man," as he told the Jews, (Acts xxii. 3), and hence not beyond these things. He knew what it was to be perplexed and cast down like the rest of us.

Second, there was the spiritual exercise and experience expressed in the words, "Always bearing about in the body the dying of the Lord Jesus." The dying of the Lord Jesus was abidingly impressed upon the mind of the Apostle, so that he bore it about with him continually. But these words seem to convey more than this, for as a consequence the dying of Jesus laid its finger, so to speak, upon every faculty and every member of his body, controlling all his ways. It laid its finger, for instance, upon his tongue, repressing many an utterance that would have been unworthy. The thing was not perfect with him, as we know. Yet it was characteristic with him, marking him normally, in spite of occasional deviations and failures.

Third, there was God's disciplinary action which he describes as being "alway delivered unto death for Jesus' sake." God permitted many a thing to come upon him, such as that episode at Ephesus, which he described in chapter i. as "so great a death," by which he was delivered to death in his experiences amongst opposing men. In this way the inward and spiritual experience of which he speaks in verse 10, was supplemented by outward experiences, sent of God to further help him in his service. By these things he lived, and his light the more brightly shone.

We have only noticed so far one side of the matter. The other side is concerned with the wonderful results, with the way in which the surpassing excellence of the power of God was displayed in and by means of these things. Though circumstances were continually against him yet he was not distressed, not in despair, not forsaken, not destroyed. Obviously a sustaining power was working in him which counteracted all that was working against him. He was rather like one of those self-righting lifeboats, pounded by the stormy seas and even overturned, which nevertheless comes up, the right side up, when the thundering billows have passed. It was indeed the power of the divine life in Paul that accomplished this.

Again, whether the action of faith and love in his own experience, leading him to bear about in his body the dying of Jesus, be in question, or whether God's disciplinary actions in keeping with that experience be in question, the same end was achieved, and a wonderful end it was. The life of Jesus was made manifest in his body, his mortal flesh. In verse 2, referring to his service, he had spoken of the *manifestation* of the truth. Again in verse 6, still referring to his service, he had spoken of the *shining forth* of the knowledge of the glory of God in the face of Jesus Christ. Now we have something additional to this, for the *manifestation* of the life of Jesus is not just service. It is character. In his unconverted days Saul of Tarsus manifested *himself*, as a man of imperious energy and self-will, in his mortal flesh. Now all was changed. The dying of Jesus was so applied to him that the Saul character was effectually stilled in death, and *the life of Jesus* manifested.

Nothing less than this is true and proper Christian testimony. Behind preaching and service lies the life. Christ in His glory should be clearly manifested *in the preaching*, but that manifestation will only reach to its maximum of power and effect as Christ is manifested *in the life*. And this is as true in regard to ourselves today as it was for the Apostle Paul. Without a doubt here lies one of the main reasons for the ineffectiveness of so much modern preaching, even though the preaching itself is correct and sound.

Verse 10 and 11, then, show us that, as the result of death working in Paul, life wrought in him, and the life of Jesus was lived by him. Verse 12 shows that there was a further result—life wrought also in those to whom he ministered, and notably the Corinthians. Some years before life had worked to their conversion. Now he was rejoicing to see further evidence of life in their genuine repentance as regards their wrong-doing, and their affection for himself in spite of his rebukes. And lastly he looked forward to the resurrection world where they together with him would be presented in due season. Verse 14 mentions this.

The words, "I believed, and therefore have I spoken," are quoted from Psalm cxvi. 10. If that Psalm be studied it will be seen that the circumstances of the Psalmist when he wrote were very similar to those of Paul. He had been confronted by death and tears and falling, but had been delivered; and now he had the confidence that he would "walk before the Lord in the land of the living:" that is, he had the resurrection world in view. Believing that, he was able to open his mouth in testimony. Now

Paul was just like that. He had "the same spirit of faith." The resurrection world was full in view for him.

Is it fully in view for us? It should be. Life and incorruptibility have come to light by the Gospel: and that which was known partially to the Psalmist may be known in full measure by us. It is only as we live in the light of resurrection that we can be content to bear about in our bodies the dying of Jesus; and only as we do that is the life of Jesus manifested in our bodies, and does life work in others whom we may serve.

Paul's ministry and service are still in view in verse 15, and the "all things" of that verse refer to the treasure with which he had been entrusted, the mercy that carried him in triumph through the persecution and discipline, the resurrection world which lay at the end. All these things were not matters purely personal to Paul, but through him were for the sake of the whole church of God. Consequently the Corinthians had an interest and a share in it all, and could add their thanksgivings to Paul's to the greater glory of God. We too may join in the thanksgiving though nearly nineteen centuries have passed; for what great blessing has reached us through his inspired epistles which sprang out of these experiences, written for our sakes as well as for the Corinthians. We too shall be presented with Paul and the Corinthians in the resurrection world.

There is nothing like having the resurrection full in view as an antidote against fainting. That glorious hope sustained the Apostle and it will sustain us. In the last verse of 1 Corinthians xv., we see how it inspires to active labour in the work of the Lord. Here, we discover how it sustains and encourages under the severest trials which threaten the perishing of the outward man: that is, the dissolution of the body in death.

And not only is there resurrection in the future but also a work of renewal in the present. "Our outward man" is the material body with which we are clothed. "The inward man" is not material but spiritual—that spiritual entity that we each possess, and which (since we are believers) has become the subject of God's new creation work. The current usage of this phrase in the world is a total misapplication of it. A man speaks of paying attention to "the demands of the inner man" when he means having a good meal to satisfy his stomach; and thus even the inner man is turned into a part of the anatomy of the outward man. This of course is symptomatic of the fact that the spiritual does not come within the range of the natural man.

The outward man is subject to all kinds of buffetings and wear and tear, yet it *may* in the mercy of God receive a certain amount of renewal, which may stave off for a time that ultimate perishing which we call death. The inward man IS renewed day by day. This renewal is doubtless produced by the gracious ministry of the Spirit of God, who indwells us.

What an extraordinary and inspiring picture is presented to our mental vision by this passage. Here is the Apostle; he has years of strenuous and dangerous labours behind him. He is continually being troubled and persecuted and battered by men, and again and again "delivered unto death" in the providential dealings of God. Yet he is pressing forward with undaunted courage, with the light of the future glory of resurrection before his eyes; and though he is worn as to his body, and signs of decay are appearing, he is being renewed daily in his spirit so that he goes forward with unabated or even increased spiritual vigour. He felt all the trouble that came upon him, yet he dismisses it as "our light affliction."

The affliction is not only light but also only "for a moment." In Paul's case it lasted from the days shortly after his conversion, when the Jews of Damascus took counsel to kill him, to the day when he suffered martyrdom: a period covering thirty years or more. This period is only a moment to him because his mind is set on an eternity of glory. What tremendous contrasts we have here! The coming glory is weighty and not light: for eternity and not merely for a moment: and it is this in a "far more exceeding" way. It might have seemed enough to say it was exceeding. To say it is "*more* exceeding" seems almost superfluous. But, "*far more* exceeding!" Paul piles on the words. It is something excessively surpassing! He knew it, for fourteen years before he had been caught up into the third heaven and had glimpses of it. He wishes us to know it too.

The secret of the Apostle's wonderful career is found in the last verse of the chapter. The "look" of which he speaks is, of course, the look of faith. He was passing through the scenes and circumstances of earth, which were very visible, yet he was not looking at them. He was looking at the eternal things, which are not visible to mortal eyes. Here doubtless is discovered to us where much of our weakness lies. Our faith is weak like Peter's was when he essayed to walk on the waters to go to Jesus. He looked at the raging waves which were so very visible, and he began to sink. If, like Paul, we had our eyes upon Christ, upon resurrection, upon glory, we should be upheld by divine power and inwardly be renewed day by day.

CHAPTER 5

THERE IS NO real break between chapters iv. and v., for he passes on to show that if our outward man does perish, and so our earthly tabernacle house be dissolved, we are to have a house of another order which shall be eternal. The thought of what is *eternal* links these verses together. Eternal things are brought within the sight of our faith. An eternal weight of glory awaits us. And we shall need a resurrection body, which shall be eternal, in order to sustain that eternal weight of glory without being crushed by it. It is absolutely certain that such a resurrection body shall be ours. "*We know*," he says. He had established that fact in the fifteenth chapter of his first epistle; so that they knew it as well as he.

Our bodies are spoken of as houses in which we dwell, and very appropriately so. Our present bodies are only "tabernacle" or "tent" houses, comparatively flimsy structures and easily taken down. Our future bodies in the resurrection world will be of a different order, as 1 Corinthians xv. has shown us. Here we learn that they will be "not made with hands;" that is, spiritual, and not of an earthly or human order. They will be eternal, for in them we shall enter into eternal scenes. Also they will be heavenly. Our present bodies are natural and earthly and abide but for a time.

In these opening verses of chapter v. we read of being "clothed," and being "unclothed;" of being "clothed upon," and of being "naked." We dwell at present in an earthly tent, clothed in bodies of humiliation. Presently we shall be clothed in glorified bodies of a spiritual, eternal and heavenly order. All the dead will be raised; even the wicked will appear before their Judge clothed in bodies. But though clothed they will be found spiritually naked before that great white throne. If we are true Christians we shall never be found naked thus, though we may be unclothed, for that word denotes the state of those saints who are "absent from the body" (verse 5) in the presence of the Lord. Paul himself, and myriads more beside, are unclothed at the present moment, but that unclothed state, blessed though it is, is not the great object of our desire. What we do long for, while we groan in our present weakness, is this clothing upon with our house from heaven.

All those who are raised will be "clothed," but only the saints will be "clothed upon," for the reference here is to that which will take place at the coming of the Lord. The term is perhaps particularly appropriate as regards those who are alive and remain to the coming of the Lord. Such will all be changed, and so enter the resurrection state. They will in the twinkling of an eye be invested with their glorified bodies, and so clothed upon with their house from heaven. Thus in a moment mortality—which is attached to our present bodies—will be swallowed up of life.

Let us not read the two expressions, "in the heavens," and "from heaven," in a materialistic sense, as some have done. We must not conceive of our future glorified bodies as though they were a new and improved suit of clothes, already existing somewhere in heaven, and coming to us straight out of heaven. So thinking, we should find ourselves in collision with 1 Corinthians xv. 42-44, where a certain identity is preserved between the body of humiliation which is put down into the ground and the body of glory that is raised up. Those expressions indicate character rather than place. Heaven is our destiny, and we shall enter there in bodies which are heavenly in their origin and character.

We have the happy assurance of these things, and can say, "we know," because God has *spoken* and revealed them to us. But not only so, He has *acted* in keeping with what He has revealed. He has already "wrought us" for this very thing. This alludes to that spiritual work wrought in us and with us by the Holy Ghost. God by His Spirit has been the Potter, and we have been the clay. This clothing upon, of which we have just been speak-

2 CORINTHIANS

ing, is described in Romans viii. as the quickening of our mortal bodies. Our mortal bodies *shall be* quickened, but already God *has* wrought a quickening work as regards our souls, and this present work is in anticipation of the work that is yet to be done as regards our bodies. Moreover He has already given us His Spirit, as the Earnest of what is to come.

What God has wrought by His Spirit must be distinguished from the Spirit Himself, given to those who are subjects of His work. The order in this fifth verse is first, the work of the Spirit: second, the indwelling of the Spirit as the Earnest; the one preparatory to the other.

Hence the Apostle can say, "we are always confident." How could it be otherwise? We have the plain revelation of God as to it. We have the work of God in keeping with it. We have the gift of God—even His Holy Spirit—as the pledge and foretaste of it. Could anything be more certain and secure? Difficulties may throng around us, as they did around Paul. We too may groan, as burdened in our mortal bodies. But that which lies before us in resurrection is perfectly clear and sure. We too may be always confident: as confident when our sky is filled with black thunder clouds as when it is for the moment wholly blue.

For the moment we are at home in the body and absent from the Lord, left here to walk not by sight but by faith. Paul's confidence was such that he was willing—even more than willing, *pleased*— to be absent from the body and present with the Lord. This is his portion today, and the portion of all those who have died in the faith of Christ. They are absent from their bodies which have been laid in the grave, waiting the moment when they shall be clothed in bodies of glory. But even now they are present with the Lord, and in all the conscious blessedness of His presence, as the opening verses of chapter xii. bear witness.

There are those who assert that assurance and confidence as to one's future is bound to have a disastrous effect on one's behaviour. That idea however is definitely negatived by verse 9. Were it a true idea we should read, "We are confident, I say . . . wherefore we"—take our ease and are indifferent and careless. The exact opposite is what it does say—"wherefore we labour . . . ." The word here is not the usual one for "work." It has the sense of "being zealous," or even "ambitious." The very confidence we have stirs us to an earnest zeal; and this is our ambition that come what may, whether life or death, we may be "accepted of Him," or, "agreeable to Him." We are "accepted in the Beloved" as Ephesians i. tells us. Now we want to be agreeable, or well-pleasing, to Him.

This desire to please the Lord is surely an instinctive one in every heart that loves Him; yet all too often it does not burn as it should. So the Apostle now brings in another fact that is calculated to stir it to greater vehemence. When He comes Christ will set up His judgment seat. It will not be like a criminal court: that is reserved for the occasion when the great white throne is established, as we see in Revelation xx. It will be

135

more like a naval prize court, when the judges sit to adjudicate as to captures during naval warfare, and the actions of officers and men come up for review, and prize money is awarded in many cases.

Before that judgment seat we must all appear; that is, we must all be manifested. Everything must come into the light in the presence of our Lord. Would we wish it to be otherwise? If there were left episodes of our lives, some of them marked by failure and shame, as to which the Lord had never had anything to say to us, would there not be a sense of reserve? Would not our otherwise bright eternity be clouded over in part by the feeling that some day they might be dragged into the light? Solemn though that judgment seat must be, it is yet a matter for rejoicing that it is to stand at the very threshold of the eternity of glory that awaits us. Before it we ourselves are to be manifested, and consequently all that we have been and done will come under the scrutiny of our Lord. That will mean seeing eveything as through His eyes, and getting His verdict. It will mean the unravelling of every mysterious episode that has marked our way; the discovery of the why and wherefore of innumerable trying experiences; together with a full understanding of the amazing grace of our God, and the efficacy of the Priesthood and Advocacy of Christ.

It will also mean reward or loss, according to what has been done "in the body;" that is, in the whole of our lives of responsibility here. This is what we see also in 1 Corinthians iii. 14, 15; only there it is distinctly a question of the character of our work as servants of the Lord. Here it is more general and comprehensive, being a question of all our actions and ways.

The thought of that judgment seat evidently carried the mind of the Apostle on to the fact that before the Lord Jesus ultimately all men will stand, whether saved or unsaved. And as he thought of these latter, and recognized what the terror of it would be for them, he was moved to warn and persuade them. He was moved also in another direction more personal to himself and the Corinthians: moved to live in such a way as to be manifested to God, and also in the consciences of his fellow-Christians.

The word for "manifest" really occurs three times in these two verses, but at the beginning of verse 10 it is translated, "appear." Substitute "be manifested" there, and the connection becomes plain. If we live our lives in the remembrance of the certainty of being manifested before the judgment seat, we shall be careful to maintain open, honest, manifested dealings with God now. When we sin we shall at once humble ourselves in confession before Him, and attempt to conceal or palliate nothing. Further we shall, like Paul, not attempt to appear other than we are in the eyes of our fellow-believers. We shall be open and transparent in all our dealings with them, and not desire or seek a cheap reputation for a devotedness or sanctity which we do not possess. There were some in Paul's day who were doing this, as verse 12 bears witness.

Are we living in the light of the judgment seat? A great question this! Let each answer it in his own conscience before God. Depend upon it, if we are we shall be characterized by lives of devotedness, unworldliness and zeal. We shall be transparent before both God and man. And we shall be keen to persuade men as Paul was. We shall earnestly seek the salvation of souls to the glory of God.

The Apostle Paul was marked by a very fervent zeal. It produced within him a great desire to be acceptable to the Lord, to be open and transparent with his brethren, and to persuade men in view of the coming judgment. His zeal was such that sometimes it carried him clean outside himself, and men labelled him as fanatical, as Festus did when he called out, "Paul, thou are beside thyself." But Paul was no fanatic, for when thus beside himself it was "to God;" that is, God was the Object before him; he was outside himself because God was so truly inside—"he that dwelleth in love dwelleth in God, and God in him" (1 John iv. 16).

We may find it difficult to understand this being "beside ourselves," and still more difficult to explain it. That may be because it is an experience almost, if not entirely, unknown to us. Very possibly we move in circles where zeal of the Pauline stamp would be looked upon as fleshly energy from the spiritual standpoint, and quite bad form from the social point of view. How great then is our loss!

But Paul was not always in an ecstasy Godward. He also knew well how to look out with sober-minded wisdom upon the interests of his Lord. Then he cared in a calculating way for the people of God, the Corinthians among them. And in this, as much as in the other, the love of Christ was the power that wrought within him and constrained him. That love had been expressed in His death, and it exerted its pressure on Paul, both in his affections toward God and His saints, and also as guiding his judgment. Constrained by the love, he was able to judge aright as to the significance of the death in which the love was expressed.

Christ "died for all." Here we have His death stated in its widest extent. He did not die for the Jew merely nor for any lesser circle than "all." This is a fact in which we may well rejoice, but what does it imply? This, that all were in a state of spiritual death: all were but dead men before God. This was the *implication* of His death.

But what was the *purpose* of His death? Its purpose was to provide a way of life for at least some, and to alter the whole character of life for these living ones.

Verse 15, you notice, begins with His death and ends with His resurrection. The intervening words set forth the design and purpose connected with those two great facts. They were in order that those who have been quickened into life might find in the risen Christ the Object and End of the new life they live. In our unconverted days we each of us had ourselves as the object and end of our lives. Everything was made to revolve around and contribute to self. Now things are to be entirely different with us, and everything in life is to revolve around and contribute to the interest and glory of Christ. Such at least is the Divine purpose and intention for us.

Verse 16 springs out of this, as the first word, "Wherefore," bears witness. Because Christ is no longer among us in the life of this world, and because we also now live in connection with Him, a new order of things has come in. Even Christ Himself is known by us in a new way. Paul had not been amongst those who knew Christ "according to flesh" in the days of His flesh. But even if he had been, he would have known Him thus no longer. But also we know *no man* after the flesh. That is not because men are not in the old condition according to flesh; for the great mass of them are. It is because of the subjective change wrought in ourselves. The Christian learns to look at men in a new way, not because of what has been wrought in them but because of what has been wrought in himself.

What has been wrought is stated in verse 17—a work of new creation in Christ. As newly created in Christ we find ourselves in a new world. We are not there yet as regards our bodies. That awaits the coming of the Lord. But we are there as regards our minds and spirits. Even today our spirits move amid things totally new, things utterly unknown in our unconverted days; also even the old things of this present creation, amongst which we move, are viewed by us in a new way.

This truth needs to be thoroughly digested by all of us. How much difficulty arises amongst Christians because they know and have dealings with one another according to flesh, that is, on the old basis and after the manner of the world. Then it is the easiest and most natural thing possible to drop into parties and cliques, to have our likes and dislikes, to be tremendously friendly with this or that fellow-believer until some disagreement arises, when an equally tremendous antagonism breaks out. All that kind of thing, even the friendship and the pleasantry and the apparent concord, rests on a wrong basis. It is according to flesh, and not according to new creation and the Spirit of God. If all saints knew one another upon the new basis what a transformation would come over the aspect of things that at present prevails in the church of God.

Verse 18 adds a further fact. We are reconciled to God *by* Jesus Christ, as well as being a new creation *in* Christ. Now reconciliation involves the removal of all that is offensive to God in us and about us, including that enmity of heart that kept us away from Him. As the fruit of reconciliation God can look down upon us with joy and complacency, and we can look up to Him with confidence and responsive love.

When Christ was here, God was in Him with reconciliation in view for the whole world. He came to bring men to God, not to arraign them before God, bringing them to book as regards their sins. This we see strikingly exemplified in John viii. 11. But God's overtures to men in Christ, with reconciliation in view, were rejected and He was put to death. It is one of the chief wonders of the Gospel that notwithstanding this His death became the basis of the reconciliation that is being announced today.

We believers are now reconciled to God; and as reconciled ourselves we have a part in the ministry of reconciliation. When the Apostle wrote, "We are ambassadors for Christ," he probably was thinking of himself and his fellow-labourers and the other apostles, for they were in a special sense put in trust with the Gospel; yet his words have an application to every believer. The church of God is like a divine embassy in the hostile world, and each of us has to remember that we are a part of that embassy, and that our attitude towards men has to be in keeping with the word of reconciliation that we carry. At the end of verse 20 we get as in a nutshell what the word of reconciliation is. The words, "you," "you," and "ye," are not in the original. "God as it were beseeching by us, we entreat for Christ, Be reconciled to God" (N. Tr.).

And if, when we thus entreat men, they turn to us asking on what basis such a reconciliation is possible, we can answer in the words of the last verse. The basis lies in God's own act, accomplished in the death of Christ.

There is a profound depth in verse 21 that defies all our feeble attempts at explanation. That God should make Christ to be a sacrifice for sin might be explained in terms of those Old Testament sacrifices that furnish a type of His sacrifice. But that God should make Him, who knew no sin, TO BE SIN for us baffles all explanation. Again, we might offer some explanation of how we are justified, of how righteousness is imputed to those who believe. But how we may in Him be MADE THE RIGHTEOUSNESS OF GOD is beyond us. Sin wholly characterized us, and all that we were He was made when He died on the cross. Righteousness wholly characterizes God, and that which He is we are made in Christ.

On the one hand then, all that we were is removed, and all that God is has been established, and we established in it. Here evidently is a perfect and unchallengeable basis for the reconciliation that we enjoy, and that we are privileged to proclaim to others.

Let us pause at this point to observe how the Apostle has been led through a considerable digression, from about verse 7 of chapter iv., springing out of the reference there made to the circumstances pressing in upon himself as a minister of the new covenant and the vessel of the light. The digression is completed at the end of chapter v., and again we see him as a minister, but this time of the word of reconciliation. The word of reconciliation doubtless goes beyond the terms of the ministry of the new covenant, and it is helpful to distinguish the one from the other. Yet we must not divide them as though there were two gospels. The one gospel of God is so great and comprehensive that it may be considered in these varied ways.

As WE OPEN chapter vi., we find Paul making a personal application and an appeal to the Corinthians concerning these things. Paul and his companions were fellow-workers in connection with the ministry (the words, "with Him," are to be omitted); and they had faithfully brought the word, whether of new covenant grace or of reconciliation, to the Corinthians. Now their beseeching was that the grace of the Gospel should not be received in vain by them. Grace is received in vain if it does not work out to its legitimate end and effect. In the epistle to Titus we are told how grace teaches us to live in a sober, righteous and godly way, and the Corinthians were very defective in these things; so the exhortation was needed by them, as also it is needed by us.

Verse 2 is parenthetical and in brackets. The first part of it is a quotation from Isaiah xlix. 8. The words quoted are addressed prophetically to the Messiah, who was to be rejected, and yet become a light to the Gentiles and salvation to the end of the earth. In spite of His rejection He should be heard and helped of Jehovah; and the hour when He should be heard and helped would be the time accepted and the day of salvation. The latter part of the verse points out that we are living in that very hour. He has been heard in resurrection, and with His resurrection the day of salvation has begun. It will continue until the day of Judgment supervenes. That of course is the reason why grace has visited us at all. We are not to receive it in vain.

Having exhorted us thus, the Apostle does not for the moment carry his beseechings further (he does this, we believe, from verse 11 onwards) but again turns aside to speak of the features that had characterized himself and his companions. He had said a good deal as to these in chapter iv., and one may be tempted to wonder why he should be led to recur to the matter here. We cannot but think that the reason is that the character, the behaviour, the whole spirit of those who are God's ministers is of the utmost importance. It has an effect upon their ministry which is simply incalculable by us. Reading the Acts of the Apostles, we see what exceptional power marked the ministry of Paul. It was of a type that either brought very great blessing or stirred up the fiercest opposition: it could not be ignored. The power of God was with him; that was the explanation. But why was the power of God with him in this exceptional degree? because he was characterized by the features mentioned in verses 3 to 10 of our chapter.

First there was the studied avoidance of all that would give offence, for he knew well that any blemish discernible in the servant would be put down as a black mark against his service. The great adversary is continually striking blows against the work of God; first by enticing the workmen into offences, and then by giving the offences wide publicity so as to discredit his work. Sometimes, sad to say, Christians play into his hands by acting as his publicity agents. They noise abroad their brother's failure to the blame of the ministry of the Gospel.

It is not enough however to avoid offence. There must be the commendation which flows from good. This was found very abundantly with the Apostle, for he was marked by much patience, or endurance, and that in the presence of a whole host of adverse and trying circumstances, which he summarizes under nine heads. Most of these nine things are clearly specified in the history of the Acts—such as afflictions, stripes, prisons, tumults, labours. The rest were not absent, as we can see reading between the lines. Through all these things he went with endurance, pursuing the ministry of grace.

And then he himself was marked by grace, in keeping with the grace he proclaimed. Verses 6 and 7 speak of this. Again we find the matter summarized under nine heads, beginning with pureness and ending with the armour of righteousness on the right hand and the left. Purity and righteousness stand like sentinels, right and left, before and behind; and protected thus, knowledge, longsuffering, love, truth, are found in the energy of the Spirit, and in the power of God. What a beautiful blending of spiritual graces is found here. The servant of God who is armed with righteousness, and yet is full of longsuffering and kindness and love unfeigned, must be like a polished sword in the hand of the Holy Ghost.

We have in these verses then, first, the negative virtue seen in the absence of offence. Then, the commendation springing from endurance under all kinds of opposing forces. Third, the positive virtues connected with both righteousness and love. And now lastly, the paradoxical state of affairs that resulted from the contradiction found between his state as to outward appearance and his state in inward reality. Once more we find nine heads under which the paradox is set forth.

If one looked merely on the surface appearance of things from a worldly standpoint, that which would have met the eye would have been dishonour. Here was a man who had thrown away all his brilliant prospects. Evil reports continually circulated about him. He appeared to be a deceiver, unknown and unrecognized by the men of religious repute. His life appeared to be a living death. Even God seemed to chasten him. Sorrow continually surged around him. He was poor, and possessed practically nothing. What a story!

There was another side to the story however. There was honour, and a good report from God. Sometimes there may have been a good report from his converts; but that was a small matter compared with his joining the company of those others who obtained "a good report through faith," as Hebrews xi., tells us. He was a true man, and well known on high. He was entering into that which is really life. He was inwardly always rejoicing. He was so serving as to enrich a great multitude. He was like a man rolling in spiritual riches, for he possessed all things. Again we say, What a story! Only this time there is another tone in our voice.

This amazing servant of God was the leader of that little band of men who were spoken of as, "These that have turned the world upside down," (Acts xvii. 6)—and no wonder! The ingredients of spiritual power are found in the verses we have just considered. Let us inwardly digest them very well, and may they be a blessing to us in this day of abounding evil in the world, and small faith and devotedness amongst the people of God.

Twice already had the Apostle spoken of the ministry of exhortation which was his, "beseeching" men (v. 20, vi. 1). These exhortations were of a more general nature; but in verse 11 he comes to one of a very personal sort, addressing the Corinthians in direct fashion. It is evident that at this point he found his mouth opened and his heart free to bring them plainly face to face with the error which lay at the root of so much that was wrong in their midst. They had not realized that if they remained yoked with unbelievers they would of necessity be dragged into much of their evil ways.

Paul did not bluntly bring them to book on this point directly he opened his first epistle. Whence came the tendency to split into parties and schools of opinion? Whence the immorality, the love of litigation, the carelessness about idolatry, the disorder in their meetings, the speculative errors as to the resurrection? From the flesh doubtless; but also as imported from the world around them, for Corinth was full of things of that kind. We may learn a valuable lesson from Paul's wise action. In his first epistle he contented himself with meeting the errors which lay on the surface, waiting until that letter had had its effect before he exposed the underlying causes. Now however, a suitable spiritual atmosphere had been produced. He had been able to direct their thoughts to the ministry of reconciliation. God and the world are in the sharpest possible antagonism, and therefore *reconciliation* with the One must involve *separation* from the other. Hence the opportune moment to speak plainly on this point had arrived.

The Apostle Paul was the man of large heart. The Corinthians were saints of narrow affections. "Straightened," means narrowed, and "bowels," signifies affections. Quite remarkable—do you think not? The average man of the world would assess matters just the other way round, and not a few Christians would agree with him. They would dub the separate Christian as, the "narrow-minded man," and praise the easy-going one of worldly type, as the large-hearted man. But, as a matter of fact it is the separate believer who finds his centre in Christ, and so enters into the largeness of His interests. The worldly believer is limited by this little world and narrowed down to selfish interests. Paul exhorted the Corinthians to be *enlarged* by *separation* from the world.

Verse 14 contains an allusion to Deuteronomy xxii. 10. The word literally is "diversely yoked" though of course if two, of diverse nature and form, such as the ox and the ass, were put together the resultant yoke would prove to be unequal. Any yoking together of the believer and the unbeliever must be unequal because they are *diverse* in their very nature and character—the one, born of God, a child of light; the other still in the

Adamic nature, a child of darkness. The yoking together of two, so wholly diverse, must prove disastrous.

It is a question, be it noted, of a *yoke*. The believer is left in the world, and comes into contact with all sorts, as is indicated in 1 Corinthians v. 9, 10. While mixing thus with all sorts he is to be careful to avoid being yoked with any. The most intimate and permanent yoke that the world knows is that of marriage. A believer may yoke himself with an unbeliever by a business partnership. Before he is through with it he may suffer much spiritual loss and the Lord's Name be dishonoured; since he has to share in the responsibility of evil things wrought by the unconverted partner. But at least he can get out of it in process of time, even if at financial loss to himself. But marriage he cannot get out of save by death—his own or his partner's. And there are many other yokes besides those in marriage and in business, though not so strong and enduring. We are to shun *all* of them.

Consider what the believer stands for—righteousness, light, Christ, the temple of God. The unbeliever stands for unrighteousness (or lawlessness), darkness, Belial, idols. Now what possible yoke, or fellowship, or agreement, can there be between the two? None whatever. Then why take up a position which involves an attempt to bring together things which are as the poles asunder? The unbeliever cannot possibly fit in with the things which are the very life of the believer. *He has not got the life which would enable him to do so.* The believer can entangle and damage himself with the things of unrighteousness which occupy the unbeliever, for though born of God *he still has the flesh within him.* Yoke the two together, and what must be the upshot?

No deep understanding is needed to answer that question. The one can only travel in *one* direction: the other can travel in *either* direction. The way of the unbeliever prevails, though the believer may be dragged very unwillingly, and hence act as a kind of brake on the wheels.

The exhortation then is that we come out from among the unbelievers and be separate, not even touching what is unclean. The believer cannot be too careful to avoid every kind of connection and complicity with what is evil; and that because of what he is in his individual character as a child of light, and also what he is collectively with other believers as the temple of the living God. Being the living God, He not only dwells in the midst of His people but He walks in their midst, observing all their ways. And holiness becomes his house for ever.

Some of us may say to ourselves, "Yes, but if I obey this injunction and consequently break these or those links, I shall suffer a great deal of loss and be in a very difficult position." That is very possible. But such a contingency is foreseen. The world may cast you out, but God will receive you, and be a Father to you. The last verse of our chapter does not refer to proper Christian relationship which is established in Christ, which is expounded by the Apostle in Galatians iii. 26 to iv. 7; but rather to that practical "fathering" of the believer which he needs when suffering from

143

the world. If we may so put it, with all reverence, God Himself will play the part of Father to him. Hence we are said to be His sons and daughters. When it is a question of proper Christian relationship we all, whether male or female, are His sons.

And notice this; the One who is pledged to play the Father's part is the Lord, Almighty. Here then we have brought together His three great Names—Father, Jehovah, Almighty. He is Jehovah, the unchanging One, faithful to His word. He wields all power. And the value of both Names He brings into His fatherly care. We need not be afraid to cut all links with the world, cost what it may.

An interesting and encouraging contrast between this verse and Ephesians vi. 12 may be pointed out. There are "the rulers of the darkness of this world," or, more literally, "the world-rulers of this darkness"—Satanic authorities and powers, no doubt, who dominate this world of darkness. We might well fear them were it not that we are under the protection of the Lord Almigthy. The word translated, Almighty, is literally the All-ruler. The *world-rulers* may be great, but they are as nothing in the presence of the *All-ruler;* just as this world, though great to us, is very small when compared with all things—the mighty universe of God.

CHAPTER 7

WE HAVE THEN these striking promises from the lips of God. If we are separate from the world, and face whatever loss that may involve, we shall find God acting as Father toward us, and we shall enter consciously into the good and sweetness of the relationship in which we are set. Now having such promises we are exhorted (as we open chapter vii.) to purify ourselves, and thus perfect holiness in the fear of God. Notice that it says, "from *all* filthiness of the flesh and spirit." This is a very important word, and very sweeping. Our attention has just been directed to the necessity of a purification from all fellowship with the world in outward things. Yet if we merely practised separation in outward things, confining ourselves to that, we should just become Pharisees; a most undesirable thing. The separation we are to practice goes much deeper. All filthiness or pollution of the flesh is to be avoided, and all filthiness of the spirit too.

Both forms of separation are called for; the inward and the outward too. The outward without the inward is just hypocrisy. The inward without the outward is at best a very defective thing. At the worst it descends to the plight in which Lot was found in Sodom, though not himself descending to the shocking morals of that city. Abraham was in the happy path of God's will; clean outside the place as well as free from the evil. There are the pollutions of the world: the pollutions of the flesh: the pollutions of the spirit: the last of the three the most subtle of all, because the most refined form of sin. May God awaken us to great carefulness as to it. Holiness when carried to its perfection covers all three. But we are to be carrying it on towards its perfection even now. May God help us to do so.

2 CORINTHIANS

The Apostle had delivered his soul thus as to the Corinthians, and was conscious that the threatened breach between himself and them had been averted in the mercy of God; and those from outside, who had fomented trouble and had been his detractors, had lost something of their power. The Corinthians, under the influence of these men, had been inclined to turn their backs on Paul. Things however were now changed, and he can say simply, "Receive us." They knew the integrity that had ever characterized him, and the fervent love towards them that was in his heart; he was identified with them in his affections whether in life or in death. Moreover, confident now as to their affection for him, he was filled with encouragement and joy. He could tell them now of the happy experience that was his, when tidings of the effect of his first epistle reached him.

Verse 5 picks up the threads of happenings from chapter ii. 13. One can read from one verse to the other as though nothing came between them. He had left Troas, in spite of the door for the Gospel opened of the Lord, because he had no rest in his spirit as to the Corinthians; yet when he got into Macedonia conditions were even worse. There were not only fears within but also fightings without. One can imagine a little perhaps of what he felt as he plunged deeply, and yet more deeply, into sorrows and troubles. Suddenly however Titus appeared, bringing good news as to the effect of his first epistle, which ministered to him great comfort. He had the companionship of Titus, and the assurance that God had intervened in His mercy.

His first epistle had been used to effect two things: first, a thoroughgoing repentance as to the evils he had denounced; second, a revival of their affection for himself. There was of course a very distinct connection between them. As they realized the error of their ways so they saw that his plain and faithful remonstrances were actuated by love; and responsive love was kindled in their hearts towards him. For a time he had been tempted to regret that he ever wrote the letter, but now that its good effect had been manifested he could only rejoice.

This scripture shows us very clearly what genuine repentance really is. It is not exactly sorrow for sin, though godly sorrow of that sort is an ingredient of it. Verse 11 shows what repentance involved in their case, and with what zeal and fear they cleared themselves. Repentance of a right sort is repentance to salvation; that is, it means deliverance from the thing repented of. Mere sorrow for sin, when confronted with its consequences, is the kind of which the world is capable, and it only works death and not salvation. Judas Iscariot is a sad example of this.

One great thing, then, that had come out of all the troubles at Corinth and the sending of the first epistle had been a mutual expression of love as between Paul and the saints there. Verse 7 mentions, "your fervent mind toward me;" and verse 12, "our care for you in the sight of God." It was no small thing to put things right as between the one who did the injury and the one who was injured, but it was even greater to bring into display that love which is the fruit of the Divine nature in the saints.

A striking feature of this chapter, from verse 5 and onwards, is the way in which all these happenings are traced to the hand of God. Having sent his first epistle, Paul was agitated and cast down in spirit to the point of regretting that he had written it—even though, as we know, it was a letter inspired of God. Then at last, when things seemed at their lowest, Titus appeared with good news as to its effect upon the Corinthians. This was the mercy of God intervening to comfort the downcast Apostle, as also it had been the mercy of God effecting a godly repentance in the hearts of the Corinthians. The word, "godly," occurring three times (verses 9, 10, 11), is really in each case, "according to God." God had intervened, and this was the real basis and cause of Paul's comfort and joy.

Moreover Titus had come back thoroughly refreshed and joyful. This evidently had far exceeded Paul's hopes. There had been much anxiety as to them, and many things to blame, as the first epistle shows; and yet the way in which they had received him had gone beyond his expectations. True he had boasted of them to Titus. He had spoken of them with warmth of affection and with assurance of their reality. And now all had been found as he had said. The Apostle's distress had been turned into exultant joy and thankfulness.

In all this we see how God delights to lift up and encourage His tried servants. The God who thus acted with Paul is just the same today. Why are we not filled with greater and more implicit confidence in Him?

The Corinthians had received Titus "with fear and trembling;" they had been marked by obedience. Paul's letter had come to them with an authority that was Divine. In it he had called upon them to recognize that the things he wrote to them were "the commandments of the Lord." Being the inspired Word of God, it had authenticated itself as such in their consciences, and it commanded their obedience. Nowadays some would like to persuade us that we have no logical reason for accepting any given scripture as the Word of God unless we are prepared to receive it as authenticated by "the Church," unless it carries the imprimatur of pope and cardinals. Nothing could be farther from the truth. It was not so at the beginning, and is not so today. The Word of God is self-authenticating in the hearts and consciences of those who are born of Him.

The obedience of the Corinthians to the Word of the Lord gave the Apostle full confidence as to them. He could say with joy, "I have confidence in you in all things." Are we inclined to look upon this as a rather exuberant overestimate on his part, the fruit of the revulsion of feeling he had undergone? It was not so at all. It was the expression of a sober judgment. Saints may be very defective and blameworthy as to many things, but if they recognize the Word of God when they hear it, and yield obedience to its instructions, one need have no fear as to them. All will be well.

2 CORINTHIANS

It was not that they had any fear of Titus, or that Paul's letters, though weighty and powerful, put the fear of Paul upon their spirits. It was rather that in spite of all their errors they did tremble at the Word of the Lord, when they heard it.

Are we equal to the Corinthians in this respect? Our day is peculiarly marked by disrespect for the Word of God. In many quarters, professedly Christian, the Bible is looked upon as subject matter for criticism. Let us beware lest we catch the infection of it. Would Paul have confidence in us as to all things? Only if he saw that we too were marked by subjection and obedience to the Word of God.

CHAPTER 8

HAVING OPENED HIS HEART to the Corinthians, both as to his own experiences and as to their need of separation from the world of unbelievers, and having expressed his joy in their obedience to the Word of God, and the confidence as to them which this gave him, Paul now felt ready to write to them more particularly concerning the collection then being made amongst the various Gentile assemblies for the benefit of poor saints in Jerusalem. He had alluded to it briefly in the closing chapter of his first epistle. He now refers to it at length in chapters viii. and ix. of this epistle; and in urging the Corinthians to liberality he brings out some very important instruction.

There has been a very remarkable display of the grace of God in the assemblies of Macedonia, and it has been put permanently on record, so that not only the Corinthians but ourselves might be stirred up by it. Some of us might be inclined to think that a recital of the devotedness of others, with a view to stirring up sluggish saints, would be an appeal to rather low-down motives and not a worthy proceeding. Here however we find the Spirit inspiring the Apostle to do this very thing. So we never need be afraid of telling how the grace of God has wrought in others. Such recitals not only reveal the grace of God to us as a real and practical thing, but also they serve to convict us of our own shortcomings: and both these results are much to be desired.

The giving of the Macedonian believers was remarkable. Paul himself could bear witness that they gave according to their power. This in itself was a big thing. It means that having righteously discharged all their proper living expenses, they then gave up to the limit of their ability. They did more than this however. They gave beyond their power; that is, they denied themselves what might be considered proper living expenses in order to give to the Lord and His people. And this they did in the most willing-hearted way, begging Paul to accept the money and undertake the responsibility of having it distributed to the saints. They had caught the spirit that was exemplified when the tabernacle was to be made, and it was reported to Moses, "The people bring much more than enough for the

147

service of the work, which the Lord commanded to make" (Exodus xxxvi. 5).

And there is more even than this; for they exceeded Paul's expectations in another direction. They began their giving at the right point by first giving themselves to the Lord. Yielding themselves to the Lord, they necessarily yielded to Him all that they had. Thus their possessions they regarded as the Lord's, to be used at His direction; and consequently they carried out the will of God in placing themselves and their possessions in the hands of Paul.

This, without a doubt, is the only true way to look at this matter of giving. God does not merely claim our superfluity but *all that we have*, because He claims *us*. When we see this, we at once become conscious how far our standard of giving falls below the standard set by the Macedonians. They were characterized by a liberality that was enhanced by their deep poverty and the fact that they were in the midst of a time of much affliction. What moved them to their liberality was the abundance of their spiritual joy. They had by faith so real and joyous a grasp of the things of heaven, that they could afford to be liberal with the things of earth.

Is liberality in giving a characteristic feature of modern Christian life? We fear there can be only one answer to that question. What devices are resorted to in many quarters in order to raise funds! What advertisements and appeals are issued! What lamentable stories as to shortness of funds! Doubtless a great deal of the trouble arises from people taking up causes and launching enterprises to which they were never called by God. Still, it also indicates that many a believer is withholding more than is meet, and it tends to spiritual poverty—to themselves as well as others. There are exceptions no doubt, in the cases of some who acknowledge their stewardship and give largely according to their means, and of some very few who have given with a liberality that is astonishing. But they are the exception, and not the rule.

We are more like the Corinthians than the Macedonians, and we need to be stirred up, as they did, by this shining example. So Paul had begged Titus during his recent visit to carry the matter to completion. Giving is spoken of as a *grace*, you notice, and this indeed it is, if rightly considered and carried out. It becomes a potent method of expressing the working of the grace of God in blessing. If our own hearts are filled to overflowing with blessing from God, we are bound to overflow ourselves in giving to others. Verse 7 is a very gentle and tactful rebuke to the Corinthians—and, we believe, to ourselves also. Whether we can be said to abound in faith and in all diligence may be doubted, but we evidently do in utterance and knowledge. Is it not true that we know in our heads, and we utter with our lips, a good deal more than we express in the form of large-hearted giving?

2 CORINTHIANS

Verse 8 shows that the Apostle did not wish to be understood as issuing a command on the subject. If we gave only because we were commanded of God to do so, our giving could no longer be spoken of as grace. It would be done under the compulsion of law. No, the forwardness and zeal of the Macedonians was to be a stimulus merely, and the giving for which he asked was to be an expression and proof of the sincerity and genuineness of their love. Love always delights to give.

The working of the grace of God in other Christians may act as a *stimulus* to us, but nothing short of the supreme working of the grace of God in Christ can supply us with the mainspring and *motive* we need, if we are to be characterized by the grace of generous giving. To that mainspring we come in verse 9.

How often verses which are like sparkling gems lie embedded in the discussion of matters which seem very ordinary and even common-place! This is a case in point. The Corinthians had been quite ready to consider the making of this collection. They had willingly taken up the idea a whole year before, and yet they had so far failed to bring it to completion, and actually give the money. What would bring them to the point? What, but the fresh sense of the grace of the Lord Jesus Christ?

This marvellous verse is an epitome of the New Testament. "Though He was rich," carries us back into the depths of His Godhead glory before His incarnation; the glory that is unfolded in the opening verses of John's Gospel and elsewhere. "Yet for your sakes He became poor," opens out into the wonderful story of His life, sufferings and death, as recorded in all four Gospels. "That ye through His poverty might be rich," indicates the wealth of blessing and glory into which we are introduced by Him and in Him, as unfolded in the Epistles and the Revelation. And the whole story is the supreme expression of GRACE; which consists in the down-stooping of Divine love to meet man's need, not merely according to the need that is met, but according to the love that meets it.

Having used this grace as a powerful lever to move and uplift the hearts of the Corinthians, the Apostle turned to enunciate a few important principles that are to govern the Christian in his giving. In the first place, we are to give out of that which *we have;* not that which we used to have, or that which we hope to have in the future. We are to live and act in the present, trusting in God as regards the future.

For, in the second place, he did not contemplate the Corinthians being always, or in every matter, in the position of givers. The time would come when they would be receivers, and the flow of gifts would be toward them instead of out from them. Indeed, if Romans xv. 25-27 be read, it will be evident that there had already been a rich flow of spiritual giving from Jerusalem to Corinth. Now there was to be a flow of giving in material things from Corinth to Jerusalem. The thought of God is that among His people there should never be a vacuum, but rather *a flow of supply* according to the need.

Verse 15 quotes Exodus xvi. 18, in support of this. Reading Exodus, one might suppose that the verse simply meant that each gatherer of the manna was able to rightly gauge his appetite and gather accordingly. The way the verse is quoted here shows however that there is more in it than that, since it is cited in support of the principle of sharing with others what God may have entrusted us with.

Verses 16 to 24 are occupied with details concerning the administration of the funds collected, which was to be in the hands of Titus and two other brethren. Though the circumstances then existing have passed away, there are points of abiding interest which we ought to notice. Paul had exhorted Titus to take up this service, and he on his part did so with willingness and alacrity. He did not count a service of this kind as beneath him. Nor did the unnamed brother who was a gifted evangelist; nor the second unnamed brother, of verse 22, who was a man of diligent zeal in many things, though not perhaps a man of gift in the gospel, nor an apostolic delegate like Titus. All three evidently recognized that to be bearers and administrators of funds, which were given as an expression of Divine love working in the hearts of saints, was no mean service.

Again, it is evident from verse 19 that the churches that gave the money chose the man who was to have the handling of the money on their behalf. This is in accord with the choosing of the seven men of honest report to "serve tables," as recorded in Acts vi. So long as men provide the wherewithal, it is within their competency to select those who shall administer their bounty. In contrast to this, we do not read of saints selecting those who are to fill the office of elder, bishop, or overseer. But that is because such are called to exercise their spiritual functions on God's behalf, not man's. Hence God and not man must choose. We read of those whom the Holy Ghost had made overseers. The most that man can do is to recognize those whom the Holy Ghost has appointed.

Further, everything had to be done honestly as before God, and also in the sight of men. It is not enough that the thing shall be handled in a way that is right before the God who knows all things. It must also be obviously right before the eyes of men who only see a very little way, but who are often very critical of what they do see. Verses 20 and 21 show this. So these men were marked by carefulness that all should be so handled as to be to the glory of the Lord, remembering that they were messengers of the churches, which are spoken of as "the glory of Christ." Let us remember that this is the proper character of every true assembly. We shall not think lightly of such, if we do remember it.

CHAPTER 9

IN THE FIRST FIVE verses of chapter ix., Paul renews his appeal to the Corinthian saints. They had been so very forward a year before, when the matter had been started, that he had even boasted of them to the Macedonians, who had now out-stripped them altogether in actual performance. Let them now really act, and act at once, so that their contribution might be seen to be a gift of the heart, and not something extracted from them almost as a matter of extortion. This fresh appeal is followed from some fresh considerations calculated to back it up. More important principles connected with the matter of giving are brought to light.

For instance, giving is *sowing;* hence the laws of sowing and reaping apply to it. If seed be scattered with a sparing hand there is a scanty harvest: if with a bountiful hand, a bountiful harvest. It cannot be otherwise whether in nature or in connection with the things of God. In giving to others we are sowing *grace;* and the Apostle reminded them, "God is able to make *all grace abound* toward you" (verse 8). Verses 10 and 11 also speak of the harvest of blessing that will be reaped especially in things spiritual.

But the giving to be really pleasing to God must be *cheerful giving.* If done grudgingly, or because one is pushed into it, there is not much value in it in the sight of God. Every man will purpose in his heart according to the state of his heart. If our hearts are right, and enlarged by dwelling in the love of God, we shall give not only bountifully but cheerfully also. We shall give after the style of God Himself; and God loves those who are like Himself.

As we give we are sowing not only grace but *righteousness* also. Psalm cxii. 9 is quoted, in which the man is described who is characterized as "good," and "upright," and "that feareth the Lord." Such a one disperses of his substance and gives to those in need, and his kind giving is not spoken of as grace but as righteousness that will remain for ever. Are we accustomed to look upon giving in this light? We have received so much from God that it is only *right* that we should take the place of givers, if God has entrusted us with a supply of either material or spiritual things. If we do not give, but rather hoard up or expend upon ourselves and our pleasures what is given to us, we are positively unrighteous. Let us take time to mark, learn, and inwardly digest this fact, so that our lives may be ordered in keeping with it.

Moreover the results of large-hearted and cheerful giving are so very blessed. There is the supplying of "the need of the saints." This in itself is a very good thing. Who, that has seen the comfort and joy of some poor saint, when relief has reached them through the liberality of their brethren, could doubt it. Beyond this, however, God is glorified. The action "is abundant also by many thanksgivings to God." The saint, who has been helped and relieved, gives thanks to God again and again for the gift and those who ministered it to him. Presently too those who gave find themselves so blessed and enlarged of God that they begin to give thanks that they were ever privileged to give. We have, you will remember, the very best authority for saying that, "It is more blessed to give than to receive." And finally the poor saints, who have nothing to give in return, do repay what is given by an answering affection and by earnest prayer. The givers reap the blessing which flows from the love and prayers of those whom they have helped.

What a marvellous train of happy results is attached to giving! No wonder it is enumerated amongst the "gifts" of Romans xii., or that elsewhere we read, "To do good and to communicate forget not." What spiritual enlargement flows out of it! And conversely, how often is spiritual poverty the direct result of the neglect of it! If believers are stingy in their handling of material things, the holy government of God will leave them poor and straightened in spiritual things.

All giving by the Christian flows from that which has been given to him from God. Hence the Apostle cannot close his exhortation on this theme without leading our thoughts to God's supreme gift from which all our giving flows. It is so great a gift as to be beyond all our powers of expression or description. We can only utter thanks for it.

God has given "His only-begotten Son." We read also of "the Holy Ghost, whom God hath given to them that obey Him;" and again that, "the gift of God is eternal life." And other such-like verses there are. We believe that here in the mind of the Spirit all these great gifts are treated as *one gift*, which demands eternal thanksgiving from us.

As we add our hearty, Amen, to the thanksgiving, let us see to it that we have such a lively sense of the greatness of the gift that we diligently practise the grace of giving ourselves.

CHAPTER 10

THE LAST FOUR CHAPTERS of this epistle are mainly concerned with matters of a more personal sort, that lay between Paul and the Corinthians. To write so much of such matters may appear to be egotism on the part of Paul. Paul himself speaks of it as his "folly" (xi. 1). Still what he wrote is as much inspired as the rest of the epistle, and as full of profit also. Much that is of deep importance for all saints, and for all time, is embedded in these chapters; and we gain immensely by having it presented to us, not from a theoretical standpoint, but as a matter of actual practice, worked out as between the Apostle and some of his fellow-believers.

During Paul's absence from them, the Corinthians had been influenced and sadly misled by other workers who had visited them. Some of these may have been true but ill-instructed believers of Judaizing tendencies; but others were "deceitful workers" (xi. 13), real agents of Satan. Anyway they had done their best to discredit Paul, making all kinds of charges and insinuations against him. They said, for instance, that though he might be able to write "weighty and powerful" letters, when he appeared on the scene he was weak and insignificant in appearance and his speech was uncultured and contemptible. From this they deduced that he possessed no particular authority, and his instructions might be disregarded. This particular insinuation Paul takes up and meets at the beginning of Chapter x.

He pleads guilty, with the utmost frankness, to being "base" or "mean" in his outward appearance. He was quite undistinguished to look at: when converted he took the name Paul, which means "Little." Now he was absent from them, and he was bold toward them. But further he expected presently to visit them, and he besought them so to carry themselves that he need not come amongst them with bold and powerful discipline which might be to their discomfiture. This he besought them by "the meekness and gentleness of Christ"—a very delicate yet powerful lever!

Meekness is not weakness, neither is gentleness that pliable softness that can be twisted in any direction. Meekness and self-assertiveness stand in contrast to each other: so do gentleness and harshness. Meekness is a matter of *character*—the Lord Jesus said, "I am meek and lowly *in heart*" —and so it comes first. Gentleness is more a question of one's *manner*. He who is meek in character will be gentle in manner. He who is self-assertive in character will be harsh in manner. Supreme meekness and supreme gentleness were found in Christ; and yet no one was bolder than He, when it was a question of maintaining the right or opposing the evil. In a very large measure the Apostle was following His steps, and hence boldness as well as meekness and gentleness were found in him.

True to this character, Paul beseeches the Corinthians rather than issuing peremptory commands to them. There were some however who thought of him as though he were a man who walked according to the flesh. This led him to give us the important statement that follows as to the character of both his walk and warfare. Verse 3 is instructive, inasmuch as both senses in which the word *flesh* is used are brought together in it. We walk *in* the flesh; that is, in the bodies of flesh which we have derived from Adam. But we do not war *after* the flesh; that is, according to the Adamic nature which is connected with our bodies.

In so saying Paul of course referred to himself and his co-workers, and also he stated what normally should be true of every Christian. But is it true of us? Do we recognize the true character of the flesh—that is, of the Adamic nature—and treat it as a condemned thing? It is normal for Christians to walk "after the Spirit" (Rom. viii. 4), but that is not mentioned here, only inferred.

The point here is not exactly our walk, but rather our warfare. Is the believer then called to warfare? He is: and to warfare of a very aggressive sort. His weapons however like the warfare are not fleshly but spiritual.

Every servant of Christ gets involved in warfare. All evangelistic labour has that character, for the Gospel is preached that it may overthrow human pride and bring men to the feet of Christ. All the teaching imparted within the assembly has to overthrow merely human thoughts. And, evil teaching having invaded the Christian profession, there must of necessity be contention for the faith, which partakes of the character of warfare. All warfare however tests us, for it is very easy to slip into the use of purely natural and fleshly weapons. The practiced political speaker, who wants to swing men round to his point of view, has many weapons in his armoury—argument, ridicule, graphic exaggeration, and the like. But he contends merely with other human beings, and upon equal terms.

Our warfare is upon another plane altogether. With us there are "strongholds" to be overthrown. Who holds these strongholds? The great adversary himself. He it is who has entrenched himself in human hearts, so that they are filled with "imaginations" or "reasonings," so that they exalt themselves on high against the knowledge of God, and are filled with lawlessness. All these lofty thoughts have to be brought low into captivity to Christ, so that lawlessness is exchanged for obedience to Him. What weapons are sufficient to produce that result?

Merely human weapons must be perfectly futile. Fleshly weapons can no more subdue flesh than Satan can cast out Satan. Spiritual weapons alone can prevail; and they must be used in a way that is according to God, if they are to be effectual.

What spiritual weapons are at our disposal? In this passage the Apostle does not pause to specify, though the succeeding verses seem to show that he was specially thinking of those powers of discipline which were vested in him as an Apostle, powers peculiar to himself. There are however, spiritual weapons which all may use: those for instance, which were mentioned by the Apostles in Jerusalem when they said, "We will give ourselves continually to prayer, and to the ministry of the Word" (Acts vi. 4). Every saint can pray, and every saint can in some way speak forth the Word

The Apostles recognised the extreme value of both these weapons, and refused to allow anything, however good in itself, to divert them from wielding them. Again and again have servants of God found themselves face to face with some human fortress of pride and unbelief like unto Jericho. And yet when encircled by prayers of faith a moment has come when the Word of God has been sounded out as from a ram's horn, and the walls of unbelief have crashed, the stronghold has been overthrown. The Lord Himself indicated another spiritual weapon when He spoke of a certain kind of demon which only could be cast out by prayer and fasting. Fasting is a weapon but very little used in these days.

Would to God that we all were alive to these things! Take for instance the preaching of the Gospel. Do we recognize that the work involves conflict of this order? If we did we should simply flock to the prayer meetings for the Gospel—that is, if we have any heart for the glory of Christ, any love for the perishing souls of men. As things are, a tiny group of two or three, or perhaps half a dozen, usually turn up for the prayer meeting, and the majority of those who attend the preaching do so in the spirit of those who have come to hear a nice address, which they expect to "enjoy," as if the enjoyment of saints were the chief end of the Gospel service. If once we caught the spirit that breathes in the verses before us, our prayer meetings, our Gospel meetings, and many other meetings, would speedily be transformed.

The Apostle made a very personal application of these things to the Corinthians. The discipline that he was empowered to exercise was, as we have said, a spiritual weapon, and they might very soon be feeling its sharp edge. The word translated, "destruction" in verse 8, is the same as that translated "pulling down" in verse 4. The word "overthrowing" is possibly better in both places. There is the power of God to overthrow strongholds of unbelief, and the same power can, if the sad necessity arises, overthrow carnal and disobedient believers. Yet the normal and proper use of that power is for the edification, or building up of the saints.

The Apostle had authority, given to him of the Lord, and power in keeping with that authority. The Corinthians, not being very spiritual were inclined to concern themselves a good deal with outward appearance (see verse 1, margin). Paul might be mean to look at, but let them remember that he was Christ's, and that at least as much as those who were his opponents and detractors, and he had an authority which they had not. Let them know too that when present amongst them they would find him to be just what his letters evidently were—weighty and powerful. Here we have, thrown in by the way, a tribute to the effect that his inspired writings had upon the people of his own day. They were the Word of God, and they authenticated themselves to be such in the hearts of those who had any spiritual sensibilities. They do just the same today. We recognize them as far too weighty and powerful to be the mere word of man.

In speaking thus of his authority Paul was not for one moment entering into a kind of competition with those who opposed him. They were anxious to commend themselves, and so get a footing with the Corinthians; and in doing this a spirit of competition got among them, and they began "measuring themselves by themselves, and comparing themselves among themselves," which was a very unwise proceeding. In so doing they got no higher than themselves. It was all self. One man might be distinguished by this feature, another by that; but in comparing themselves with one another they never rose up to God, and to the measure which He had ordained.

In verse 13 Paul continues to use the word, "measure," but with a rather different significance, coupling it with the word "rule" which occurs again in verse 15, and also in verse 16, where it is translated "line." It almost looks as if he were alluding to God's work in creation, as stated in Job xxxviii. 5, where God Himself asks, of the earth, "Who laid the measures thereof, if thou knowest? or who hath stretched the line upon it?" He is a God who works by measure and by line, whether in creation or in the administration connected with His grace. Now God had measured things out and appointed a line or rule in connection with Paul's apostolic service.

From other scriptures we know what the measure and rule of Paul's service was. He could say, "I am ordained a preacher, and an apostle . . . a teacher of the Gentiles in faith and verity" (1 Tim. ii. 7). The line allotted to him was a very extensive one. The whole Gentile world was within the circumference of his measure. Of course then he had not stretched beyond his measure in coming to the Corinthians; his measure reached even to them. They came well within the scope of his apostolic commission.

Indeed, Paul's eye of evangelistic zeal looked beyond Corinth to more distant regions beyond them, where he expected yet more abundantly to preach the Gospel. In the epistle to the Romans he speaks of having fully preached the Gospel of Christ from Jerusalem round about unto Illyricum, the district we now know as Albania, on the shores of the Adriatic; and ultimately he went to Rome. The true evangelist always has his eye on "the regions beyond."

We must not fail to notice the short clause in verse 15, "when your faith is increased." There was a connection between the increasing of their faith and the enlargement of Paul's own service, at all events as regards the geographical spread of it. As long as they were feeble in faith their whole state would be feeble, and this would have its effect upon Paul's activities and service. When he saw them strong in faith he would be the more free to push on from them into the regions beyond. In this way the state of the saints affects the activities of the servant of God. We are members one of another, and not even an apostle can be wholly unaffected by the state of others. This fully applies to us today, of course. God help us each to diligently and conscientiously enquire as in His presence whether we are helping to enlarge or to contract the work of His servants. One or the other it must be.

Several of the remarks which the Apostle makes in these verses were intended to point out that the men opposing him, and endeavouring to turn the Corinthians from him, were working on very different lines. They were boasting of things without their measure. They held no commission from the risen Lord, as he did. They were not pushing out into the regions beyond, and suffering the privations and persecutions that were involved in such labour. They were "boasting . . . of other men's labours" for they were meddling with his work; or as he puts it in verse 16, "boasting in another man's line of things made ready" to their hands.

It is very noticeable how false religious cults often have this feature strongly marking them. They find their happy hunting ground amongst other people's converts. They boast in that which after all is the work of others.

The boasting of the Apostle was not in man, nor even in work. As in the first epistle, so here he declares, "He that glorieth, let him glory in the Lord." If the Lord gives the measure and the rule it is well. If the Lord prospers the work so that men are brought to faith in Christ, and in due course their faith is increased, again it is well. But even so our only boasting must be in the Lord, whose servants we are.

And, on the other hand, the commendation which comes from the Lord is the only commendation worth having. Men may push themselves forward, and commend themselves, as Paul's opponents were doing, but it is all worthless. It is very natural for us to "receive honour one of another, and seek not the honour that cometh from God only" (John v. 44), but it is very fatal. To have the Lord's commendation when the great day of the judgment seat arrives, is worth everything. Let us live our lives as those who have their eyes upon that day.

CHAPTER 11

IN THE LIGHT of the coming day, when the Lord will commend His servants, the commendation of oneself in the presence of one's fellows appears to be but folly. Paul acknowledges this in the first verse of our chapter. He had been speaking about himself in the previous chapter, and he goes on to do so more fully in the chapter before us, but all with a view to assuring the Corinthians of the reality and genuineness of his apostolic mission. He pleads guilty to this "folly" and asks them to bear with him in it.

There was indeed a very good reason for it. His detractors brought their charges and insinuations against him not merely out of opposition to himself. There was an ulterior motive. They depreciated Paul because they aimed thereby at undermining, in the minds of the Corinthians, the truth of the Gospel that he had brought them. They would overthrow Paul's credit as a preliminary step towards overthrowing the Gospel that he preached, and that accomplished, Christ would lose His pre-eminent place in their hearts.

The thought of this stirred the Apostle very deeply. Elijah had been very jealous for the Lord God of Hosts in his day, and here we find Paul jealous with a jealousy which was of God on behalf of Christ. When the Gospel he preached is truly received, it fairly wins the heart of the convert for Christ, so really so that he could say, "I have espoused you . . . that I may present you as a chaste virgin to Christ." This is figurative language, but it is quite transparent as to its meaning. Paul so preached, and we all ought so to preach, that the hearts of those who believe are wholly captivated by Christ. But that is only the beginning.

We should also make it our aim, as Paul did, that each convert might retain this single-eyed devotedness to Christ all through life until the moment arrives for presentation to Christ in glory. Each believing heart should wear the "chaste virgin" character, untouched and unsullied by any other master-passion or absorbing love. Alas! how few of us bear that character in any measure. How many there are who are easily diverted from Him, and spend much of their energy in pursuit of other loves! It is possible to turn from Him to pursue things which are really quite opposed to Him; but to turn from Him to pursue things subsidiary to Him, and therefore quite good in their way, is an even greater snare. May God help us to beware of it.

Verse 3 is very important as exposing before us the way in which the great adversary lays the snare for our feet. In chapter iv. we were instructed as to the way in which he blinds the minds of those who believe not. Here we find that when some have believed, and so as to them his blinding tactics have failed, he is still pertinaceously active and aims at beguiling them, as once he beguiled Eve. When he acts with subtilty as the serpent he is more dangerous than when he opposes as a roaring lion.

The devil in the guise of a serpent deceived Eve in a very subtil and crafty way. Step by step he corrupted her mind as to God, and led her to act apart from and independently of her husband. In similar fashion he works today. He aims at diverting us from simplicity and from true subjection to Christ. The rendering of the New Translation is, "your thoughts should be corrupted from simplicity as to the Christ."

The words, "corrupted from simplicity," are very suggestive, and worth pondering deeply. In man's world things proceed from the simple to the complex. The earliest printing machines, for instance, were very simple affairs. In the course of several centuries they have become marvellous machines of great complexity. So in the ordinary way, confining ourselves to the affairs of men, we should speak of things being developed and improved from their original simplicity. But here we are dealing with what is extraordinary and outside the affairs of men. God's thoughts are not our thoughts, nor are His ways our ways. It is well to get this firmly settled in our souls.

The works and ways of God are marked by simplicity. His simplicity is perfect. We cannot improve upon it. We may attempt to alter it, but then we only corrupt it. The Gospel is the essence of simplicity. It sets Christ before us as the One who is the expression of all that God has to say to us, as also He is the One who has wrought the necessary work of redemption, and in whom we now stand before God. It brings us into complete subjection to Him. But Satan is a master of craft and subtilty. Using these men who were the opponents of Paul, he did not totally deny the Christ whom Paul preached. Verse 4 is clear evidence of this. If they could have come with another gospel, announcing another Jesus, and conferring another spirit, there might have been something to say on their behalf, especially if it could have been an improvement on what they had already received.

Instead of denying Christ they came under the pretence of adding something to Christ. A fuller idea of their position may be gleaned from the epistle to the Galatians, where we find them adding the law to Christ: teaching that, though we may be justified by Him, we are put under the law in order that holiness may be promoted. That Christ should be made righteousness to us they were prepared to admit, but that He should also be made sanctification seemed to them much too simple.

It is not otherwise today. The tendency to hanker after the elaborate, the abstruse, the complicated, the far-fetched is always with us. The intellectual men of the world find the Gospel far too simple, and they stumble at it. The trouble is however that believers, whose strong point is their intellect, always have a tendency in the same direction, unless they walk in the spirit of self-judgment as regards intellectualism. If they do not maintain self-judgment, all their elaborations, their deep and abstruse thoughts, only eventuate in something that corrupts from simplicity as to the Christ.

The mind is a very important part of a man, and Satan's acutest beguilements are aimed at it. It is far from being the whole of a man: his affections and his conscience have a very large place. The trouble is that the intellectual person is very apt to give a much larger place to his mind than Scripture gives to it, and to forget that God reveals His truth to us, not for our intellectual enjoyment, but that it may command our hearts, appeal to our consciences and govern our lives. Let that be properly realized, and we at once find plenty to occupy our spiritual energies in the profound simplicities of the truth, and any itching desire we ever had for mere complexities and novelties and obscurities forsakes us.

"Simplicity as to the Christ!" That is what we need. To know Him: to love Him, as united in heart to Him: to adore Him: to serve Him: that is it! If our minds are thus stayed upon Him in uncorrupted simplicity, all else will be added unto us, and we shall be maintained in the fervour of "first love." It was just at this point that decline set in, as witnessed in Revelation ii. 4. So here: Paul knew well that if Satan succeeded in his beguilings at this point, he would succeed all along the line.

So, once more, in defending his Gospel from the subtle attack of Satan through men who were, however unwittingly, serving him, he had to make plain the reality and power of his apostleship in contrast to features that marked them. He was indeed an apostle, and not in the least inferior to those who were most prominent among the twelve.

From verses 6 to 9 we gather that the Apostle had been belittled not only because his speech was not highly polished but because he had taken no monetary help from the Corinthians whilst amongst them. In alluding to this his language was tinged with irony. He had abased himself in order to exalt them. Was this an offence, a sin? He had accepted help from other churches, notably the Macedonian, and he speaks of this as robbing, or spoiling, them—still the language of irony, of course. He had done the Corinthians the greatest possible service without the least cost to themselves. And he boasted thus, not in the spirit of emulation as though he did not love them, but just because he did love them, and he desired to deliver them from the fascination which the opposers exercised over them by reason of the foolish boasting in which they indulged so freely.

This leads the Apostle to speak with great plainness about the opposers. They were false apostles, for they never had been sent of the Lord as the true apostles were. They were workers right enough, but deceitful ones,

2 CORINTHIANS

since they transformed themselves into what they were not. In this they partook of the character of him whom they served, and according to their deceitful works will be their end.

It is very important that we should remember that Satan so commonly transforms himself into an angel of light, and his servants into servants of righteousness. That being so, we must expect sin and error to frequently present themselves in a pleasing and delightful guise. Again and again we find the advocates of error to be quite nice men. It is unsafe to receive the message because the man who brings it appears so good, so charming, so eloquent, so like an angel of light. The only safe test is, Does he bring the doctrine of Christ, the true Gospel? If he does, receive it by all means, even if he is a bit uncouth, a poor speaker, or of ugly appearance. "Prince Charming" is all too often a servant of Satan in plain clothes.

Such was the character of some—if not all—of those who were opposing Paul. Hitherto he had not said much as to them, but now the time had come to stand up to them and expose them, and this he does very effectually here. They were always boasting concerning themselves, and they did it with a view to self-exaltation. They were marked by a spirit which was the exact opposite of Paul's. He abased himself in order to exalt those whose blessing he sought (verse 7): they exalted themselves and did not scruple to exploit those whom they professed to serve. They brought them into bondage, they devoured them by getting their money, they even smote them on the face. Very possibly smiting on the face was not literal, but in the sense of being rude to them in haughty fashion, or, as we should say, browbeating them. The Corinthians being carnally-minded had evidently been impressed with their domineering manner. Had they been more spiritual they would have seen through it.

Still as these men acted in this way Paul felt that he should take up their challenge. If they wished to institute a kind of competition as to who had the highest credentials, he would speak somewhat further as to his. This boasting was all foolishness, but since they had started it he would speak, and again in verse 19 he uses irony. The Corinthians were enriched in all knowledge and so took the place of being wise, and seemed to suffer gladly the fools who boasted so much; for, he says, you do indeed suffer when these boasting men domineer over you and brow-beat you as they have been doing.

The boastings of these men apparently centred around two points: first, their natural origin as true-blooded Hebrews and Israelites, the seed of Abraham according to the flesh; second, their dignity as servants of Christ, which they claimed to be. As to the former matter, for what it is worth, Paul was not one whit behind them. He could say, "So am I" without the least hesitation.

But when it comes to the second matter he does not say, "So am I," but rather, "I am more," for he completely outshone them. The phrase he uses has been translated "I above measure so," for there was really no com-

160

parison between them: and he proceeds to speak, not of the triumphs he had won, but of the sufferings he had endured.

Let us take time to really digest the significance of this. Had we been in Paul's shoes, should we not almost for a certainty have proceeded to talk of the mighty power of God that had been manifested in our service? We should have had much to say about the mighty signs and wonders that had been manifested, the striking conversions, the wonderful transformations of life and character that had been recorded. Would it have occurred to us to recount the buffetings, the troubles, the sufferings, we had endured? We think not. To tell the truth there would have been hardly anything of that sort to tell.

We are not saying that the servant of Christ should never speak of that which the Lord may have done through him in the way of blessing. There are times when he may profitably do so, as we see by reading Acts xiv. 27, and xv. 12. We do say however that when it is a question of one's credentials, of producing facts which prove beyond all question that one is a genuine servant of Christ, then the record of one's sufferings is far more convincing. Signs and wonders may be produced by a power other than that of the Spirit of God: nothing but absolute devotion to the Lord will enable one to serve with patient persistence through years of toil and suffering.

There are modern religious movements whose main stock-in-trade is the recounting of the wonders they can produce, either in healings, or in tongues, or in the realm of habits and character—"life-changing" as it is called. Of fidelity to Christ, and of suffering for His Name, they have little if anything to say, for it seems non-existent in their scheme of things. They often know quite a lot about high-pressure meetings, and even first-class hotels, but nothing about the labours and perils and infirmities that marked Paul. And as for the rest of us, who do not wish to recount our own doings, successful or otherwise, how little are we like to him.

He was more than a servant of Christ, as he tells us in verse 23. He was an apostle of Christ and actively engaged in filling up "that which is behind of the afflictions of Christ in my flesh" (Col. i. 24). As far as the record given to us in Scripture is concerned, he stands alone amongst the people of God in his sufferings. An Abraham, a Moses, a David, a Daniel, each had their own special and distinctive characteristics which marked them out as pleasing God, but not one of them approached Paul in this. Labours, stripes, prisons, deaths, journeyings, perils of all descriptions, weariness, painfulness, watchings, hunger, thirst, fastings, cold, nakedness, care—what a list! It covers pretty well the whole range of human suffering, whether of body or mind.

From the Acts of the Apostles we can identify a few of the experiences of which he speaks. For instance, "once was I stoned," that was as recorded in chapter xiv. He speaks of being "in deaths oft," and one occasion was in the riot in the Ephesian theatre, recorded in chapter xix, for he speaks of this as "so great a death," in the first chapter of our epistle. But on the other hand we must remember that when he penned this list his experiences were not over. He had been shipwrecked thrice, one of the occasions involving a night and a day in the deep; being washed about in the waters of the Mediterranean, we suppose that means; but as yet the shipwreck recorded in Acts xxvii. had not taken place. That must consequently have been number four, at least.

The most wearing sufferings of all were, we venture to think, those that he speaks of last—the care of all the churches. To bear with the feebleness of the weak, to listen again and again to the complaints of the offended, to correct the foolishness of saints, and contend for the truth against false brethren, all this must have been the most testing thing of all. Yet he did it.

The incident with which he closes the chapter seems symbolic of the whole drift of his life of service. He was "let down," and that in a very undignified way. If secular history is to be trusted the lettings-down never ceased until he knelt by the headsman's block outside the imperial city, Rome. But it was just these lettings-down and the sufferings they involved which put upon him the brands of the Lord Jesus, and marked him out as a servant of Christ in surpassing measure.

<h3 style="text-align:center">CHAPTER 12</h3>

THE REMARK WITH which the Apostle opens chapter xii. again indicates that this speaking about himself was repugnant to him, though he found himself impelled to do it. The New Translation renders it, "Well, it is not of profit to me to boast," so his thought may have been that what he had to say about himself brought no profit or credit to him. The beatings, the perils, the hunger, the thirst, the nakedness, the infirmities, of which he had just spoken were not the kind of experiences which are considered profitable, according to the standards of the world. And now that he proceeds to speak of what he had received of the Lord, in the form of visions and revelations, there was still no credit to him; for it was not exactly as an apostle that he received them, and much less as a man in the flesh, but as "a man in Christ."

In making this distinction we are not splitting hairs, for Paul himself makes it, and lays very definite stress upon it. Note how verses 2-5 carry on the thought, "A man in Christ . . . such an one . . . such a man . . . such an one . . ." These heavenly revelations were given to *such a man as that.* Who and what then is this "man in Christ"?

Without any question Paul was alluding to a marvellous experience in his own history, but he carefully eliminates the personal element from his story in order to impress us with the fact that the experience was only possible for him inasmuch as he was "such a man" as "a man in Christ." Eliminating the personal element he was able thus to abstract in his mind that which he was in the very essence of his being by the work of God in new creation. Elsewhere he has told us that, "We are His workmanship, created in Christ Jesus unto good works" (Eph. ii. 10); and in our own epistle he has already said, "If any man be in Christ, he is a new creature" (v. 17). It is evident therefore that every true believer in the Lord Jesus is "a man in Christ." Consequently every one of us ought to be very eager to take in its significance.

By natural birth we are men in Adam: that is, we enter upon his life, and are of his race and order, inheriting his sinful characteristics; though in different individuals they come out in different ways and degrees. By the grace of God in new creation the believer enters upon the life of the risen Christ, and is of His race and order. The new life he has received has its own characteristics, even those which in all their perfect beauty were seen in Christ Himself. True, in various individual believers these characteristics are only seen in differing ways and degrees, and only partially in the best.

But that is because each individual believer, while under observation in this world, still has the flesh in him, and *that*, whenever permitted to operate, obscures and contradicts the features of the life of Christ. Still our many failures must not be allowed to obscure the fact that a "man in Christ" is what each of us is; and that by an act of God.

When the Lord comes, and we are "clothed upon with our house which is from heaven," the last link that we have with the first Adam will have disappeared. Our very bodies then will be of a new creation order. There will be nothing about us which is not new creation, and hence all need for abstract thinking in connection with this matter will have passed away. We shall no longer have to differentiate and speak of "such an one," for there will be no other kind of "one" entering into the question. How glorious that will be!

Still at present we have to speak as Paul speaks here; and how delightful it is to find that a man in Christ can be caught up into Paradise, even the third heaven, and yet feel at home there and receive communications from God, of a character beyond anything that could possibly be known in this world. How great a contrast for the Apostle between such an experience as this and all those experiences he endured in his life of service, of which we have just been hearing. In them he was "let down," and that in the most undignified way. In this he was "caught up," and that to Paradise. Such an experience must have been in itself a big recompense for his sufferings, and it was only a foretaste of greater things and eternal, which were to come. No wonder he spoke to us, in chapter iv., of the "far more exceeding and eternal weight of glory," which awaits us.

That glory awaits us when we too are caught up as predicted in 1 Thessalonians iv. 17. When all the saints are thus caught up—the Apostle Paul amongst them—they will be clothed in bodies of glory; there is no shadow of uncertainty as to that. There was uncertainty about this experience of Paul's as he tells us twice over. He did not know whether it was supernatural experience, in the nature of a vision, granted to him while still in the body; that is, still a living man in this world: or whether he was out of the body; that is, that he died, his spirit passing into the presence of the Lord, and then subsequently he was brought back to life here. This remark of his, coupled with the date he gives us, makes it quite possible that the experience was granted to him when he suffered the stoning recorded in Acts xiv. He must have been in an insensible condition for some time; since all thought him dead, and his apparent lifeless body was dragged out of the town.

The wonderful experience was his, though he was uncertain what exactly was his condition when he had it. Incidentally this shows us that the "falling asleep" of a saint does not mean the sleep of the soul. If the death of a saint involves his total unconsciousness until the coming of the Lord, then the Apostle would have been in no uncertainty. He would have said, "I must have been in the body for I was conscious: had I been out of the body I should have had no consciousness at all."

This man in Christ was caught up to the third heaven; that is, the immediate presence of God, of which the holiest in the tabernacle was a type. We have boldness to enter into the holiest by the blood of Jesus, and Paul found that as a man in Christ he had free access into the third heaven, which he identifies with Paradise, into which the thief went with Christ. During his sojourn there he found himself in touch with a range of things entirely outside anything known in this world. He heard, "unspeakable words, which it is not lawful for a man to utter."

This does not mean that he heard mysterious utterances quite unintelligible to him, but that the things he heard, and doubtless understood in some degree, were so exalted as to be beyond us in our present condition. The things spoken about in the third heaven cannot be communicated to us. We have no language in which they can be expressed. And further, if it were possible to convey to us a little of that "eternal weight of glory" it would only crush us in our present condition of weakness. Hence Paul was not allowed to utter the things he heard, even if he could have found words in which to clothe the things revealed. This vision and revelation from the Lord was a special privilege conferred upon him, and for his own illumination and strengthening.

In all this there was nothing in which Paul could boast, as he makes so plain in verse 5. Circumstances had been permitted to push him into a position where he was constrained to speak of this wonderful experience, as to which he had kept silence for fourteen years, yet even so, though there was much that he might mention keeping strictly within the bounds of truth (which was more than his opponents always did), he would say nothing except as to his infirmities.

This leads him to reveal the fact that when he resumed his active life in this world he came under a special disciplinary dealing on God's part, of a kind that was designed to deliver him from dangers that threatened. The flesh in Paul was unchanged as to its evil tendencies even after such an experience as this. How easy for him to be lifted up with pride and self-exaltation, and thus invite a sorrowful fall. So the thorn in flesh was given to act as a kind of counterpoise. Paradise and its unspeakable words on the one hand, but the thorn and its buffetings on the other.

It is said that "thorn" hardly gives in any adequate way the sense, and that "stake" would be better. We do not think much of thorns and easily extricate them, but a stake in the flesh is a far more serious thing and thoroughly crippling in its effects. What in particular Paul alluded to we do not know, though a good deal of discussion has centred round the point. Probably it is purposely left vague in order that all our thought may be concentrated on the fact that any affliction, even of the most damaging kind, may be turned into an occasion of spiritual preservation and gain.

The thorn, whatever it was, affected his body for the good of his soul. Its action is described as a "buffeting." It came from Satan, for it is described as "a messenger," or "an angel" of Satan, and it is his mode of attack when a devoted and faithful saint is in question. He blinds the minds of the unbelieving as we were told in chapter iv. He aims at corrupting the simple and unestablished, as chapter xi. showed. But for Paul who had been caught up into the third heaven a different line of attack was followed, and the devil dealt him heavy blows that fell upon his body.

We should have said rather that the devil was permitted to deal him heavy blows, for all that happened was beneath the hand of God. It was with Paul as it had been long before with Job: three causes are discernible. The third causes were fire from heaven, whirlwind, evil men, in the case of Job, and the thorn in the flesh in the case of Paul. Behind these in each case lay the power and animus of Satan; but behind him as the first cause there was the hand of God. Job's safety and blessing lay in his turning away from the third causes, and even from the second cause, that he might accept all from the hand of God; and so too it was with Paul.

Very naturally Paul betook himself to prayer. It was *intense* prayer: he not only requested but besought. It was *repeated*, for he besought the Lord thrice. Yet for all that his desire was not granted. Instead of having the thorn removed he received the assurance of abundant grace; such grace that the thorn would become an asset rather than a liability, a means of blessing rather than a hindrance. The Lord answered his prayer, but not according to his thought. He gave him rather that which was better. The grace bestowed more than counterbalanced the thorn.

We must lay great stress in our minds upon the little word, "MY." The thorn was a messenger of Satan, but the grace was Christ's. The Lord's reply to Paul was, "*My* grace is sufficient for thee." The Lord and His grace are infinite, sufficient for ten thousand times ten thousand of His saints—surely then sufficient for Paul, or for any one of us, no matter what we may have to face. But He added, "My strength is made perfect in weakness."

If the thorn served to augment and emphasize Paul's weakness it thereby opened the way for a fuller and more perfect display of the grace of the Lord.

Without a question all this is right in the teeth of our natural thoughts. We should connect the thought of power and strength with every kind of mental and bodily fitness. We should say—I will glory in my fitness that the power of Christ may rest upon me. When I am tuned up to concert pitch then I am strong. Our thoughts however are wrong: the Divine way is right. We may wish to present ourselves to the Lord for service saying, "Just as I am; young, strong, and free . . ." Paul has to learn to come saying, "Just as I am; old, battered, weak . . ." It is very certain that the Lord accomplished a great deal more through Paul than He is ever going to do through you or me.

The thorn in the flesh, then, worked good in two ways. First, it checked that tendency to pride that otherwise might have overcome Paul and wrought such mischief. Second, it cast him so fully upon the Lord that it became a medium through which abundant supplies of grace were received by him.

This being so, the Apostle had learned to take pleasure in these various forms of adversity. In Romans v. he tells us how he boasted in tribulations because he knew what they were designed to effect in the sphere of Christian character. Here he takes pleasure in tribulations because he had discovered them to be the way by which the power of Christ became operative through him in service. The very weakness into which he was plunged made him a suitable medium for the outflow of that power.

And in this, as well as in other things, Paul was a pattern to us who follow him. This was God's way at the beginning of the dispensation, and it is still His way at the end. Fashions and customs and many other things which lie upon the surface of affairs do indeed vary, but the underlying facts and principles do not vary. Consequently there is no other way of power for us. Does not this fact go a long way to explain the lack of power so sadly evident, and so often deplored, today?

Having let us into the secret, as to the revelations he had from the Lord on the one hand, and the discipline which came upon him from the Lord on the other, the Apostle utters his closing appeal. He ought really to have been commended of the Corinthians seeing they were his converts, instead of which he was forced into defending his apostleship before them. Though nothing in himself, he was behind the very chiefest apostles in nothing. As to this he could appeal to his whole career, and more particularly to his life and service when amongst them.

Paul's estimate of himself was—I am nothing. Let us be instructed by this. We sometimes sing,

"O keep us, love divine, near Thee,
That we our nothingness may know."

The desire is a good one. We never do realize our nothingness more effectively than when we are filled with divine love. In the passage before us the confession "I am nothing," follows the setting forth of the all-sufficient grace of Christ.

Yet this man who was nothing had been called to apostleship in surpassing measure, and the signs of it were very evident; not only in wonders and mighty deeds but also and firstly in patience—a patience which he was now displaying in abundant measure in his dealings with the Corinthians. When he was in their midst he carefully abstained from being in any way a financial burden to them, though he had taken help from other churches. He speaks again with a tinge of irony in saying, "forgive me this wrong." He purposed to continue on the same lines. Inasmuch as he was their spiritual father he proposed to provide for them, rather than counting upon their providing for him.

Verse 15 is very beautiful. Paul was indeed a father in Christ, his heart well saturated with divine love, hence he could love the unloving, even as God does. The natural tendency of our hearts is just the opposite of this. We are perhaps kindly disposed towards certain persons, and show them various favours. They receive all, but are cool and unappreciative. We are annoyed, and declare we will have done with them! But it was not thus with Paul. Even if things got so bad that their response only decreased as love increased, he would go on expressing his love in the most practical way of all. He would spend and be spent for them. A little of this lovely spirit we see in 1 Samuel xii. 23. A good deal more of it we see in the passage before us. But the thing itself is seen supremely in God Himself, as displayed by the Lord Jesus Christ.

The same spirit had been seen in those associated with the Apostle in his labours, as Titus and others. Yet this loving spirit did not mean indifference to evil, and a condoning of things that were not right; and so there follow very plain words as to the sin which he feared was still to be found amongst them, which would merit very severe judgment if he again came into their midst.

Sin breaks out in many ways, but two forms of it were very prevalent at Corinth, as verses 20 and 21 bear witness. First, there were all those disturbing features that spring from self-assertiveness and the envy and jealousy thereby generated. Second, self-gratification and the licentiousness that springs from it, in its varying forms. The Apostle feared that both these things were still rife at Corinth and unrepented of; and that if he came on this proposed third visit he would be full of grief in their midst and have to act in judgment. We may observe that he speaks of his humiliation and sorrow (xii. 21) before he speaks of his authority in judgment (xiii. 2).

2 CORINTHIANS

CHAPTER 13

AS AN APOSTLE he had special authority and power in this direction. When once the apostles had passed off the scene the only discipline possible was that exerted by the church or by the saints collectively; and that so often in these days appears to be singularly ineffectual. There are of course reasons for this. One reason is that it has been so often perverted to ends of a personal or party nature that the whole idea of it has fallen into disrepute. Another is that even when discipline has been rightly inflicted it has been done in a harsh judicial spirit instead of in the spirit of humiliation and sorrow which marked the Apostle here. We have made it the cold, heartless discipline of the court of law instead of the warm, affectionate discipline of the family circle.

Still, discipline there has to be: the discipline of God's house, which is not prejudiced nor unreasoning but founded on well established facts. Hence when Paul came he intended that every word should be established in the mouth of two or three witnesses. All should be sifted with impartiality, so that if some reports were not based upon fact their falsity might be exposed, and their weight fall not upon the head of the accused but upon the head of the accusers. Some may have sinned by licentiousness as Paul feared; but others may have sinned by "backbitings" and "whisperings" of false accusations, because their hearts were filled with envy. All would be made manifest and judged, as we see in the opening verses of chapter xiii. We venture to think that, if today there were as much zeal in bringing discipline to bear against the backbiters and whisperers as against the licentious, it would be for the spiritual health and well-being of the church of God.

Paul's authority as an apostle had however been questioned, and the Corinthians had very foolishly given ear to these questionings. They were the last persons who should have done so, or should have had any doubts as to whether Christ had spoken through him. Since they had entertained such doubts, some kind of answer was needed, and a very crushing one Paul was able to give. He had simply to say, "Examine yourselves, whether ye be in the faith." Since they were his converts, the fruit of his labour, they themselves were the proof—unless indeed they were reprobates, just worthless frauds. If they were but frauds then indeed Christ might not have spoken in Paul; but if they were true men He most certainly had.

Verse 5 has sometimes been taken apart from its context and turned into a plea for continual self-inspection, and even doubt as to one's own salvation. This is because the parenthesis extending from the middle of verse 3 to the end of verse 4 has not been noticed. If we connect the early part of verse 3 with verse 5 the sense is quite clear. There is again a touch of irony in Paul's words, for the doubts they had foolishly entertained as to Christ speaking in him really recoiled upon their own heads. If indeed Christ had *not* spoken *in Paul* then—since they had professed conversion

168

under his *speaking*—Christ would *not* be found *in them*. But if Christ was indeed found *in them* it was conclusive proof that Christ had spoken *in him*.

It is quite possible of course that in speaking thus the Apostle wished to convey to them the fact that he was not too sure of the genuineness of some of them, and thereby he desired to stir them up and exercise their consciences. At the same time he was quite confident as to the majority of them.

This is evident if we consider the parenthesis, the first words of which tell us that Christ had not been "weak" toward them but rather "mighty in you." Looking back to the work that had been wrought when first he came among them, Paul was full of confidence that the power of Christ had been in it. The whole path of Christ on earth had been characterized by a "weakness" which culminated in His crucifixion. Yet He is alive in resurrection by the power of God. Now that which marked the path of the great Master marked also the path of the servant, who was following in His life and way. Weakness also characterized the external life and service of the Apostle but under the surface the power of God was vitally present with him.

The words at the end of verse 4 are remarkable—"by the power of God *toward you*." These words indicate that what was in the Apostle's mind was not that he would live in resurrection in the time to come, but that, as associated with the living Christ, he would display in the present the power of that life towards the Corinthians. Christianity is marked by the power of a new life which operates in blessing. Nothing short of *that*, whether it be creed or ceremony or work, will do.

The whole passage shows once more that what God looks for is reality and power. It emphasizes also that, as far as outward appearances go, weakness has been stamped upon the true saints and servants of God from the beginning, even when the Gospel was winning its earliest and greatest triumphs. We need not therefore be surprised if weakness is stamped upon us today. The thing to be concerned about is that we may judge and refuse all that would jeopardize that power.

The self-abnegation of the Apostle again comes strikingly to light in verse 7. He prayed that they might do no evil, and so be manifestly approved and not reprobate; and this, not that it might approve his work amongst them, and so be for his glory, but that they might do what is right, and so prove beyond all question that they were not reprobates. If that were so he would be content, even though he appeared to be a reprobate himself. That he was not a reprobate he knew very well, and he trusted they knew it too, as he says in verse 6.

So also we see his self-abnegation in verse 9. He was not only content but glad to be weak if it but led to spiritual strength in those to whom he ministered; the great object before him being the perfecting of the saints. He longed to see them led forward to completion—to full growth in

Christ. As for himself, he knew that all the power in which he served was Divine in its origin, and so was only available for so long as he was labouring for the truth and in the truth. If he had turned against the truth he would instantly have been shorn of *that* power. There are powers antagonistic to the truth, but in the long run they cannot prevail. Hence against the truth he was powerless, whilst for it he was powerful.

In all this a note of sharpness or severity has not been absent, and in verse 10 we have the explanation of why he had written in this strain. He anticipated being amongst them for the third time and desired to overthrow and clear away the evil by means of this letter, and so have only the happy work of building up what is good when he came. He had authority given of the Lord, but it was primarily for building up. Overthrowing is necessary, as we saw when reading the early part of chapter x., but only in view of building up, which is the great thing the Lord desires for His people.

Verse 11 gives us *the closing desires*. If we are perfected, of good comfort (or encouraged), of one mind, and at peace, we shall indeed do well. It is easy to see that these were things much needed by the Corinthians. But we need them just as badly. The church of God today, as a whole, is in a condition very similar to them. There is plenty of immaturity, of discouragement, of disunity, of strife: indeed these things seem very much to flow one out of the other. They are met and countered by a true ministry such as Paul's; and maturity, encouragement, unity and peace are promoted. May it be so with us, and we too shall know the presence of the God of love and peace.

Verses 12 and 13 give *the closing salutations*. Verse 11 being fulfilled in them, there would be no difficulty amongst themselves, no jealousies and strifes and evil speakings, which would prevent their saluting one another in holiness. The spirit of faction, the desire to boast of being of Paul or Peter or Apollos, would be cast out. Moreover "all the saints" saluted them, for their affections had not been alienated from them by reason of their blameworthy condition of unspirituality. The saints elsewhere had not formed a party against them, or what is even worse, fallen themselves into parties as the result of hearing about the schisms at Corinth. *All the saints* saluted them, in spite of their failures.

Verse 14 gives *the closing benediction*. Here we have indicated the great realities which are calculated to produce the things desired in verse 11— grace, love and communion, proceeding respectively from the three Persons of the Godhead. Let us notice in passing that the Lord Jesus, who is so often spoken of as the Second Person, is put in the first place here, just as the Holy Spirit is put in the first place in 1 Corinthians xii. All such terms as First, Second or Third Person must therefore be used with a considerable measure of reserve.

2 CORINTHIANS

The grace of the Lord Jesus was *known* by the Corinthians, as the Apostle had acknowledged in chapter viii. It is another and a further, thing for it to be *with us all*. Then we shall *all* be pervaded by its blessed influence. So with the love of God; and so too with the communion of the Holy Spirit. In this benediction the grace is put first, for if that fails with us all will fail.

Heaven will be filled with the love of God and the communion of the Holy Spirit, but we shall not need grace—at least, not as we need it here. It is in the circle of the church on earth that all kinds of trials and testings occur. It is here that we have to do with perverse men and trying brethren, all the while possessing wayward hearts ourselves. Nothing but the grace of the Lord Jesus Christ can preserve us in a way that is pleasing to God. But the grace of the Lord *can do it*.

And if the grace of the Lord does preserve us, then the love of God and the communion of the Holy Spirit may have full course and be with us all. The Spirit being holy the communion which He inspires must be holy. We shall be found in happy partnership and fellowship as to the whole range of things which He reveals to us, even the deep things of God.

The love of God *shines upon us* as His children, even when our practical condition is not at all pleasing to Him. But when it is *with us all* its benediction is felt throughout the great circle of all saints. Indeed it overflows that circle and goes out to the world beyond. A lovely picture is thus presented of what the church is according to the thought of God: a circle governed by grace, overflowing with love, and filled with a holy communion concerning the things of God.

We cannot say that the church is that practically; but we can say that it may and should be that. We can say also that if any of us approximate to this, even in a small degree, we shall be greatly blessed, and be a benediction to others.

So may it be then with all of us.

www.ingramcontent.com/pod-product-compliance
Lightning Source LLC
La Vergne TN
LVHW011351080426
835511LV00005B/239